The Royal Commission on Historical Manuscripts

Guides to Sources for British History
based on the National Register of Archives

6

Papers of
BRITISH CHURCHMEN
1780 – 1940

London   Her Majesty's Stationery Office

HMSO BOOKS

HMSO publications are available from:

HMSO Publications Centre
(Mail and telephone orders only)
PO Box 276, London, SW8 5DT
Telephone orders 01-622 3316
General enquiries 01-211 5656
(queuing system in operation for both numbers)

HMSO Bookshops
49 High Holborn, London, WC1V 6HB   01-211 5656 (Counter service only)
258 Broad Street, Birmingham, B1 2HE   021-643 3740
Southey House, 33 Wine Street, Bristol, BS1 2BQ   (0272) 24306/24307
9-21 Princess Street, Manchester, M60 8AS   061-834 7201
80 Chichester Street, Belfast, BT1 4JY   (0232) 238451
71–73 Lothian Road, Edinburgh, EH3 9AZ   (031) 228 4181

HMSO's Accredited Agents
(see Yellow Pages)

and through good booksellers

Preface

This sixth volume in the Commission's series of *Guides to sources for British history* arose out of a wider survey of all kinds of records relating to religion and religious thought about which information had been assembled in the National Register of Archives. These initial investigations, whilst uncovering substantial amounts of information, revealed many gaps in the Commission's knowledge which it subsequently set out to fill. As a result of this research the Register has itself been considerably enriched. It soon became apparent that the surviving papers of individual churchmen were of such quantity and interest as to fill a volume themselves, leaving treatment of institutional records for later consideration.

It would not have been possible to prepare the volume without the assistance of numerous private and institutional custodians and their honorary archivists, many of whom gladly gave much time to the Commission's staff, and of individual scholars and archivists in record repositories who generously shared the results of their own enquiries with the compilers. Their major contribution is evident from the text of the volume and is most gratefully acknowledged.

The investigation and compilation of the guide was undertaken by Dr NW James, Dr Isabel Kenrick and Mr LA Ritchie under the direction of Dr Susan Willmington.

BS SMITH
Secretary
6 January 1987

Quality House, Quality Court,
Chancery Lane, London WC2A 1HP

Contents

Introduction

This guide describes the papers of over 800 churchmen and women active during the period 1780-1940, selected on the basis of their significance for the study of British ecclesiastical history. The opening date was chosen in order to include the papers of those who took part in the eighteenth-century movements which laid the foundations for the great religious upheavals of the following century. Amongst these are, most notably, papers of the first Methodists (John Fletcher, Vincent Perronet, Charles and John Wesley), the Anglican evangelicals (John Newton, Henry Venn) and the leaders of Independent and Unitarian congregations (William Bull, Timothy Kenrick, Joseph Priestley). The closing date was adopted so as to bring the survey as near to the present as possible whilst excluding the papers of living people and those still closed to scholars.

The main focus is on the papers of the ordained clergy or recognised ministers of the various Christian denominations whose biographical details are traceable in standard works of reference. Colonial churchmen and missionaries have not been included except where their papers illustrate a substantial part of their career spent at home (RH Codrington, GA Selwyn) or shed light on the domestic ecclesiastical scene (Samuel Gobat, Wilfrid Parker). Churchmen who left only antiquarian or literary papers have also been omitted and such papers occurring in fuller collections have been summarily treated. Laymen have been included only where their papers are of particular significance to religious affairs and they do not have entries in other published or projected guides in the series. Among them are a small number of lawyers whose practice was primarily ecclesiastical (LT Dibdin, JR Hope-Scott).

As in previous volumes the survey was concerned with the papers that remained with an individual at the time of his or her death and therefore outgoing letters preserved among the papers of recipients were normally excluded. Initial research quite quickly revealed certain patterns of survival. In the case of all denominations other than the Roman Catholics papers were discovered to have passed for the most part from family custody into institutional keeping either as direct gifts or loans or through the collecting initiatives of individual repositories. The precise route along which papers had travelled could not always be traced but where papers are known to have come from a family this fact is recorded. Amongst the most important of such collections are those formed by Lambeth Palace Library and Pusey House, Oxford (Anglicans), the John Rylands Library (Methodists), New College London and its predecessors, now in Dr Williams's Library (Independents and Congregationalists), Manchester College, Oxford (Unitarians) and New College, Edinburgh (Church of Scotland). In view of this institutional collecting activity direct approaches were made to descendants only when the existence of papers in their possession was known from other sources (JH Monk, HRL Sheppard). But in the case of Roman Catholics a systematic approach was made to diocesan archives and religious houses which were expected and proved to be the natural resting place for groups of private papers.

Many of the papers found in institutional ownership were entirely or partly uncatalogued. Some of them also incorporated a significant number of an individual's autograph letters collected from other sources and added to his personal papers. When these have been brought together with an archive (JH Newman, EB Pusey, John Wesley) they have been described. Uncatalogued collections were surveyed by the Commission's staff when practicable but a number could not be inspected with the result that some entries may be uneven or incomplete.

Papers fall mainly within the categories traced in earlier volumes in the series, that is correspondence, diaries, journals and working papers. Sermons are also noted, but only where they form part of a larger collection. With the major exception of the presbyterian churches in Wales and Scotland, inheritors of a long preaching tradition, sermons do not appear to have survived in great quantities.

Official papers relating to the formal administration of the churches, both national and local, have normally been excluded where they form part of distinct administrative archives. In the case, however, of both Anglican and Roman Catholic bishops and dignitaries official and personal papers are often intermingled. Where information was full enough for identification, correspondence with individual clergy, parishes and religious orders has been noticed as it frequently contains much information of general historical interest, but details of the financial and legal records of parish, cathedral, diocesan and provincial administration have not been incorporated, nor have pastoral letters and circulars. Correspondence between bishops and representatives of government has also been noticed for the same reason as has that between Roman Catholic bishops and the papal curia and their agents in Rome, usually referred to for convenience as correspondence 'with Rome'.

The diversity of the material that was found is illustrated by the following figures. Papers were traced for 351 Anglicans, 60 of them mainly of Irish, Scottish or Welsh interest, 195 Roman Catholics, 55 Methodists, 48 Scots presbyterians, 34 Independents or Congregationalists, 32 Unitarians, 30 Quakers, 28 Calvinistic Methodists, 20 Baptists and 14 others. The tendency for churchmen's papers to become dispersed is shown by the total of 266 institutions in which they were traced, including Roman Catholic archives in the custody of diocesan bishops. It is known from contemporary biographies based on personal papers (WD Maclagan, Francis Paget, Robert Rainy, William Stubbs) that only fragments of some collections have survived while others have disappeared altogether. In one instance (Francis Kilvert) papers are known to have been deliberately destroyed, whilst the text provides numerous examples of collections of which it may reasonably be presumed a major part has been lost. But papers also continue to emerge unexpectedly and the Commission would welcome further information to add to that uncovered by this survey.

Access to privately owned papers

Privately owned collections of papers deposited on loan in libraries, record offices and other public institutions are normally available for research without restriction. Special conditions, however, may sometimes apply to their use, particularly if they are to be cited in published works. All enquiries on this point should be addressed to the institutions concerned.

Permission to see other privately owned collections whether held by institutions or individuals should be sought from their owners in writing. Details of their locations may, where appropriate, be obtained from the Commission. Applicants are reminded that such papers can normally be made available for use only at considerable personal inconvenience and expense to their owners, and that access for the purposes of research is a privilege not a right. The conditions of access to individual collections were those prevailing in December 1986.

Published reports of the Royal Commission on Historical Manuscripts are cited with the initials HMC. Lists available for consultation in the National Register of Archives are cited by their number there, eg NRA 16303.

Papers of
British churchmen
1780-1940

[1] **ACTON, Charles Januarius** (1803-1847)
Cardinal 1842.

Corresp and papers 1827-46, mainly letters to him
with some draft replies, rel to the English, Welsh
and Scottish districts 1835-45, general English
affairs 1837-45, Malta 1840-6 and Canada 1844-9
(4 vols); corresp with Italian religious foundations
from 1839 (1 bundle); English and French
corresp from 1827 and misc papers (2 bundles);
judicial and administrative papers, treatises and
notes (1 vol, 1 bundle).
Vatican Archives, Rome (Spogli Acton).

Collected letters from Acton, mainly to his
brother FRE Acton 1820-36 (154 items) and his
mother 1821-37 (84 items).
Westminster Diocesan Archives (St Edmund's
College Ware, series 15). NRA 16303.

[2] **ACTON, Sir John Emerich Edward Dalberg**
(1834-1902), 8th Bt 1837, 1st Baron Acton 1869
Regius professor of modern history, Cambridge
1895-1902.

Collected MSS, historical notes and transcripts,
some family and personal papers, letters to him
rel to *Cambridge Modern History* 1896-9 (c850
items).
Cambridge University Library (Add 4607-5021,
5347-8, 5381-710, 5751-76, 6443, 7726-32, 7892).
Bequeathed and purchased 1903.

Corresp (c11 boxes) incl corresp with JJI von
Döllinger (1 box) and letters from WE Gladstone
(1 bundle) and Richard Simpson (5 bundles);
notes on the Vatican Council etc (1 box);
historical and misc papers (6 boxes).
Cambridge University Library. Purchased 1973.
NRA 20501.

[3] **AGAR, Charles** (1736-1809), 1st Earl of
Normanton 1806
Bishop of Cloyne 1768-79; archbishop of Cashel
1779-1801, of Dublin 1801-9.

Corresp and papers 1767-1809 (14 boxes) rel to
political, personal and ecclesiastical affairs, incl

letters to him 1767-1809 (1,197 items) and letter
book 1800-3 (1 vol), accounts of the state of the
dioceses of Cloyne, Cashel and Dublin and
Glendalough 1755-1809 and visitation charges.
Hampshire Record Office (21M57). Deposited
1957. NRA 8798.

[4] **AITKEN, John** (1726-1816)
Minister of St Vigeans 1754-1816.

Journal 1761-1816.
St Andrews University Library (MS 37224).

[5] **ALEXANDER, Samuel Joseph** (1841-1936)
Quaker minister.

Corresp and misc papers 1855-1908 (c80 items).
Society of Friends Library, London (Temp MSS
75/3).

[6] **ALFORD, Henry** (1810-1871)
Dean of Canterbury 1857-71.

Notebook 1846 (1 vol); *Poetical works of Henry
Alford* with MS illustrations, annotations and
appendix of unpublished poems (1 vol).
Canterbury Cathedral Library (Addit MSS 84-5).
Presented by his great-grandson, David Alford
1960.

[7] **ALLANSON, Peter [Athanasius]** (1804-1876)
Provincial of the northern province of the English
Benedictine Congregation 1858-76.

History of the English Benedictine Congregation
(3 vols); constitutions (1 vol); *acta capitulorum
generalium* (2 vols); records (5 vols); biographies
of English Benedictines (2 vols) with index (1
vol).
Ampleforth Abbey (MSS 154-67).

[8] **ALLON, Henry** (1818-1892)
Congregational minister of Union Chapel,
Islington 1852-92.

Letters from Henry Alford, Walter Besant, EA
Freeman, RH Hutton, Humphry Sandwith and
others c1856-91 (c345 items).
Dr Williams's Library, London (24.110). NRA
13168.

[9] **AMHERST, Francis Kerril** (1819-1883)
Bishop of Northampton 1858-79.

Financial corresp with the diocese of Nottingham,
papers rel to parish visitations, missions and the
building of Northampton cathedral, with other
papers (1 box); papers rel to the Vatican Council
1870 (1 box).
Bishop of Northampton.

Letters from his family (2 bundles), his brother
William and other clergy (6 bundles); collected
letters incl an account of the Vatican Council
1870.
Society of Jesus, London.

[10] **AMHERST, William Joseph** (1829-1869)
Jesuit historian.

Corresp and papers, with those of his family,
1792-1880 (24 vols, 9 bundles) incl corresp with
Poor Clares (1 bundle), Charles and Arthur
Langdale, John Morris and William Turner (1
bundle); family corresp (4 bundles); notebooks
and drafts for a history of the church in England
1748-1850, *The old English catholics* and an
unfinished third volume of *The history of catholic
emancipation*; diary 1856-7; autobiography (1
bundle).
Society of Jesus, London.

[11] **AMIGO, Peter Emmanuel** (1864-1949)
RC bishop of Southwark 1904-49; archbishop *ad
personam* 1937.

Corresp and papers rel to the episcopal
interregnum in Southwark 1903-4 and the
consistorial case 1903-10 (6 boxes); letters from
FA Bourne 1905-35 (2 boxes); misc corresp and
papers (23 boxes) incl papers rel to George Tyrell
and Maude Petre, Irish affairs, the Spanish civil
war, Ronald Knox's NT translations 1940-4,
military chaplaincies in the first and second world
wars and biographical papers; interview diaries
etc 1919-49 (c11 vols); visitation diaries 1909-49
(c7 vols); papers of S Banfi as his secretary (3
boxes).
Southwark Diocesan Archives. NRA 27760.

[12] **ANDERSON, Robert** (1768-1837)
Minister of Old Greyfriars, Edinburgh 1804-37.

Corresp with JPE Voute 1810-23 (78 items);
letters from Herman Geffroy 1827-8 (16 items),

G Hyne 1819-27 (29 items) and Henry Porter
1812-14 (28 items); letters to him and his brother,
Charles 1800-37 (24 items); corresp with his
brothers 1800-29 (31 items); corresp and papers
rel to Waterhead, Lanarks c1775-1846 (53 items);
notebook 1806; lecture notes (24 items); essays
(10 items); papers, mainly bonds and discharges
(20 items).
Scottish Record Office (GD 1/821).

[13] **ARMITAGE, Elkanah** (1844-1929)
Congregational minister, Oldham and Rotherham.

Diaries 1872-1908, 1911-27 (4 vols).
Revd HA Wilson.

[14] **ARMSTRONG, George** (1792-1857)
Unitarian minister of Lewin's Mead Chapel,
Bristol 1838-56.

Letters from Lord Brougham 1844-55 (13 items);
commonplace books 1818, 1829 (2 vols); diaries
1837-55 (6 vols).
Manchester College, Oxford. NRA 19870.

[15] **ARNOLD, Thomas** (1795-1842)
Headmaster of Rugby School 1827-42; regius
professor of modern history, Oxford 1841-2.

Diaries and travel journal 1826-42 (6 items);
letters to Edward Hawkins, AP Stanley, his
family and others c1828-42 (c100 items); misc
papers incl sermons 1838-9 (1 vol).
Rugby School. Presented by his grand-daughter,
Miss Dorothy Ward. NRA 5282.

Diaries and travel journals 1816-42 (10 vols);
letters to his wife Mary and family, to George
Cornish, Edward Hawkins, Edward Stanley and
others 1810-41 (c140 items); misc family letters
and papers 1799-1863 (c30 items).
Brotherton Library, Leeds University. Mainly
purchased from his descendant, Mrs Mary
Moorman 1966. NRA 10085.

Family corresp and misc papers 1812-1919 (c114
items).
Trinity College, Dublin (MS 5102). Presented
1971. NRA 24100.

[16] **ASPLAND, Robert Brook** (1805-1869)
Unitarian minister.

Notebooks (50 vols) incl notes on puritanism and
dissent (24 vols).
Manchester College, Oxford. NRA 19870.

[17] **ASTLEY, Richard** (1785-1855)
Minister of High Street Unitarian Chapel,
Shrewsbury 1831-53.

Letters to him c1807-53 (c135 items); letter book
1826-33 (1 vol); journal 1814-26 (1 vol);
architectural notebook (1 vol).

Shrewsbury Public Library (Astley papers). NRA 7293.

[18] **ATMORE, Charles** (1759-1826)
Wesleyan methodist minister.

Corresp 1783-1826 incl letters from John Wesley 1783-90 (4 items), John Pawson 1784-1805 (104 items) and others (*c*20 items); journal of conferences 1794, 1797, 1800, 1801, 1806, 1808, 1809; autobiography; misc papers 1786-1815 (3 items).
Methodist Archives, Manchester.

[19] **AYCKBOWM, Emily** (1836-1900)
Founder of the Community of the Sisters of the Church.

Corresp and papers incl letters from EW Benson *c*1895, notes and commentaries on the Rule (*c*10 vols), diary and addresses.
St Michael's Convent, Ham Common, Richmond.
Closed to research.

[20] **BACKHOUSE, Edward** (1808-1879)
Quaker minister.

Journals, mainly rel to travels in Europe, 1856-77 (6 vols, 1 bundle); sketch books 1825-63 (4 vols); genealogical notes on the Backhouse family 1653-1809 (1 vol).
Durham County Record Office (D/Wa). NRA 25375.

[21] **BACKHOUSE, Hannah Chapman (née Gurney)** (1787-1850)
Quaker minister.

Family corresp *c*1805-50 (*c*1,000 items), incl letters rel to her North American visits 1831, 1834-5; corresp rel to Friends' affairs (3 bundles); personal and household accounts etc 1817-50 (11 vols, 9 bundles); American journals 1831-2; papers rel to the death of HG Backhouse 1836 (1 bundle).
Department of Palaeography and Diplomatic, Durham University. Deposited by DM Backhouse 1982.

Family corresp and papers with those of her husband Jonathan *c*1801-49 (*c*210 items); journals 1802, 1804-24 (5 vols).
Department of Palaeography and Diplomatic, Durham University. Deposited by Lt-Colonel MRC Backhouse 1949, 1958. NRA 0628.

Corresp with members of the Backhouse, Gurney and Hodgkin families 1826-50 (*c*280 items), incl letters from John Hodgkin 1843-50 (102 items).
Durham County Record Office (Hodgkin papers). Deposited by Miss Lois Hodgkin 1966. NRA 12281.

[22] **BACKHOUSE, Jonathan** (1779-1842)
Quaker minister.

Corresp, incl letters from his wife Hannah and rel to Friends' and business matters, *c*1819-37 (250 items); commonplace book 1795; personal and household accounts 1811-42 (7 vols).
Department of Palaeography and Diplomatic, Durham University. Deposited by DM Backhouse 1982.

Family corresp and papers with those of his wife *c*1801-49 (*c*210 items); literary anthology 1797 (1 vol).
Department of Palaeography and Diplomatic, Durham University. Deposited by Lt-Colonel MRC Backhouse 1949. NRA 0628.

Letters from his wife 1841-2 (72 items) and others 1823-42 (17 items).
Durham County Record Office (Hodgkin papers). Deposited by Miss Lois Hodgkin 1966. NRA 12281.

[23] **BAGGS, Charles Michael** (1806-1845)
Rector of the English College, Rome 1840-4; vicar apostolic of the western district 1844-5.

Letters to him 1836-43; papers as vice-rector, rector and agent for the English vicars apostolic.
English College, Rome (Scritture 74, 77-78 *passim*).

Corresp and papers as vicar apostolic, mainly letters to him (*c*75 items).
Bristol Record Office (Clifton diocesan records).

[24] **BAGSHAWE, Edward Gilpin** (1829-1915)
Bishop of Nottingham 1874-1901.

Corresp with and reports to Rome 1875-1901 (*c*53 items); diocesan financial corresp 1874-98 (38 items); reports on visitations *c*1880-7 (*c*40 vols) and 1892-7 (1 box); preparatory papers for diocesan synods 1874-1901 (2 boxes); diary 1874-1901 (1 vol).
Bishop of Nottingham. NRA 27317.

Autobiography 1847-74 (1 vol).
The Oratory, London. NRA 16631.

[25] **BAILLIE, Donald Macpherson** (1887-1954)
Professor of systematic theology, St Andrews 1935-54.

Corresp, diaries, notebooks, lectures, sermons and literary MSS 1890-1955 (18 boxes).
St Andrews University Library.

Commonplace book (1 vol); lectures (1 vol).
New College, Edinburgh.

[26] **BAINES, Peter Augustine** (1786-1843)
Vicar apostolic of the western district 1829-43.

Corresp and papers 1822-43 (*c*900 items) mainly letters to him, with a few draft replies, personal

financial papers and papers rel to Prior Park
College, Bath.
Bristol Record Office (Clifton diocesan records).

Diary 1817-18.
St John's Presbytery, South Parade, Bath. See *Post
reformation catholicism in Bath*, i, ed JA Williams,
Catholic Record Society, Record series 65, 1975.

Diary 1820-1; misc papers rel to Prior Park
College.
Bishop of Clifton.

[27] **BANDINEL, James** (1814-1893)
Rector of Emley 1862-81; honorary secretary of
the Association for Promoting the Reform of
Convocation 1881-7.

Corresp, mainly rel to his career, his writings and
the Oxford movement, incl letters from William
Palmer, AP Stanley and others; sermons and
poetry (1 vol).
*William R Perkins Library, Duke University,
Durham, N Carolina.* NRA 25903.

[28] **BARBERI, Dominic** (1792-1849)
Passionist missionary to England.

Letters from JD Dalgairns, JH Newman, George
Spencer, NPS Wiseman and others 1832-47 (c50
items); collected letters from him 1841-9 (14
items); sermons, lectures, retreat notes (c12 vols
and items).
*Archives of the English Province of Passionist
Fathers, London.*

[29] **BARDSLEY, Samuel** (d 1818)
Senior preacher of the Wesleyan methodist
connexion.

Corresp 1767-1812 incl letters from John Allen,
John Pawson, Joseph Sanderson, Richard Seed,
Richard Swan, John Wesley and others (85
items); diaries 1765-6 and letter books 1772-6 (4
vols); fragments of diaries 1776-7, 1797 (1 vol);
misc accounts (1 item).
Methodist Archives, Manchester.

[30] **BARING-GOULD, Sabine** (1834-1924)
Rector of Lewtrenchard 1881-1924.

Corresp and agreements with publishers c1870-
1920 (1 bundle); papers rel to his ecclesiastical
appointments 1864-81 (1 bundle).
Devon Record Office (TD 166). NRA 27785.

Sermon notes 1866-83; extracts from parish
registers of Devon and Cornwall (19 vols).
West Devon Record Office. Formerly in Plymouth
City Library. Partial list: NRA 7947.

[31] **BARNES, Ernest William** (1874-1953)
Bishop of Birmingham 1924-53.

Corresp and papers to 1924, mainly as master of
the Temple and canon of Westminster (4 files);
corresp and papers 1902-53, mainly as bishop of
Birmingham, (139 files) incl corresp with clergy
and diocesan officials (15 files), rel to disputes
with clergy and parishes over eucharistic doctrine
etc (37 files), to Birmingham affairs and
institutions etc (37 files) and to his writings,
broadcasts etc 1902-52 (15 files); engagement
diaries 1904-53 (50 vols); mathematical papers (29
files); misc published articles etc (101 items).
Birmingham University Library. Deposited by his
family. NRA 26562.

[32] **BARNETT, Samuel Augustus** (1844-1913)
Vicar of St Jude, Whitechapel 1873-94 and
warden of Toynbee Hall 1884-96; canon of
Westminster 1906-13.

Collected letters to his brother Frank and his wife
1883-1913 (459 items); letters to his mother and
family describing his travels 1879-80 (66 items);
letters from him and his wife during their journey
around the world 1890-1 (260ff); sermon notes
1875-88 (19 vols, 3 items); lecture notes, articles,
etc 1884-1907 (4 vols, c35 items); travel diaries,
Ireland and America [1856], 1867 (2 vols); misc
papers 1867-1913 (c65 items).
Greater London Record Office. Collected by his
wife and presented by SHG Barnett 1968. NRA
12596.

Letters to him and his wife from Octavia Hill rel
to her social work etc 1873-1906 (95 items).
British Library of Political and Economic Science
(Coll misc 512). Purchased at Sotheby's 12 Dec
1967, lot 475. NRA 15880.

Papers and misc letters to him rel to the National
Church Reform Union 1871-1913 (4 vols).
Lambeth Palace Library (MSS 1463-6).

[33] **BARRINGTON, Shute** (1734-1826)

Bishop of Llandaff 1769-82, of Salisbury 1782-91,
of Durham 1791-1826.

Letters to him and his agent R Burn, with draft
replies, mainly 1817-18, and misc papers rel to
his translation to Durham and earlier precedents
1676-1818 (109 items); corresp with Burn and
others about patents, etc c1764-1816 (15 items).
Durham University Library (MS Accessions 450,
452).

Corresp and misc papers (c170 items), incl letters
from JD Carlyle about MSS in Greek monasteries
1799-1801.
Suffolk Record Office, Ipswich (HA 174).

Letters and papers mainly rel to the restoration of
Salisbury cathedral 1788-9 (1 bundle).
Wiltshire Record Office (Salisbury diocese).

P Stewart, *Guide to the records of the bishop. . . of Salisbury*, 1973.

[34] **BARROW, John** (1735-1811)
RC mission priest, Claughton-on-Brock 1766-1811.

Personal and pastoral corresp and papers 1766-1811 (14 bundles, *c*48 items), incl corresp rel to the establishment of a college for priests in the north 1796-1808 (1 bundle) and to the general fund for clergy (2 bundles).
Lancashire Record Office (RCCl/1). NRA 14963.

Corresp with Robert Bannister, Thomas Eyre, William Gibson, Robert Gradwell and others 1798-1809 and misc papers (*c*60 items).
Ushaw College, Durham (Barrow papers). NRA 13674.

[35] **BATHURST, Catherine Anne** (1825-1907)
Dominican.

Letters to her from JH Newman rel to her religious vocation, to tractarians and RC converts and the establishment of her Dominican houses etc 1853-87 (*c*80 items).
St Dominic's Convent, Stone (H/JHN 1-82). NRA 27580.

[36] **BEARD, Charles** (1827-1888)
Unitarian minister.

Letters to him from John Kenrick, JH Thom and others 1846-86 (45 items).
Mrs J Jephcote. NRA 22203.

[37] **BEARD, John Relly** (1800-1876)
Unitarian minister.

Letters from Sir John Bowring, William Gaskell, Henry Morley, William Mountford, Albert Réville and others 1835-74 (*c*260 items).
John Rylands University Library of Manchester (Unitarian College Manchester MSS).

[38] **BEDFORD, John** (1810-1879)
Wesleyan methodist minister.

Letters to him 1833-67 (12 items); journals of conferences 1849, 1850, 1871, 1873 (8 vols).
Methodist Archives, Manchester.

Private minute book of Wesleyan centenary conference, Liverpool 1839.
Bolton Metropolitan Borough Archives (ZZ/46).

[39] **BEECHAM, John** (1787-1856)
General secretary of the Wesleyan Methodist Missionary Society 1831-55.

Corresp 1829-53 incl letters from Jabez Bunting 1829-44 (20 items), William Lord 1853 (11 items) and others (*c*170 items); misc papers rel to New Zealand 1838 and West Africa 1842.
Methodist Archives, Manchester.

[40] **BELL, George Kennedy Allen** (1883-1958)
Bishop of Chichester 1929-58.

Corresp, diaries and papers (over 320 vols) incl corresp and papers rel to the German churches and ecumenical conferences (over 80 vols), the atomic bomb (*c*6 vols), the World Council of Churches (over 8 vols) and church unity in southern India (*c*6 vols) and diaries and journals (*c*100 vols).
Lambeth Palace Library. Presented by his widow.

Corresp and papers rel to the Community of the Holy Cross, Hayward's Heath 1929-57 (6 vols).
Lambeth Palace Library (MSS 3066-71).

Misc warrants, diplomas and addresses 1919-57 (14 items).
West Sussex Record Office (Add MSS 5922-35). NRA 10519.

[41] **BELSHAM, Thomas** (1750-1829)
Unitarian minister.

Letters from Theophilus Lindsey and his wife, Joseph Priestley and others 1775-1823 (*c*100 items).
Dr Williams's Library, London (12.12-13, 57-8, 80, 24.107). NRA 13168.

Letters to him 1793-1807 (3 items); theological lectures (23 vols), lectures on pneumatology (2 vols) and electricity 1783 (1 vol); notes on ecclesiastical history and the NT (2 vols); sermons.
Manchester College, Oxford. NRA 19870.

[42] **BENNETT, Richard** (1860-1937)
Calvinistic methodist historian.

Letters from MH Jones 1910-30 (163 items), EE Morgan 1905-23 (29 items) and others 1878-1931 (407 items); diaries 1877, 1881, 1891, 1918-19; notebooks containing extracts, historical notes etc; articles, addresses, transcripts of the Trevecca letters, misc papers.
National Library of Wales (Presbyterian Church of Wales MSS, General Collection). NRA 28345.

[43] **BENNETT, William James Early** (1804-1886)
Priest in charge of St Paul, Knightsbridge with St Barnabas, Pimlico 1843-51; vicar of Frome Selwood 1852-86.

'Directory for the celebration of Holy Communion' (1 vol); English mass book, with notes on liturgical practices (1 vol).
Lambeth Palace Library (MSS 1922-3). Purchased 1966.

[44] **BENSON, Christopher** (1789-1868)
Master of the Temple 1826-45.

Corresp and misc papers 1826-45 (85ff).
Inner Temple Library (vol 20). J Conway Davies,
Catalogue of manuscripts ... of the Inner Temple, iii,
1972.

Copies of letters from him on theological issues,
church government etc 1844-61 (82ff).
Lambeth Palace Library (MS 2792).

[45] **BENSON, Edward White** (1829-1896)
Master of Wellington College 1859-72; bishop of
Truro 1877-83; archbishop of Canterbury 1883-
96.

Corresp and papers rel to the affairs of
Wellington College 1852-85 (3 vols, *c*900 items)
incl papers rel to governors' meetings etc 1853-67
(2 vols).
Wellington College, Berks. See David Newsome, *A
history of Wellington College 1859-1959*, 1959.

Corresp and papers mainly rel to Truro diocese
and cathedral 1876-96 (*c*300 bundles and vols
passim).
Cornwall Record Office. Deposited by the dean
and chapter of Truro.

Home and foreign corresp 1883-96 (148 vols);
subject files 1887-96 (26 vols) incl those rel to the
bishopric of Natal 1887 (5 vols), the Clergy
Discipline Act 1893 (5 vols) and Lord Halifax and
reunion 1895 (1 vol); letter register 1880-96 (1
vol); press cuttings with indexes 1882-99 (6 vols).
Lambeth Palace Library. See *Index to the letters
and papers of Edward White Benson ...*, 1980.

Letters from WE Gladstone, Lord Salisbury and
others 1843-96 (65 items), letters from his wife
Mary and his family *c*1850-73 (3 bundles); letters
to his wife 1846-1911 (34 bundles).
Bodleian Library, Oxford (Dep Benson). NRA
16904.

Letters to him and papers rel to alterations in the
printing of the prayer book 1890-6, with his notes
(1 vol).
British Library (Add MS 36656). Presented by his
son AC Benson 1902.

Diaries 1871-96 (16 vols); notebooks and diaries
1849-93 (23 vols); typescript copies of his corresp
(11 vols).
Trinity College, Cambridge. Presented by AC
Benson 1924.

Personal book of Lincoln chapter minutes as
chancellor 1876-7 (1 vol).
Lincolnshire Archives Office (D & C A/4/18).
Deposited by the chancellor of Lincoln Cathedral
1976.

Papers rel to the Lambeth Conference 1878
(25ff); notes of debates at the Conference
attributed to him (1 vol).
Lambeth Palace Library (MSS 1919, 1947).

[46] **BENSON, Joseph** (1749-1821)
Methodist minister; editor of the *Methodist
Magazine* 1804-21.

Corresp 1768-1821 incl letters from John Wesley
1768-72 (8 items), Christopher Hopper 1773-94
(10 items), William Smith 1774-9 (56 items), John
Pawson 1791-1806 (94 items), Keith Keysall rel to
sacramental controversy 1793-1811 (12 items) and
others (*c*420 items); pocket book and accounts
1806 (1 vol); misc papers, incl drafts of letters
and corresp in Latin from 1794 rel to expulsion of
undergraduates from St Edmund Hall Oxford.
Methodist Archives, Manchester.

[47] **BENSON, Richard Meux** (1824-1915)
Founder of the Society of St John the Evangelist
1866, superior 1866-90.

Letters from members of the Society and others
1854-1911 (4 boxes) incl Samuel Wilberforce
1862-5 (*c*15 items); letters to him and papers rel
to the Indian mission *c*1854-88 (3 boxes); letters
from him collected by the Society (8 boxes, 3
bundles, *c*60 items); theological and devotional
papers 1850-1902 (11 boxes); biographical and
misc family papers etc 1915 (3 boxes).
*Society of St John the Evangelist, St Edward's
House, Westminster.*

[48] **BENSON, Robert Hugh** (1871-1914)
Member of the Community of the Resurrection,
Mirfield 1898-1903; RC 1903.

Letters from his mother 1889-1918 (2 bundles)
and to his family 1882-1913 (1 bundle); literary
and devotional MSS (16 items); diary 1896-7.
Bodleian Library, Oxford (Dep Benson). NRA
16904.

[49] **BERESFORD, Lord John George de la
Poer** (1773-1862)
Archbishop of Armagh 1822-62.

Personal and official corresp 1823-62 (722 items);
accounts and misc papers 1787-1863 (65 bundles
and items).
Public Record Office of Northern Ireland (D664).
Presented by Arthur Pack-Beresford *c*1954. NRA
19564.

Corresp and papers rel to estates inherited from
his maternal grandfather, Henry Monck, 1801-54
(3 bundles).
Public Record Office of Northern Ireland (Armagh
diocesan registry DIO 4/13/10-12). NRA 23891.

Papers rel to the government and endowment of
Belfast Academical Institution 1822-8.
Public Record Office of Northern Ireland. See
Deputy Keeper's Report 1926, Appendix D.

Official corresp and papers 1822-65 (11 vols, 15
bundles).

Armagh Diocesan Registry. Copies in Public Record Office of Northern Ireland (T 2772). NRA 20493.

Corresp and papers rel to tithes, visitations, episcopal promotions etc c1823-44 (141 items). *Representative Church Body Library, Dublin* (MS 178). Copies in Public Record Office of Northern Ireland (T 2772). NRA 20493.

Corresp 1825-55 (71 items) and misc papers 1830-7 (24 items) rel to tithes, clerical relief, patronage etc. *Representative Church Body Library, Dublin* (MSS 183, 185). NRA 27251.

Corresp and papers rel to Trinity College Dublin and educational affairs 1828-59 (c880 items). *Trinity College, Dublin* (MSS 2770-4). Acquired from Denis Pack-Beresford 1925-38. NRA 20075.

Letters from Nathaniel Alexander, JH Singer and Edward Stopford, bishops of Meath and other clergy 1842 (147 items). *Meath Diocesan Registry*. Copies in Public Record Office of Northern Ireland (T 2772). NRA 20493.

Corresp rel to Down, Connor and Dromore dioceses 1823-60 (c100 items) incl letters from James Saurin 1827-38 (7 items) and corresp with Richard Mant 1823-43 (c30 items). *Down, Connor and Dromore Diocesan Library, Belfast*. NRA 28017.

Misc letters and papers rel to tithe composition in Cloyne diocese etc 1794-1854 (26 items). *Dean and Chapter of Cloyne*. Copies in Public Record Office of Northern Ireland (T 2772). NRA 20493.

Misc corresp and papers rel to Ossory, Ferns and Leighlin diocese 1825-42 (13 items). *St Canice's Cathedral Library, Kilkenny*. NRA 29204.

[50] **BERINGTON, Charles** (1748-1798)
Bishop coadjutor of the midland district 1786-95; appointed vicar apostolic of the midland district 1795.

Letters to him 1790-8 rel to the blue books and his appointment as vicar apostolic (c30 items) and administrative and financial matters (c25 items). *Archbishop's House, Birmingham*. NRA 8129.

Corresp 1791-8 rel to the Catholic committee and his appointment as vicar apostolic etc (c100 items). *Archbishop's House, Birmingham* (St Mary's College Oscott). NRA 8129.

[51] **BERINGTON, Joseph** (1743-1827)
RC priest, Buckland, Berks 1793-1827.

Corresp with Hannah More 1809, letters from Joseph Nightingale 1811 and John Kirk 1826 (14 items); theological drafts and sermon notes 1791-1825 (c50 items).

Archbishop's House, Birmingham (St Mary's College Oscott). NRA 8129.

Corresp with the Throckmorton family 1789-1827 (25 items); letters to him 1771-1826 (18 items). *Warwick County Record Office* (Throckmorton MSS). NRA 0741.

[52] **BERNARD, John Henry** (1860-1927)
Archbishop of Dublin 1915-19; provost of Trinity College, Dublin 1919-27.

Corresp and papers 1890-1927, mainly rel to Trinity College, (c760 items); letters from provost George Salmon 1891-1903 etc (2 vols and loose items); notebooks 1887-1927 (3 vols); scrapbooks c1923-7, nd (2 vols); address books 1865-1911 (2 vols); papers rel to the Irish Convention 1917 (2 boxes); press cuttings and misc papers. *Trinity College, Dublin* (MSS 2381-93, 2986-7, 3509, 4973, 5872). Mainly deposited in 1927. NRA 20074.

Political corresp with AV Dicey, David Lloyd George and leading southern Irish unionists 1910-26 (1 vol); general corresp 1912-25 (2 vols); literary MSS, proofs, speeches and press cuttings 1912-25 (1 vol). *British Library* (Add MSS 52781-4). Bequeathed by his widow 1940.

[53] **BEWICK, John William** (1824-1886)
Bishop of Hexham and Newcastle 1882-6.

Letter books as vicar general, treasurer and bishop 1860-86 (4 vols); misc letters to him (c30 items). *Northumberland Record Office* (Hexham and Newcastle diocesan archives). NRA 28236.

[54] **BICKERSTETH, Edward Henry** (1825-1906)
Bishop of Exeter 1885-1900.

Corresp and papers 1845-1901 (66ff) incl corresp with WE Gladstone 1874-89 (21ff) and rel to evening communion 1884, 1893 (16ff). *Lambeth Palace Library* (MS 2961). Presented by his great-grandson, the Rt Revd JM Bickersteth 1977.

[55] **BICKERSTETH, Edward Monier** (1882-1976)
Secretary of the Jerusalem and the East Mission 1915-35.

Corresp (9 boxes). *Bodleian Library, Oxford*.

Papers as secretary of the Jerusalem and the East Mission. *St Antony's College, Oxford*.

B

[56] **BICKERSTETH, Samuel** (1857-1937)
Vicar of Leeds 1905-16; canon of Canterbury
1916-37.

Corresp and papers rel to the division of Ripon
diocese 1907-17 (437ff).
Lambeth Palace Library (MS 2948). Presented by
his grandson, the Rt Revd JM Bickersteth 1977.

[57] **BILSBORROW, James Romanus** (1862-
1931)
Archbishop of Cardiff 1916-20.

Corresp and papers (2 files).
Archbishop of Cardiff.

[58] **BIRDSALL, John [Augustine]** (1775-1837)
President-general of the English Benedictine
Congregation 1826-37.

Account of Lamspringe abbey, Hanover 1801-2
with diary of events of 1779-1832 (1 vol); diary of
journey from Lamspringe to Liverpool 1826 (1
vol); 'Account of contest between the Rt Revd
Bishop Baines and the English Benedictines'
(100pp) with misc letters from PA Baines 1823.
Downside Abbey.

[59] **BIRT, Henry [Norbert]** (1861-1914)
Monastic historian.

Collections and papers rel to English Benedictine
history, mainly after 1780 (70 boxes);
transcriptions and notes on MSS (32 vols).
Downside Abbey (Edmund Bishop papers).

[60] **BISHOP, Edmund** (1846-1917)
Liturgiologist and historian.

Corresp 1867-1917 (23 boxes); collected letters to
and papers of EC Butler and JG Doland rel to
Benedictine constitutional reform (2 boxes);
transcriptions, notes and drafts (243 vols) incl
personal diaries and travel journals from 1867,
'secret archives' of Downside movement c1887-
1906 (18 vols) and notebooks and misc
transcriptions by FA Gasquet (c30 vols); misc
bibliographical notes, drafts, corresp on book
purchases etc (2 boxes).
Downside Abbey.

[61] **BISHOP, William Chatterley** (1853-1922)
Rector of Orsett 1900-15.

Corresp 1880-1922 (1 vol); liturgical notes (3
vols); press cuttings and misc notes 1882-c1896 (1
vol); misc letters to him.
Lambeth Palace Library (MSS 1926-30, 1934-5).
Purchased 1962.

[62] **BLACKBURN, John** (1791-1855)
Congregational minister; editor of the
Congregational Magazine.

Corresp with Thomas Binney, George Hadfield
and others, some rel to the *Congregational
Magazine*, 1800-53 (5 vols).
Dr Williams's Library, London (New College
L52/1-6). NRA 13042.

[63] **BLAIKIE, William Garden** (1820-1899)
Professor of apologetics and pastoral theology,
New College, Edinburgh 1868-97.

Notes of the proceedings of the convocation of
November 1842, compiled in 1846 (1 vol);
sermon notes (1 vol).
New College, Edinburgh.

[64] **BLAIR, William** (1830-1916)
Minister of Leighton Church, Dunblane.

Diaries 1848-91 (5 vols); visitation journal 1852-3
(1 vol); commonplace books 1851, 1853 (2 vols);
notebooks etc 1847-c1880 (16 vols); sermons
1853-1903 (17 vols); lectures 1857-66 (6 vols).
National Library of Scotland (Acc 3334).
Purchased 1962. NRA 27989.

[65] **BLAKESLEY, Joseph Williams** (1808-1885)
Vicar of Ware 1845-72; dean of Lincoln 1872-85.

Letters from members of the 'Apostles' and
others 1825-85 (328 items).
Trinity College, Cambridge (Add MS a 243).

Letters from Edward Fitzgerald 1880-2.
Cambridge University Library. Deposited 1979.

Scrapbooks of his newspaper articles and book
reviews.
Trinity College, Cambridge. Deposited 1982.

Papers mainly rel to the living of Ware 1845-73 (1
bundle).
Hertfordshire Record Office (D/P 116 3/4).

[66] **BLOMFIELD, Charles James** (1786-1857)
Bishop of Chester 1824-8, of London 1828-56.

Letter books as bishop of London 1828-55 (60
vols) mainly rel to diocesan affairs, but incl letters
rel to the Bennett controversy, Gorham judgment,
Hampden case, papal aggression etc (3 vols);
corresp and papers rel to individual parishes
1828-55 (8 vols); visitation returns (5 vols).
Lambeth Palace Library (Fulham papers).

Misc corresp 1816-34, incl some with George
Spencer 1826; notebook and letter book 1825-6 (1
vol).
Private. Microfilms in Lambeth Palace Library
(MS Films 19-20).

[67] **BLOXAM, John Rouse** (1807-1891)
Fellow of Magdalen College, Oxford 1836-63;
rector of Upper Beeding 1862-91.

Historical collections and personal papers (50 vols
and bundles, 188 items), incl letters from JH
Newman [1838]-1885 (157 items) and collections
rel to Newman 1801-87 (3 vols), letters from
Ambrose Phillipps de Lisle 1841-57 (1 vol), AW
Pugin c1841-5 (188 items) and MJ Routh 1842-
c1851 (1 vol) and diary as vice-president of
Magdalen 1847 (1 vol).
Magdalen College, Oxford (Old Library MSS 304-
824 *passim*).

[68] **BOGUE, David** (1750-1825)
Congregational minister, Gosport, Hants.

Papers incl diary 1799-1817 (1 box); sermons (4
boxes); lecture notes (10 vols, 4 boxes).
New College, Edinburgh.

[69] **BONAR, John James** (1803-1891)
Minister of St Andrew's Greenock 1835-43; Free
Church of Scotland minister, Greenock from
1843.

Letters from his family 1829-75 (1 vol), Horatius,
James and William Bonar 1829-75 (428ff),
William Cunningham 1828-44 (36ff) and JB
Patterson 1828-35 (32ff).
National Library of Scotland (MSS 15996-8).
Presented by the trustees of JJ Bonar 1974. NRA
27278.

[70] **BOOTH, William** (1829-1912)
Founder of the Salvation Army.

Corresp 1892-1912 (4 boxes); letters to WS Crown
1871-8 (69 items); letters, incl copies, to Elijah
Cadman from him, WB Booth and GS Railton
1876-1913 (97 items); diary 1910-12 (3 vols);
addresses, notes, printed and biographical
material (9 boxes); press cuttings rel to his death
1912 (1 vol).
Salvation Army International Headquarters, London.

[71] **BOUCHER, Jonathan** (1738-1804)
Vicar of Epsom 1785-1804.'

Corresp 1759-1803 (216 items) incl letters from
William Stevens 1777-1803 (90 items) and Charles
Daubeny 1798-1803 (28 items) and letters to John
James 1759-81 (53 items).
East Sussex Record Office. NRA 11600.

Letters from WA Drummond rel to Scottish
episcopalian affairs etc c1789-c1804 (1 bundle).
Scottish Record Office (GD 230). NRA 10137.

[72] **BOURNE, Francis Alphonsus** (1861-1935)
Bishop of Southwark 1897-1903; archbishop of
Westminster 1903-35; cardinal 1911.

Official papers 1903-35 (500 boxes).
Westminster Diocesan Archives.

Papers rel to the foundation of St John's
Seminary, Wonersh (2 boxes); misc papers (1
box).
Southwark Diocesan Archives. NRA 27760.

Corresp and papers as a student 1869-79, incl
European travel notes (12 items); family papers
1845-97 (c90 items).
Ushaw College, Durham (Bourne papers). NRA
13674.

[73] **BOURNE, Hugh** (1772-1852)
Founder of the primitive methodist connexion.

Journals 1803-21, 1842-52 (23 vols); self review
1800 (1 item); autobiographies c1844, 1845,
1850-1 (3 vols); prayers nd.
Methodist Archives, Manchester.

[74] **BOWDEN, Henry George [Sebastian]**
(1836-1920)
Oratorian.

Papers (1 box); diaries and notes 1898-1917 (24
vols); engagement diaries 1902-18 (10 vols).
The Oratory, London. NRA 16631.

[75] **BOWDEN, John Edward** (1829-1874)
Oratorian.

Corresp and papers, with collections for his *Life
and letters* of FW Faber 1869, incl letters from
Faber 1848-63 (123 items), JH Newman 1835-69
(18 items) and WA Hutchison 1850 (14 items);
family corresp and papers 1848-72, particularly
concerning Faber's illness and death 1862-3.
The Oratory, London. NRA 16631.

[76] **BOWDEN, John William** (1798-1844)
Ecclesiastical writer.

Letters to him and his wife Elizabeth from JH
Newman 1822-86 (2 vols).
The Oratory, London. NRA 16631.

Family papers.
The Oratory, Birmingham. NRA 27809.

[77] **BOYD, Archibald** (1803-1883)
Dean of Exeter 1867-83.

Estate, testamentary and misc family corresp and
papers 1825-1907 (26 bundles).
Devon Record Office (1926 13/BO). NRA 6747.

[78] **BRADBURN, Samuel** (1751-1816)
Methodist preacher.

Letters from John Wesley 1776-9 (9 items),
Charles Wesley 1786-7 (5 items) and others 1776-
1816 (10 items); collected letters from him, with
family papers, sermons etc (c50 items); diaries
and memoranda books 1774-1815 (5 vols); copies
of hymns and rules in preaching, indexes to
hymns (4 vols).
Methodist Archives, Manchester.

Collections of hymns (1 vol).
London Library. NRA 20043.

[79] **BRADFORD, Henry** (1843-1923)
Baptist minister of Union Church, Northampton
1884-1912.

Corresp and misc papers 1874-1934 (638 items),
mainly letters rel to the establishment of Union
Church from Sir William and Lady King-Hall (87
items), Edward Wilkinson (47 items) and others
(299 items).
Northamptonshire Record Office. Deposited by
Miss KF Bradford 1962-5. NRA 11858.

[80] **BRADLEY, George Granville** (1821-1903)
Dean of Westminster 1881-1902.

Corresp as dean 1882-1902 (c200 items).
Westminster Abbey (WAM 59329-59477, 61729-73
and *passim*).

[81] **BRAITHWAITE, Anna** (1788-1859)
Quaker minister.

Letters to her and her husband Isaac 1801-52 (98
items).
Society of Friends Library, London (Temp MSS
114). Presented by AW Braithwaite 1971.

[82] **BRAITHWAITE, Joseph Bevan** (1818-
1905)
Quaker minister.

Misc corresp and papers 1834-1903 (c50 items);
private memoranda books 1865-76, 1882-1905 (4
vols); commonplace book (1 vol).
Society of Friends Library, London (MS Vols s 293-
6, 358).

[83] **BRAITHWAITE, Martha (née Gillett)**
(1823-1895)
Quaker minister.

Extracts from memoranda books 1837-42 (1 vol);
journals 1842-95 (30 vols); European travel
journal 1875 (1 vol).
Society of Friends Library, London (MS Vols s 301-
32).

[84] **BRAITHWAITE, William Charles** (1862-
1922)
Quaker minister.

Diary of Five Years Meeting 1912 (1 vol); travel
diaries 1883-1920 (5 vols); notes and papers rel to
a new map of Friends' meetings c1891 (1 vol, 1
bundle).
Society of Friends Library, London (MS Vols s 91,
333-8, Temp MSS 106/2). Mainly deposited by
AW Braithwaite 1958.

[85] **BRAMSTON, James Yorke** (1763-1836)
Vicar apostolic of the London district 1827-36.

Corresp and papers as vicar apostolic (7 boxes)
incl corresp with Rome and pastorals (2 boxes),
corresp with other bishops and London district
clergy (1 box), with other clergy incl John Kirk
and John Lingard (1 box), with clergy abroad and
emigré clergy (2 boxes); letters from NPS
Wiseman and PA Baines at Rome 1829-36 (c50
items); diary, Rome 1815.
Westminster Diocesan Archives (A69-75, W1/2,
2/4/1, Z42). NRA 28616.

Diary of journey to Rome 1814-15 (1 vol).
Westminster Diocesan Archives (St Edmund's
College Ware, series 15). NRA 16303.

Letters to him rel to Gibraltar 1835-6 (1 bundle).
Southwark Diocesan Archives. NRA 27760.

[86] **BRANSBY, James Hews** (1783-1847)
Unitarian minister.

Corresp (3 vols).
John Rylands University Library of Manchester
(Unitarian College Manchester MSS).

[87] **BRIGGS, John** (1788-1861)
President of Ushaw College 1832-6; vicar
apostolic of the northern district 1836-40, of the
Yorkshire district 1840-50; bishop of Beverley
1850-60.

Corresp and papers as a student and mission
priest 1805-33 (3 bundles); corresp and papers
1833-60 (c2,800 items) incl letters from Thomas
Grant from 1836 (60 items) and letter books as
bishop of Beverley.
Bishop of Leeds.

Corresp and papers 1833-56 (c50 items) incl
letters from Ralph Platt 1810, George Newsham
and George Brown 1841-51; papers rel to affairs
of the northern district, restoration of the
hierarchy and the establishment of the diocese of
Beverley.
Ushaw College, Durham (President's archives and
passim). NRA 13674.

Letters to him mainly rel to mission funds (c55
items).
Northumberland Record Office (Hexham and
Newcastle diocesan archives). NRA 28236.

[88] BRIGHT, William (1824-1901)
Regius professor of ecclesiastical history, Oxford 1868-1901.

Letters from HP Liddon 1861-90 (3 vols); diaries rel to his friendship with WH Seary 1873-1901 (2 vols); antiquarian notebooks c1882-7, nd (3 vols); financial and legal papers 1830-1911 (15 vols, 2 boxes).
Bodleian Library, Oxford (MSS Eng lett d 300-2 and *passim*). NRA 16752.

[89] BRINDLE, Robert (1837-1916)
Bishop of Nottingham 1901-15.

Corresp and papers 1902-15, incl letters from Rome 1902-15 (12 items), financial corresp 1902-3 (1 box), general corresp 1902-13 (15 items), sermons and addresses 1860-1915 (c24 items).
Bishop of Nottingham. NRA 27317.

[90] BRISCOE, Thomas (1813-1895)
Fellow of Jesus College, Oxford 1834-59; vicar of Holyhead 1857-95.

Letters from DL Lloyd, John Williams 'Ab Ithel' and other scholars and churchmen 1850-94 (1 vol).
National Library of Wales (MS 7939).

[91] BROADHEAD, Joseph (1860-1929)
Vice-president of Ushaw College 1910-29; monsignor.

Letters mainly from Raphael Merry del Val 1900-29 (102 items).
Ushaw College, Durham (Merry del Val papers). NRA 13674.

[92] BRODRICK, Charles (1761-1822)
Archbishop of Cashel 1801-22.

Personal, family and ecclesiastical corresp and papers c1780-1822 (c25 vols) incl letters from William Bennet 1802-20 (1 vol), John Jebb 1801-22 (1 vol), TL O'Beirne 1803-22 (1 vol) and Richard Woodward 1787-94 (1 vol).
National Library of Ireland (MSS 8861-95). See *Manuscript sources for the history of Irish civilisation*, 1965.

Corresp and papers 1782-1824 (6 vols).
Surrey Record Office, Guildford (1248/14-19). NRA 1351.

Letter book Apr-July 1784.
The Town Clerk, Midleton, Cork. See *Manuscript sources for the history of Irish civilisation*, 1965.

[93] BROOKE, Charles (1777-1852)
Provincial of the Society of Jesus in England 1826-32; superior of Stonyhurst College 1832-45.

Collected letters to him; letters from Thomas Glover; historical notes and transcripts for a

history of the English province since 1635 (2 vols); diary notes for 1777-1852.
Society of Jesus, London.

[94] BROWN, George Hilary (1786-1856)
Vicar apostolic of the Lancashire district 1840-50; bishop of Liverpool 1850-6.

Letters to him as bishop (13 boxes *passim*); corresp and papers rel to financial and other district and diocesan affairs (2 boxes) incl letters from Thomas Grant 1840-8 (c30 items); misc letters to him (c100 items); engagement diary 1840-50 (1 vol).
Lancashire Record Office (Liverpool archdiocesan records).

[95] BROWN, James (1812-1881)
RC bishop of Shrewsbury 1851-81.

Diary 1850-81 (1 vol).
Bishop of Shrewsbury.

[96] BROWN, John (1754-1832)
Minister of the Burgher Church, Whitburn, West Lothian 1776-1832.

Letters from ministers and schoolmasters in the Highlands and Islands about translations of the catechism and tracts into Gaelic 1805-26 (c60 items).
New College, Edinburgh.

[97] BROWN, Richard (1806-1868)
Rector of St Peter's RC church, Lancaster 1840-68.

Papers rel to the building of St Peter's 1845-63 (3 bundles, c10 items); commonplace book on RC church affairs in Lancaster from 1865; papers rel to parochial affairs etc (c4 bundles); personal and church account books 1845-68 (3 vols).
Lancashire Record Office (RCLn). NRA 19475.

Diary 1825 (1 vol).
English College, Rome (Scritture 122).

[98] BROWN, Thomas Joseph (1798-1880)
Vicar apostolic of the Welsh district 1840-50; bishop of Newport and Menevia 1850-80.

Corresp and papers of or rel to him (20 files) incl corresp rel to diocesan affairs, relations with Rome and other bishops, corresp with HE Manning from 1865, accounts etc.
Archbishop of Cardiff.

[99] BROWN, William Francis (1862-1951)
RC rector of St Anne, Vauxhall 1892-1951; auxiliary bishop of Southwark 1924-51.

Papers (5 boxes), incl material rel to the Education Acts 1902-8, 1936-44, his apostolic

visitation of Scotland 1917, and the Education (Scotland) Act 1918, draft essays, Scottish consistorial papers, misc papers, personal memoranda and autobiography.
Southwark Diocesan Archives. NRA 27760.

[100] **BROWNLOW, William Robert** (1830-1901)
Bishop of Clifton 1894-1901.

Letters from Rome (1 vol *passim*); misc papers incl pastoral letters (1 vol); letter books 1894-1901 (2 vols).
Bristol Record Office (Clifton diocesan records).

Letters from JH Newman (2 bundles); scrapbooks 1860-94 (3 vols).
Bishop of Clifton.

[101] **BUCKLAND, William** (1784-1856)
Dean of Westminster 1845-56.

Letters from churchmen 1833-49 (60ff).
Bodleian Library, Oxford (MS Eng lett d 5).

Letters from Sir Robert Peel 1836-49 (55 items).
Beinecke Library, Yale University, New Haven (Osborn collection MS d 61). NRA 18661.

Corresp 1818-54 (*c*300 items).
Royal Society.

Scientific, personal and family corresp and papers etc 1800-1956 (*c*700 items).
Devon Record Office (138 M). NRA 11695.

See also HMC, *The manuscript papers of British scientists 1600-1940*, 1982.

[102] **BULL, WILLIAM** (1738-1814)
Congregational minister, Newport Pagnell 1764-1814.

Letters from John Thornton, Hannah Wilberforce and others 1763-1809 (1 vol); corresp with John Newton 1773-1804 (1 vol).
Lambeth Palace Library (MSS 3095, 3097).

[103] **BUNTING, Jabez** (1779-1858)
Wesleyan methodist minister.

Corresp 1806-57 incl letters from John Beecham, Joseph Entwisle, Robert Newstead and others (*c*2,100 items); letters of thanks from ministers received into full connexion 1812, 1836; sermon registers 1803-11 (1 vol); sermons (126 items); memoranda book 1795-1804 (1 vol); misc personal and controversial papers (1 box).
Methodist Archives, Manchester.

[104] **BURDER, George [Bernard]** (1814-1881)
Abbot of Mount St Bernard 1853-8.

Corresp and papers as abbot 1853-8 (3 boxes).
Mount St Bernard Abbey, Coalville.

[105] **BURGESS, Thomas** (1756-1837)
Bishop of St Davids 1803-25, of Salisbury 1825-37.

Corresp with churchmen and scholars 1778-1837 (7 vols) incl letters from Shute Barrington 1785-1825 (25 items), Ralph Churton 1811-28 (22 items), Charles Daubeny 1809-25 (15 items), GI Huntingford 1790-1831 (20 items) and GW Marriott 1823-33 (45 items); misc letters and papers, incl some rel to JS Harford's *Life*, 1825-40 (1 vol).
Bodleian Library, Oxford (MSS Eng lett c133-140). Purchased 1949.

Letters to him mainly on classical subjects 1779-1837 (158ff) incl letters from Thomas Tyrwhitt 1779-86 (53 items).
British Library (Add MS 46847).

Letters from archdeacons Thomas Beynon and HT Payne and others rel to an inscribed stone at Myddfai 1825 (8 items).
National Library of Wales (MS 14883).

[106] **BURGESS, Thomas** (1791-1854)
Bishop of Clifton 1851-4.

Letters from Rome (1 vol *passim*); misc papers incl pastoral letters (1 vol *passim*).
Bristol Record Office (Clifton diocesan records).

[107] **BURGON, John William** (1813-1888)
Dean of Chichester 1876-88.

Letters to him about his protest against Frederick Temple's nomination as bishop of Exeter 1869-70 (1 vol) and his appointment as dean 1875-6 (3 vols); pamphlets, sermons and related corresp 1838-82 (10 vols), incl letters from EB Pusey 1873, with copies of his replies (58ff).
Bodleian Library, Oxford (MSS Eng th d 8-21). Deposited by his descendant CH Rose 1916. NRA 27378.

Collation of three Greek gospel MSS 1853 (1 vol) and index of NT texts referred to by patristic authors compiled by or for him 1872-88 (16 vols).
British Library (Add MSS 33421-36, 39317).

[108] **BURKITT, Francis Crawford** (1864-1935)
Norrisian professor of divinity, Cambridge 1905-35.

Letters to him (*c*1,050 items), lectures, articles and misc papers.
Cambridge University Library (Add 7658).

[109] **BURTON, Edward** (1794-1836)
Regius professor of divinity, Oxford 1829-36.

Letters from theologians with some draft replies 1824-33 (3 vols).
Shrewsbury School.

[110] **BURTON, Edwin Hubert** (1870-1925)
Vice-president 1902-16 and president 1916-18 of
St Edmund's College, Ware; RC canon of
Westminster 1917.

Letters from BN Ward, mainly to him, 1897-1918
(175 items); letters and misc papers mainly rel to
the college 1885-1918 (*c*260 items); sermons,
historical, literary and theological papers (53
items).
Westminster Diocesan Archives (St Edmund's
College Ware, series 13). NRA 16303.

[111] **BURTON, George Ambrose** (1852-1931)
Bishop of Clifton 1902-31.

Letters to him 1902-28 (14 vols).
Bishop of Clifton.

Letter book 1901-30 (1 vol); appointment diaries
1905-9, 1917-31 (3 vols); sermons *c*1890 (1 vol);
addresses to him (3 vols).
Bristol Record Office (Clifton diocesan records).

Student diary 1884-90 (1 vol).
English College, Rome (Libri 824).

[112] **BUTLER, Charles** (1750-1832)
Secretary to the committee of English Catholics
for repeal of the penal laws and to the Cisalpine
Club 1782-1828.

Papers as secretary to the Catholic committee incl
minutes 1782-92 and related documents.
British Library (Add MSS 5416, 7961-2).
Presented by him.

Letter books on legal, literary and RC matters in
England and Ireland 1808-18 (3 vols).
British Library (Add MSS 25127-9). Presented
1863.

MS of 'Additions to Mr Butler's historical
memoirs of the English, Irish and Scottish Roman
Catholics' (1 vol); papers rel to Stonyhurst
College 1818-22.
Westminster Diocesan Archives (F7). Presented by
Butler to William Poynter 1822.

Family corresp 1770-5 (1 vol) incl letters from
Alban Butler 1770-3 (23 items); misc corresp and
papers 1782-1829 rel to Catholic relief acts.
Westminster Diocesan Archives (St Edmund's
College Ware, series 12.) NRA 16303.

[113] **BUTLER, Edward Joseph Aloysius**
[Cuthbert] (1858-1934)
Abbot of Downside 1906-22; president of the
English Benedictine Congregation 1914-21.

Misc corresp and papers incl letters from FA
Gasquet, Alban Goodier and Friedrich von Hügel
(9 bundles); collections rel to Benedictine
constitutional reform 1880-1900 incl letters to HE
Ford 1891-9 and papers for chapter meetings (5
boxes, 2 bundles); personal notebooks (10 vols);
theological notebooks (*c*30 vols); historical and

theological working papers incl MSS, etc of
published and unpublished works (2 boxes, *c*52
bundles and vols); corresp, etc rel to publishers
and publications (1 box, 2 bundles).
Downside Abbey.

Notebooks on the history of the Downside
movement (9 vols).
Downside Abbey (Edmund Ford papers).

[114] **BUTLER, George** (1819-1890)
Principal of Liverpool College 1866-82; canon of
Winchester 1882-90.

Corresp with his family, sermons and misc papers
of and rel to him *c*1825-90 (*c*130 items).
Northumberland Record Office (ZBU E2).
Deposited by H St Paul Butler 1966. NRA 0580.

Letters, etc to him and his wife Josephine 1816-
1907 (102 items).
St Andrews University Library (MSS 30,017-118).
Presented by ASG Butler 1963. NRA 0456.

[115] **BUTLER, Henry Montagu** (1833-1918)
Headmaster of Harrow School 1859-85; master of
Trinity College, Cambridge 1886-1918.

Corresp with his family and others; journals and
diaries 1858-1917; theological notes and misc
papers.
Trinity College, Cambridge (JRM Butler papers).

Corresp with BF Westcott 1861-97 (23 items) and
misc corresp 1860-85 (56 items); headmaster's
book 1874-85; sermons 1862, 1865 (2 items).
Harrow School. NRA 27630.

Letters from his nephew Sir SH Butler 1891-7.
India Office Library and Records (MSS Eur F
116). NRA 27526.

Letters to him 1896 (52 items).
Trinity College, Cambridge (Add MS a 67).
Deposited 1974. NRA 8804.

[116] **BUTLER, James** (d 1791)
RC archbishop of Cashel 1774-91.

Papers 1764-90.
Archbishop of Cashel. See *Manuscript sources for the
history of Irish civilisation: first supplement*, 1979.

[117] **BUTLER, Samuel** (1774-1839)
Headmaster of Shrewsbury School 1798-1836;
bishop of Lichfield and Coventry 1836-9.

Corresp and papers 1764-1839 (16 vols).
British Library (Add MSS 34583-98). Presented by
his grandson Samuel Butler 1894.

Corresp 1798-1836 (1 vol).
Shrewsbury Local Studies Library (MS 135).
Presented by Samuel Butler 1896. NRA 19299.

Diary 1836; collected letters from him as headmaster 1805-39 (45 items); misc literary papers etc, some printed (6 items).
Shrewsbury School.

[118] **BUTLER, Weeden** (1742-1823)
Preacher at Pimlico chapel 1776-1814.

Letters from clergy and others 1765-1801 (2 vols); corresp, mainly with James Neild rel to the relief of small debtors 1808-11, (2 vols); collections for his *Memoirs of . . . Mark Hildesley* with related corresp, papers etc 1745-1801 (11 vols).
British Library (Add MSS 19024-5, 19682-92, 27577-8). Presented by Thomas Butler 1852-67.

[119] **BUTLER, William John** (1818-1894)
Vicar of Wantage 1846-81; dean of Lincoln 1885-94.

Journals of parish events and related papers 1847-86 (6 vols, 94 items).
Berkshire Record Office (D/P 143).

Sermons (1 bundle) and misc papers.
Community of St Mary the Virgin, Wantage.

[120] **BUTT, John** (1826-1899)
RC bishop of Southwark 1885-97.

Corresp with the Admiralty, Colonial and War Offices 1883-95 and personal and financial papers (3 boxes); letters from the Howard family, Dukes of Norfolk 1885-97 (several bundles); engagement diaries 1872-94 (15 vols); personal diaries 1888, 1891, 1892 (3 vols); official diaries 1885-96; corresp register 1885-6 (1 vol); address to the clergy 1870 (1 vol).
Southwark Diocesan Archives. NRA 27760.

[121] **CADOUX, Cecil John** (1883-1947)
Congregational theologian.

Corresp 1900-47 (50 boxes) and papers rel to his publications.
Bodleian Library, Oxford. Acquired 1984.

[122] **CAIRD, Edward** (1835-1908)
Professor of moral philosophy, Glasgow 1866-93; master of Balliol College, Oxford 1893-1907.

Personal corresp incl letters from the Empress Frederick of Germany, Benjamin Jowett and others 1872-1906 (c140 items); letters to him, mainly as master of Balliol, 1877-1908 (c 64 items); misc letters and papers rel to him c1873-1967 (c20 items).
Balliol College, Oxford.

Letters to him, chiefly on Balliol matters, 1889-1903 (31ff).
National Library of Scotland (MS 3218).

[123] **CAMERON, Alexander** (1747-1828)
Vicar apostolic of the lowland district, Scotland 1805-25.

Corresp and papers as vicar apostolic; accounts 1794-1823 (3 bundles); papers rel to French and Spanish affairs, notes on the Scottish mission etc (10 bundles).
Scottish Catholic Archives (B 3; BL 5, 10; SM 10).

[124] **CAMERON, John Kennedy** (1860-1944
Professor of systematic theology, Free Church College, Edinburgh 1906-1944.

Autobiography c1940 incl notes rel to the Free Church of Scotland c1922 (2 vols); misc papers incl retiring speech as moderator.
National Library of Scotland (Acc 6557).

[125] **CAMM, Reginald [Bede]** (1864-1942)
Master of Benet House, Cambridge 1919-31.

Letters from RH Benson, FA Gasquet, Raphael Merry del Val, JH Pollen, GA Vallance and others c1910-25 (7 boxes, 2 bundles); diaries 1886-1918 (1 box); papers rel to Caldey abbey and St Bride's convent, Milford Haven (1 box); academic notebooks 1887-8 (1 box); memoirs of Thomas Wilkinson and Wilfrid Wallace (2 bundles); transcripts and research papers on English martyrs, rood-screens and rood-lofts (11 boxes, 3 vols); misc MSS (2 boxes).
Downside Abbey. NRA 19936.

[126] **CARLYLE, Benjamin Fearnley [Aelred]** (1874-1955)
Benedictine.

Letters received in Canada, with copies of his replies, 1921-51 (15 boxes); family corresp (5 boxes); diaries 1929-55 (13 vols); corresp registers and interview diaries 1937-c1941; constitutions for oblate brothers and 'The English Order of St Benedict' 1895 (1 vol) and other misc anglican papers.
Prinknash Abbey. See *Catholic Archives*, 5, 1985.

[127] **CARPENTER, Joseph Estlin** (1844-1927)
Principal of Manchester College, Oxford 1906-15.

Letters from James Martineau 1860-98 (74 items), PE Richards 1899-1919 (124 items) and others 1879-1926 (166 items); notebooks on the NT, historical topics etc (c15 vols).
Manchester College, Oxford.

[128] **CARPENTER, Lant** (1780-1840)
Unitarian minister.

Letters from Thomas Belsham, Mrs Newcome Cappe, Lord Ebrington, John Young and others 1799-1839 (c139 items); letters to Carpenter and others rel to his works 1805-77 (1 bundle, 8

items); letters from America 1822-39 (45 items); corresp with and rel to Rammohun Roy and his funeral 1831-3 (11 items).
Manchester College, Oxford.

[129] CARPENTER, William Boyd (1841-1918)
Bishop of Ripon 1884-1911; canon of Westminster 1911-18; clerk of the closet 1903-18.

Corresp with Queen Victoria and officials of the royal household 1883-1900 (4 vols); letters from members of the British, Prussian and Russian royal families 1884-1918 (2 vols); general corresp and index 1878-1918 (3 vols); diaries 1885-1917 (33 vols); sermons etc 1862-1918 (6 vols); misc papers 20th cent (1 vol).
British Library (Add MSS 46717-65). Presented by his daughter Mrs Mary Wentworth-Sheilds 1948.

[130] CARR, Robert James (1774-1841)
Bishop of Chichester 1824-31, of Worcester 1831-41.

Family and personal corresp mainly with George IV, the royal family, bishops and statesmen (1 bundle).
TR Fetherstonhaugh Esq. NRA 5685.

[131] CARR, Thomas (1788-1859)
Bishop of Bombay 1837-51; rector of Bath abbey 1854-9.

Letters (1 vol) and copy of his diary (18 vols).
Buckinghamshire Record Office (D/MH). NRA 0001.

[132] CARROLL, John (1838-1897)
RC bishop of Shrewsbury 1895-7.

Letter book as bishop, with letters of Edmund Knight, 1895-1901 (1 vol).
Bishop of Shrewsbury.

[133] CARRUTHERS, Andrew (1770-1852)
Vicar apostolic of the eastern district, Scotland 1832-52.

Corresp and papers, mainly as vicar apostolic, 1797-1852 (c22 bundles) incl letters from JF Kyle 1836-51 (67 items) and James Gillis 1840-4 (28 items).
Scottish Catholic Archives (ED 1).

[134] CARTER, Thomas Thellusson (1808-1901)
Rector of Clewer, Berks 1844-80 and founder of the Community of St John the Baptist, Clewer 1852.

Corresp rel to the Community of St John the Baptist etc (c350 items) incl letters from EW Benson, WE Gladstone, John Keble, HE

Manning, JM Neale, JH Newman, Henry Phillpotts, EB Pusey and others c1850-90; sermons, retreat notes etc (c15 bundles).
Convent of St John the Baptist, Clewer, Berks.

[135] CARY-ELWES, Dudley Charles (1868-1932)
Bishop of Northampton 1921-32.

Corresp as bishop with Rome and other bishops (1 bundle), with clergy and laity (6 bundles) and with parishes (113 bundles); historical collections for Peterborough (1 box).
Bishop of Northampton.

Diaries, incl travels in Europe and Australasia, 1887-92 (7 vols).
Northamptonshire Record Office. NRA 23057.

[136] CASARTELLI, Louis Charles (1852-1925)
Bishop of Salford 1903-25.

Corresp and papers 1866-1924, mainly letters to him (4 bundles, c200 items) rel to scholarly, educational and ecclesiastical concerns, from HA Vaughan 1874-7 (71 items), Columba Marmion 1903-5 (c50 items), Pius XI 1909-21 (4 items) and others; letter books 1913-24 (7 boxes, 13 vols); diaries 1866, 1871-1924 (c65 vols); MSS of translations from Sanskrit and Avestan.
Bishop of Salford.

Journals at Louvain 1876-7, Louvain and Manchester 1884, 1896 and in Belgium 1900.
Ushaw College, Durham. NRA 13674.

[137] CASWALL, Edward (1819-1878)
Oratorian.

Letters from his family and others (6 files); diaries 1846-7 (2 vols); theological and other notebooks, sermons and literary papers; community journal 1854-5 (1 vol); papers as treasurer, minister and prefect of the Little Oratory.
The Oratory, Birmingham. NRA 27809. National Library of Ireland, *Annual Report* 1951-2, p15.

[138] CECIL, Richard (1748-1810)
Minister to St John's Chapel, Bedford Row, London 1780-1810.

Diary of prayers and reflections 1806-7 (1 vol); sermons and sermon notes 1789-90, nd (3 vols); notes on preaching, reminiscences etc (1 vol); collections from his unpublished papers by J Cecil (1 vol).
Ridley Hall, Cambridge. NRA 1109.

[139] CHALMERS, Thomas (1780-1847)
Theologian.

Corresp and papers incl letters to him 1792-1847 (formerly 34 vols), corresp and papers rel to

parish work in Glasgow and West Port,
Edinburgh, church extension, convocation of
1842 etc (c2,300 items); collected letters 1792-
1847 (c700 items); journals 1803-46 (15 vols);
commonplace books, notebooks 1803-47 (10 vols);
lectures, class books etc 1802-47; sermons 1796-
1847 (c500 items); speeches 1803-47 (262 items);
corresp, notebooks etc of his wife and children
1808-1962 (c2,250 items).
New College, Edinburgh. NRA 27818.

Letters to him 1810-25 (439 items).
St Andrews University Library. RP Sturges,
Economists' papers 1750-1950, 1975.

Lectures on the *Epistle to the Romans* (25 items).
Strathclyde Regional Archives (TD 584).

[140] **CHARLES, David** (1812-1878)
Calvinistic methodist minister; principal of
Trevecca College 1842-62.

Diaries 1830-48, 1874-8 (3 vols); sermon notes
1852-78 (1 vol); estate accounts 1849-78 (2 vols);
misc family corresp and papers 1833-79.
National Library of Wales (MSS 4799-4807).

[141] **CHARLES, Thomas** (1755-1814)
Calvinistic methodist minister, Bala.

Corresp 1778-1814 (2 vols); sermons (1 vol).
National Library of Wales (MSS 4796-8).

Letters from Lady Ann Erskine 1792-1802 (8
items) and others 1788-1806 (6 items); letters
from him 1783/4, 1791 (2 items); sermons (3
items).
National Library of Wales (Presbyterian Church of
Wales MSS, General Collection). NRA 28345.

[142] **CHAVASSE, Christopher Maude** (1884-
1962)
Master of St Peter's Hall, Oxford 1929-39; bishop
of Rochester 1940-60.

Letters from his father FJ Chavasse 1895-1918
(115 items); corresp rel to the Church of England
in South Africa 1930-6 and evangelical unity
1941-3; sermons 1910-62 (15 boxes); press
cuttings 1939-62 (4 vols).
Bodleian Library, Oxford. Deposited by St Peter's
College. NRA 27561.

[143] **CHAVASSE, Francis James** (1846-1928)
Principal of Wycliffe Hall, Oxford 1889-1900;
bishop of Liverpool 1900-23.

Corresp 1869-1927 (c500 items) incl letters from
his sons Christopher c1890-1918 (c100 items) and
Noel c1890-1917 (c200 items) and rel to the
building of Liverpool cathedral 1900-26 (c100
items); essays, notebooks and lecture notes c1860-
c1900 (10 vols, 4 boxes); diaries 1862-8, 1878 (7
vols); notes at bishop's meetings 1900-20 (3 vols);

sermons 1877-1925 (29 vols); press cuttings 1900-
28 (2 vols).
Bodleian Library, Oxford. Deposited by St Peter's
College. NRA 27561.

[144] **CHEYNE, Thomas Kelly** (1841-1915)
Oriel professor of the interpretation of Holy
Scripture, Oxford 1886-1908.

Letters to him from churchmen and others
[1859]-1891 (90ff).
Bodleian Library, Oxford (MS Eng lett e 28).

[145] **CHURCH, Richard William** (1815-1890)
Dean of St Paul's 1871-90.

Letters from JH Newman (98 items); working
papers for *The Oxford Movement* (3 vols); sermons
(1 bundle).
Pusey House, Oxford.

Letters to him 1850-90, mainly rel to his efforts
to obtain copies of JH Newman's letters, (12
items) and misc papers rel to Newman.
Oriel College, Oxford.

[146] **CHURTON, Edward** (1800-1874)
Archdeacon of Cleveland 1846-74.

Corresp and papers 1831-72 incl letters to him
1841-55 (63 items), letters to Joshua Watson
1842-51 (24 items) and RI Wilberforce 1845-54
(103 items), visitation charges 1846-72 (17 items)
and sermons 1832-72 (96 items).
Pusey House, Oxford. NRA 29544.

Misc corresp 1846-50.
Magdalene College, Cambridge (Inge papers).

[147] **CLARK, George** (1777-1848)
Chaplain of the Royal Military Asylum, Chelsea
1804-48.

Corresp 1795-1839 (3 vols); commonplace book (1
vol); diary 1817 (1 vol); notes, misc papers and
copies of corresp 1804-39 (4 vols).
National Library of Wales. Presented by WD
Clark. *Annual Report* 1948-9, p20.

Sermons annotated by his son GT Clark c1805-47
(21 vols).
London University Library (MS 577). Purchased
1963, 1965.

[148] **CLARKE, Adam** (c1762-1832)
Methodist theologian.

Corresp 1786-1832 (c165 items) incl corresp with
John Wesley 1786-91 (37 items) and letters from
Sarah Wesley 1809-23 (15 items).
Wesley College, Bristol (D6/1, 2). From his papers
presented to Wesley College, Headingley. NRA
27694.

Corresp 1780-1832 incl letters from Joseph Benson and his wife (51 items) and collected letters from him (92 items); misc notes.
Methodist Archives, Manchester.

Letters to his wife and children and later family corresp rel to the publication of his biography 1739-1875 (301 items).
William R Perkins Library, Duke University, Durham, N Carolina.

Letters, mainly to his wife, 1794-1828 (59 items).
University of Chicago Library. See *National union catalog MS 64-69.*

Letters and misc papers c1808-31 (23ff) incl letters rel to his work for the Record Commission 1808-16 (4 items).
Bodleian Library, Oxford (MS Eng lett c12).

[149] **CLAUGHTON, Piers Calverley** (1814-1884)
Bishop of St Helena 1859-62, of Colombo 1862-70; archdeacon of London 1870-84.

Letters and papers 1837-75 (95ff).
Lambeth Palace Library (MS 1751).

Papers rel to Repton School 1841-85 (70ff).
Lambeth Palace Library (MS 1812). Presented by AO Claughton.

[150] **CLAUGHTON, Thomas Legh** (1808-1892)
Bishop of Rochester 1867-77, of St Albans 1877-90.

Diary c1837-63, 1887 (1 vol).
Lambeth Palace Library (MS 1835).

[151] **CLAY, John** (1796-1858)
Chaplain of Preston gaol 1823-58.

Corresp, with some of his son Walter Lowe Clay, 1821-73 (1 vol, 37 items), mainly rel to crime and prisons.
William R Perkins Library, Duke University, Durham, N Carolina (MS 1087).

[152] **CLAYTON, Charles** (1813-1883)
Secretary to the Church Pastoral Aid Society 1845-7; rector of Stanhope, co Durham 1865-83.

Letters to him, notes and misc papers 1833-79 (c130 items); notebooks etc 1833-76 (8 vols); summaries of his diaries 1833-54 (2 vols) and diaries 1876-83 (2 vols).
Gonville and Caius College Library, Cambridge. Deposited 1971.

Letters to him as secretary of the Cambridge University Missionary Association 1848-83 (12 items).
Church Missionary Society, London (Unofficial papers Acc 140). NRA 22944.

[153] **CLAYTON, Nicholas** (1730-1797)
Unitarian minister, Liverpool and Nottingham.

Letters to him, mainly from members of the Nicholson family, 1785-95 (118 items).
Liverpool Record Office (920 NIC). Purchased 1967. NRA 26481.

[154] **CLAYTON, Philip Thomas Byard** (1885-1972)
Founder of Toc H.

Corresp and papers, mainly rel to Toc H after the first world war, c1910-72 (c70 boxes).
Guildhall Library, London. Deposited 1983.

Collected corresp and papers rel to Toc H during the first world war 1914-20 (2 boxes).
Imperial War Museum. Presented 1982.

[155] **CLEAVER, Euseby** (1747-1819)
Archbishop of Dublin 1809-19.

Letter books 1798-1819 (5 vols); draft letters (6 items); letters from JB Gordon 1802 about his *History of the Rebellion* (2 items); notebook rel to Roscommon estates c1808.
Representative Church Body Library, Dublin (MS 328). Presented by RDM Cleaver. NRA 28014.

Account book 1772-84 mainly as rector of Spofforth, Yorkshire.
West Sussex Record Office (Add MS 1930).

[156] **CLIFFORD, William Joseph Hugh** (1823-1893)
Bishop of Clifton 1857-93.

Corresp 1851, 1857-70 (3 bundles) incl letters rel to the Roman Catholic Charities Act 1860; notes, transcripts, lectures, sermons c1855-90 (5 bundles, 3 vols) incl MS of his history of the bull *Romanos Pontifices*; personal mission accounts 1873-1901 (1 vol); diaries 1854-5, 1880-93 (16 vols); press cuttings etc rel to his death 1893 (1 vol).
Bishop of Clifton.

Letters from Rome (2 vols *passim*); letters from friends and clergy 1854-81 (c100 items); letter books (7 vols); misc papers 1857-89 (4 vols *passim*).
Bristol Record Office (Clifton diocesan records). NRA 21476.

Corresp 1850-94 (4 bundles); theological and historical draft essays and letters (c4 bundles); school and student notes c1830-99 (3 bundles); working papers at the Vatican Council 1869-70 (1 bundle); diary, Italy and Germany 1875 (1 vol); personal and misc papers 1866-95.
Lord Clifford of Chudleigh. NRA 20060.

[157] **CLOWES, John** (1743-1831)
Swedenborgian; rector of St John, Manchester
1769-1831.

Autobiography 1814-18 (2 vols).
Chetham's Library, Manchester (Mun A 3 51-2).

[158] **CLOWES, William** (1780-1851)
Primitive methodist minister.

Memoirs 1821-4 (1 vol); notebooks on the
beginnings of the primitive methodist connexion
*c*1836 and on relations with Hugh Bourne 1830-8
(7 vols); letters from primitive methodist missions
in Philadelphia and Upper Canada 1830-7 (*c*31
items).
Methodist Archives, Manchester.

[159] **CODRINGTON, Robert Henry** (1830-
1922)
Missionary in Melanesia 1866-87; prebendary of
Chichester 1888-1922.

Corresp 1866-1922 (6 vols); diaries and sketch
book 1869-82 (2 vols) with other misc papers rel
to Melanesia 1867-1908 (8 vols, 2 items);
European travel diaries 1859 (2 vols); diaries
1892-1922 (9 vols); lectures 1895-1915 (2 vols);
misc sermons (1 vol); letters and papers rel to his
biography 1922-6 (1 vol).
Rhodes House Library, Oxford (MSS Pac s 2–33).
NRA 28338.

Melanesian travel journals 1872-5 (3 vols).
*Melanesian Mission, Watford. See Australian joint
copying project handbook*, 8, 1984.

[160] **COFFIN, Robert Aston** (1819-1885)
Provincial of the English Congregation of the
Most Holy Redeemer 1865-82; RC bishop of
Southwark 1882-5.

Corresp and papers 1843-85 (*c*10 bundles), incl
letters from RF Douglas 1857-69, FW Faber, CB
Lans 1852-66, RG MacMillan, JH Newman 1845-
52 and Redemptorist priests at St Trond, Belgium
1860-81, copy letters to Ambrose Phillipps de
Lisle 1845-83, papers rel to Teignmouth Priory
1879, retreat notebook, letters from his family
1843 and an account of his death 1885.
*Congregation of the Most Holy Redeemer, St Mary's
Clapham.*

Letters to him *c*1880-5 (1 bundle); corresp with
the Admiralty, Colonial and War Offices 1882-5
(1 bundle); financial papers 1883 (1 bundle); diary
1882-5 (4 vols).
Southwark Diocesan Archives. NRA 27760.

[161] **COLERIDGE, Henry James** (1822-1893)
Editor of *The Month* 1865-81.

Letters from JH Newman 1862-87 (1 vol *passim*)
and others 1884 (1 bundle); corresp with EG
Bagshawe, Thomas Grant and other Jesuits

(1 bundle) and rel to his *Life of Mary Ward* 1883
(2 bundles); notebooks on ethics 1843; personal
corresp and papers (2 bundles).
Society of Jesus, London.

Journal incl theological notes 1842-5 (1 vol).
Birmingham University Library (6/i/9).

[162] **COLERIDGE, Sir John Taylor** (1790-
1876)
Justice of the King's Bench 1835-58.

Letters from Thomas Arnold 1817-42 (1 vol);
letters from his father, sister Frances and other
members of his family 1812-42 (2 vols); corresp
with Charles Dyson 1820-60 (1 vol), his uncle
George Coleridge [1805]-1826 (1 vol), and with
PM Latham and James Randall 1841-74 (1 vol);
letters to John Keble 1850-65 (1 vol) and from
Keble 1811-66 (3 vols).
Bodleian Library, Oxford (MSS Eng lett d 126-31,
133-7). Purchased from Lord Coleridge and
presented by the Pilgrim Trust 1951.

Letters from ST Coleridge, Robert Southey and
William Wordsworth with misc family papers
1794-1849 (1 vol).
British Library (Add MS 47553). Presented by the
Pilgrim Trust 1951. NRA 20966.

[163] **COLLINGRIDGE, Peter Bernardine**
(1757-1829)
Vicar apostolic of the western district 1807-29.

Corresp and papers 1806-29 incl letters from
Rome (1 vol *passim*), from William Poynter and
others (*c*1,000 items), pocket book 1822-3, wills
1816-23 (4 items) and personal accounts (*c*23
vols).
Bristol Record Office (Clifton diocesan records).

Letters to him 1802-28 (5 items); notebook 1810-
18, 1822-9 and account book as procurator 1813-
24; financial and misc papers 1803-29 (6 items);
annotated office book 1802 (1 vol).
*Archives of the English Province of Friars Minor,
London.*

Letters *c*1815 (2 vols); sermons from 1820.
Convent of the Poor Clares, Arundel (Archives of
the Franciscan Convent, Taunton). Presented by
Ambrose Burton, bishop of Clifton.

Diary 1822-3.
Bishop of Clifton.

[164] **CONNELLY, Cornelia** (1809-1879)
Founder of the Society of the Holy Child Jesus.

Corresp and papers 1837-79 (38 boxes) incl letters
from NPS Wiseman 1846-52 (22 items), Charles
Towneley 1851-69 (22 items), Thomas Grant
1856-70 (*c*300 items), GB Eyston 1857-63 (42
items), James Danell 1862-78 (25 items), and
Joseph Searle 1864-5 (22 items); letter books
1853-76 (6 vols); collected letters from her (*c*188

items); drafts of the Rule 1846-77 (8 items); spiritual notebooks 1839-48 (3 vols); commonplace book from 1844, engagement diary 1846-64, directory for superiors 1873 and notebook on Ruoert House 1852-71 (4 vols). *Convent of the Holy Child Jesus, Mayfield, East Sussex* (temporarily deposited in the Mother House, Rome 1985).

Corresp and papers of her husband, Pierce Connelly, incl corresp with her 1837-49 (*c*63 items).
Archbishop's House, Birmingham. NRA 8129.

[165] **CONWAY, William** (1815-1876)
Rector of St Margaret, Westminster 1864-74.

Family corresp 1822-1912 (650 items), diaries 1832-65 (6 vols) and misc papers.
Cambridge University Library (Add 7676). NRA 27757.

[166] **CONYBEARE, William James** (1871-1955)
Archdeacon of Nottingham 1916-36; provost of Southwell 1931-45.

Letters to him as chaplain to Frederick Temple and RT Davidson 1900-03 (*c*49 items) and letters to Temple answered by him (27 items).
Pusey House, Oxford.

[167] **COOKE, George Albert** (1865-1939)
Oriel professor of the interpretation of Holy Scripture, Oxford 1908–14; regius professor of Hebrew, Oxford 1914-36.

Diaries 1884-1939 (58 vols).
Bristol University Library. Deposited 1968.

[168] **COOKE, William** (1806-1884)
Methodist New Connexion minister.

Corresp mainly rel to the methodist new connexion in Australia, Canada and Ireland 1836-82 (221 items); general corresp of Cooke and others 1827-84 (192 items) incl corresp of and rel to Joseph Barker 1840-69 (65 items).
Methodist Archives, Manchester. NRA 25769.

[169] **COOPER, James** (1846-1922)
Regius professor of ecclesiastical history, Glasgow 1898-1922.

Diaries 1867-74, 1883-1922 (44 vols) incl letters and cuttings (715 items); corresp and papers (1 box).
Aberdeen University Library (MSS 2283/1-44). NRA 22900.

[170] **COPELAND, William John** (1804-1885)
Fellow of Trinity College, Oxford 1832-49; rector of Farnham, Essex 1849-85.

Corresp and papers 1829-80 incl letters from JH Newman 1834-85 (217 items) and from Lord Adare and AJ Beresford Hope rel to the foundation of St Augustine's College, Canterbury 1845, papers rel to Tract XC, his 'Narrative of the Oxford Movement' dictated to his nephew WC Borlase and other collected papers.
Pusey House, Oxford.

Letters from Thomas Keble 1842-69 (16 items).
Lambeth Palace Library. Deposited by the Revd Edward Keble 1966.

[171] **COPLESTON, Edward** (1776-1849)
Provost of Oriel College, Oxford 1814-28; bishop of Llandaff and dean of St Paul's 1828-49.

Letters from politicians, churchmen and literary figures 1801-48 (2 vols).
National Library of Wales (MSS 21743, 21977).

Letters from the 3rd Baron Lyttelton 1809-12 (72 items), William Gifford 1809-12 (42 items), JW Ward, afterwards Earl of Dudley 1815-21 (46 items) and others 1808-49 (24 items).
Devon Record Office (1149 M). Deposited 1962. NRA 9294.

Letters from JW Ward and others 1810-49 (87ff).
Bodleian Library, Oxford (MS Eng lett d 309). Purchased 1971.

Letters from JW Ward 1814-15 (54ff).
Lambeth Palace Library (MS 1995).

Letters from churchmen, politicians and others (1 vol).
Untraced. Sold at Sotheby's 8 Nov 1983, lot 330.

[172] **CORNTHWAITE, Robert** (1818-1890)
Rector of the English College, Rome 1851-7; bishop of Beverley 1861-78, of Leeds 1879-90.

Corresp and papers 1851-90 incl some as rector of the English College, Rome and letters to him as bishop, mainly from clergy (5 bundles); papers rel to the division of the diocese of Beverley 1878; notes on hierarchy low week meetings and records of the foundation of St Joseph's seminary, Horsforth 1878 (*c*350 items).
Bishop of Leeds.

Papers as rector.
English College, Rome (Scritture 77-78 *passim*).

[173] **COULSON, John Edward** (1806-1886)
Wesleyan methodist minister.

Letters from Jabez Bunting, John Rattenbury and others 1843-83 (312 items); diary written on mission circuit, Newcastle upon Tyne 1829-33 (1 vol).
Methodist Archives, Manchester.

[174] **COWGILL, Harry** (*c*1850-*c*1937)
Curate of St John the Evangelist, Miles Platting
1877-83; vicar of Shireoaks 1892-1927.

Letters from SF Green *c*1873-1916 (544 items),
Lord Halifax and others 1874-*c*1891 (314 items)
and Sir TP Heywood *c*1881-*c*1896 (81 items);
corresp with the bishop of Manchester *c*1877–82
(13 items); papers rel to the Miles Platting
controversy *c*1881-4, 1920 (26 items); diaries
1882-*c*1883 (2 vols) and misc papers 1871-83 (15
items).
Nottinghamshire Record Office (DD MP).
Deposited by his son, the Revd JWA Cowgill
1969. NRA 14388.

[175] **COX, Samuel** (1826-1893)
Minister of Mansfield Road Baptist Church,
Nottingham 1863-88.

Sermons 1863-5 (7 vols); notes on scripture etc (5
vols).
Nottingham University Library (Mr Co 1-12). NRA
9989.

[176] **CRAWLEY, Arthur Stafford** (1876-1948)
Canon of Windsor 1934-48.

Letters to him 1897-1919, 1929 (2 boxes); letters
from the royal family, prime ministers etc 1918,
1934-45 (1 box); letters from his wife 1902-38
(*c*550 items) and his mother 1899-1913 (244
items); letters from him to his wife and family
1894-1929 (*c*200 items, 4 boxes); diaries 1914-48
(21 vols); bills and accounts 1896-1901 (109
items); sermons 1909-1948 (1 box).
St George's Chapel, Windsor Castle. NRA 28435.

Letters from CG Lang to him and his family
1901-16.
Lambeth Palace Library. Presented by Lady
Goodman and Aidan Crawley. *Annual Report*
1983-4.

[177] **CREIGHTON, Mandell** (1843-1901)
Bishop of Peterborough 1891-7, of London 1897-
1901.

Corresp and papers as bishop of London (11
boxes) incl corresp with clergy 1897-9 (2 boxes)
and rel to parochial and clerical disputes 1896-
1900 (3 boxes).
Lambeth Palace Library (Fulham papers).

Letters from Lord Acton 1882-98.
Cambridge University Library (Add 6871).

[178] **CROKE, Thomas William** (1824-1902)
RC archbishop of Cashel 1875-1902.

Corresp and papers 1841-1902 incl corresp,
mainly as archbishop, with clergy and politicians,
notebook 1849-75, sermons, journal and personal
papers.

Archbishop of Cashel. Copies in the National
Library of Ireland.

[179] **CROLLY, William** (1780-1849)
RC archbishop of Armagh 1835-49.

Misc corresp, papers and sermons as archbishop
1835-47 (16 items).
Archbishop of Armagh. Microfilm in the Public
Record Office of Northern Ireland (MIC 451).

[180] **CUBITT, George** (1792-1850)
Wesleyan methodist minister; editor of the
Wesleyan Magazine.

Corresp 1816-46 incl letters from John Hannah
and others (111 items) and collected letters from
him (*c*50 items).
Methodist Archives, Manchester.

[181] **CULLEN, Paul** (1803-1878)
Rector of the Irish College, Rome 1832-48;
archbishop of Armagh 1849-52, of Dublin 1852-
78; cardinal 1866.

Papers as rector.
Irish College, Rome.

Misc corresp and papers mainly as archbishop of
Armagh 1850-3 (5 files).
Archbishop of Armagh.

Corresp and papers 1820-78 (*c*100 boxes), incl
general corresp, letter books 1855-78 (6 vols),
memoranda, sermons, reports, and accounts rel to
diocesan administration, relations with
government, the Catholic University, the Vatican
Council 1869-70, synods and the O'Keefe case,
and family and personal papers.
Diocesan Archives, Archbishop's House, Dublin.

[182] **CUNNINGHAM, John William** (1760-
1861)
Vicar of Harrow 1811-61.

Letters mainly from CJ Hoare 1801-17 (16 items);
diaries 1822-30 (8 vols).
Dorset Record Office (D 289). NRA 13647.

[183] **CURTIS, Patrick** (1740-1832)
RC archbishop of Armagh 1819-32.

Corresp and papers, mainly as archbishop, 1784-
1832 (25 files) incl corresp and papers rel to the
Irish College, Salamanca 1784-1830 (8 items) and
to Catholic emancipation 1829-31 (7 items).
Archbishop of Armagh. Microfilm in the Public
Record Office of Northern Ireland (MIC 451).

[184] **DALE, Robert William** (1829-1895)
Congregational theologian; minister of Carr's
Lane Chapel, Birmingham 1859-95.

Letters from John Bright 1862-82 (11 items), WE
Gladstone 1875-86 (7 items), John Morley 1875-
86 (22 items) and Henry Wace 1875-91 (35
items).
Birmingham University Library. Presented by his
grand-daughter, Mrs AB White. NRA 13202.

[185] **DALGAIRNS, John Dobrée [Bernard]**
(1818-1876)
Oratorian.

Letters to him 1842-72 (*c*420 items), incl those
from JH Newman 1842-71 (118 items), Ambrose
St John 1845-7 (12 items), FW Faber 1853-62 (8
items), Mother Margaret Hallahan 1856-67 (24
items) and RH Hutton 1870-2 (16 items); letters
from him, mainly 1845, rel to his conversion (68
items).
The Oratory, London. NRA 16631.

[186] **DALTON, John Neale** (1839-1931)
Canon of Windsor 1885-1931.

Corresp and papers 1893-1920 incl corresp rel to a
proposed official history of Windsor Castle 1901-
12, misc corresp 1896-1920, visitation notebook
rel to St George's College livings 1893-6 etc.
St George's Chapel, Windsor Castle. NRA 18513.

Letters to him concerning his *Collegiate church of
Ottery St Mary* 1903-17 (20ff).
Lambeth Palace Library (MS 1680).

[187] **DALY, Robert** (1783-1872)
Bishop of Cashel and Waterford 1843-72.

Letters to him (26 items).
National Library of Ireland (MS 17837). See
*Manuscript sources for the history of Irish
civilisation: first supplement*, 1979.

[188] **DANELL, James** (1821-1881)
RC bishop of Southwark 1871-81.

Corresp with the Admiralty, Colonial and War
Offices (1 box); personal and financial papers (2
boxes); engagement diaries 1869-72 (6 vols); mass
book 1846-77 and lists of converts 1857-68 (2
vols).
Southwark Diocesan Archives. NRA 27760.

[189] **DANSON, Ernest Denny Logie** (1880-
1946)
Bishop of Edinburgh 1939-46 and primus of the
Scottish episcopal church 1943-6.

Diaries 1900-46 (36 vols) and scrapbooks 1898-
1950 (2 vols).
Scottish Record Office (CH 12/33).

Log book as bishop 1917-46.
Bishop of Edinburgh. Enquiries to NRA (Scotland)
(NRA (S) 2702).

Papers rel to a survey of the Anglican communion
(1 box).
National Library of Scotland (Dep 172). NRA
27988.

[190] **DARBY, John Nelson** (1800-1882)
Plymouth brother; founder of the Darbyites.

Letters to him, with misc papers and some draft
replies, mainly rel to affairs of the brethren in
Great Britain and abroad 1829-82 (539 items).
Private. NRA 26471. Photocopies in the John
Rylands University Library of Manchester.

[191] **DAVIDSON, Randall Thomas** (1848-1930)
Archbishop of Canterbury 1903-28.

Corresp and papers 1848-1930 (*c*400 vols) incl
corresp with EW Benson 1882-96 (2 vols) and
Queen Victoria 1885-1900 (2 vols) and diaries and
memoranda 1903-30 (5 vols).
Lambeth Palace Library. Partly closed to research.

Corresp and papers as dean of Windsor 1877-90.
St George's Chapel, Windsor Castle. NRA 18513.

Corresp and papers rel to the controversy over the
Westminster Abbey sacristy *c*1927 (54 items) incl
letters from WF Norris (24 items).
Westminster Abbey (WAM 59159-59212).

Travel journal, Europe and the Near East 1872-3
(2 vols).
Lambeth Palace Library (MSS 1602-3).

[192] **DAVIES, Charles** (1849-1927)
Baptist minister.

Letters received 1895-1913 (1 vol); diaries 1869-
1925 (57 vols); sermons and misc papers (6 vols).
National Library of Wales (MSS 10372-435).
Presented by his son JF Davies 1936.

[193] **DAVIES, David Charles** (1826-1891)
Calvinistic methodist minister and theologian.

Letters to him and his wife 1864-1903 (39 items);
diary 1837-8 (1 vol); preaching register 1884-91 (1
vol); sermons 1851-79 (442 items); lectures and
addresses 1859-85 (*c*50 items); notes, extracts,
cuttings, etc 1861-88.
National Library of Wales (Presbyterian Church of
Wales MSS, General Collection). NRA 28345.

[194] **DAVIES, Edward Owen** (1864-1936)
Calvinistic methodist minister.

Letters to him 1893-9, 1922-36 (1,850 items);
diaries 1929-35 (10 vols); sermons 1905-36 (30
vols, 19 items); notes, addresses and misc papers.

National Library of Wales (Presbyterian Church of Wales MSS, General Collection). NRA 28345.

[195] DAVIES, John (1804-1884)
Independent minister, Glandwr 1827-63, Moriah Church, Llanwinio 1863-84.

Corresp 1823-40 (6 bundles); diaries 1827-48 (1 bundle); sermons and sermon notes *c*1821-84 (59 vols); literary and theological MSS *c*1818-81 (11 vols); misc papers (3 vols).
National Library of Wales (MSS 6196, 8613-91).

[196] DAVIES, John (1843-1917)
Calvinistic methodist minister, Pandy and Forest Coal Pit, Mon 1870-1917.

Letters to him *c*1886-1916 (2 vols); diaries 1866-1916 (18 vols); sermons 1859-1915 (29 items); notebooks, essays, misc papers, etc on pastoral and antiquarian subjects (*c*25 vols).
National Library of Wales (MSS 11356-11429). Presented by his son-in-law, B Elystan Price 1937.

[197] DAVIES, Owen (1840-1929)
Baptist minister, Caernarfon 1876-1905.

Corresp 1860-1918 (1 vol); sermons 1860-4 (6 vols); sermon notes 1904-21 (1 vol); autobiographical papers, etc (3 vols); material for *Cofiant y parch John Pritchard, Llangollen* . . . (1 vol).
National Library of Wales (MSS 19587-98). See *Annual Report* 1965-6, pp29-31.

[198] DAVIES, Richard (*c*1777-1859)
Archdeacon of Brecon 1804-59.

Corresp and papers 1780-1840.
Powys Archives.

[199] DAVIS, Timothy (1779-1860)
Minister of Oat Street Unitarian Chapel, Evesham 1819-53.

Journals incl copies of corresp 1804-58 (11 vols); misc family corresp and papers 1705-1856 (1 vol).
National Library of Wales (MSS 5487-98). Presented by his grandson Rudolf Davis 1924.

[200] DAWSON, George (1821-1876)
Minister of the Church of the Saviour, Birmingham 1847-76.

Personal and family corresp 1845-94 (1 vol); sermons 1844-76 (2 vols); lectures 1845-76 (2 vols); speeches 1844-78 (1 vol); prayers, poems, etc 1840-87 (1 vol); press cuttings 1845-95 (5 vols); papers rel to the Church of the Saviour 1846-1901 (1 vol); biographical materials collected by WW Wilson (8 vols).

Birmingham Reference Library. See *A catalogue of the Birmingham collection,* 1918.

[201] DEANE, Henry (1838-1894)
Biblical scholar.

Family corresp and misc papers 1843-92 (23 items); diaries 1858, 1882, 1884-94.
Dorset Record Office (D 359). Partial list: NRA 17604.

Letters from EB Pusey, mainly on Hebrew teaching, *c*1860-82 (1 bundle); letters to the Bidder family (1 bundle).
St John's College, Oxford.

[202] de LABILLIERE, Paul Fulcrand Delacour (1879-1946)
Dean of Westminster 1938-46.

Corresp, memoranda and misc papers as dean, mainly rel to abbey affairs and to Westminster School 1940-5 (*c*500 items).
Westminster Abbey (WAM 61229-61628, 61945-62152).

[203] DENISON, Edward (1801-1854)
Bishop of Salisbury 1837-54.

Corresp rel to the offer of Newark vicarage and the bishopric of Salisbury 1835, 1837 (2 bundles); corresp with his brother JE Denison 1825-47 (1 bundle); letters, mainly to JE Denison, rel to the bishop of Salisbury's income 1848 (1 bundle).
Nottingham University Library (OsC). Deposited by Colonel WME Denison 1964. NRA 0205.

[204] DENISON, George Anthony (1805-1896)
Archdeacon of Taunton 1851-96.

Corresp, mainly 1847-54, rel to the Gorham judgement, the National Society, Church Union affairs etc (*c*3,000 items) and other papers.
Pusey House, Oxford.

[205] DIBDIN, Sir Lewis Tonna (1852-1938)
Dean of the arches 1903-34; vicar-general of the province of Canterbury 1925-34; first church estates commissioner 1905-31.

Papers, lectures and addresses rel to ecclesiastical cases and affairs 1711-1933 (2 vols); press cuttings 1881-1928 (1 vol); list of his papers 1872-1933 (1 vol).
Lambeth Palace Library (MSS 1586-9). Presented by LG Dibdin 1958.

[206] DIGBY, Mabel (1835-1911)
English provincial 1872-94 and superior-general 1895-1911 of the Society of the Sacred Heart.

Letters from the mother house, Paris 1870-92 (4 bundles).
Society of the Sacred Heart, Roehampton.

Letters to her 1890-1911 mainly from Mother Janet Stuart (*c*5 boxes, 1 bundle).
Central Archives, Society of the Sacred Heart, Rome. Photocopies at Roehampton.

[207] **DIX, George Eglington Alston [Gregory]** (1901-1952)
Prior of Nashdom Abbey 1948–52.

Papers (8 boxes) incl corresp with churchmen at home and abroad 1934-52, papers rel to his early life and working papers rel to reunion and *The shape of the liturgy*.
Nashdom Abbey, Burnham.

Scholarly papers rel to his edition of the *Apostolic Tradition* of St Hippolytus.
Revd Professor Henry Chadwick.

[208] **DIXON, Joseph** (1806-1866)
RC archbishop of Armagh 1852-66.

Corresp and papers as archbishop 1852-66 (88 files) incl letters from his dean, Michael Kieran 1852-66 (2 files) and archdeacon, Felix Slane 1852-66 (2 files).
Archbishop of Armagh. Microfilm in the Public Record Office of Northern Ireland (MIC 451).

Notebooks rel to Scriptural exegesis (6 vols).
University College Library, Dublin. See *Manuscript sources for the history of Irish civilisation: first supplement*, 1979.

[209] **DODS, Marcus** (1834-1909)
Professor of New Testament criticism and exegesis, New College, Edinburgh 1889-1909.

Commonplace book (1 vol); NT studies, lectures and sermons (16 boxes).
New College, Edinburgh.

[210] **DODSON, Sir John** (1780-1858)
Dean of the arches 1852-8.

Papers 1807-57 (35 boxes), incl admiralty and ecclesiastical case notebooks 1807-26 (7 vols), letter books as king's (later queen's) advocate to 1851 (12 vols) and opinions as advocate-general 1834-52 (1 vol).
Bodleian Library, Oxford (Dep Monk Bretton 1-35). NRA 9224.

Corresp and papers 1820-56 (*c*90 items), incl papers rel to the case of Weston *v* Liddell on church ornament 1856 (6 items).
East Sussex Record Office (D 350). Deposited by Lord Monk Bretton 1959. NRA 21871.

[211] **DOLAN, John [Gilbert]** (1853-1919)
Benedictine.

Corresp and working papers rel to English Benedictine martyrs (1 box, 2 vols); other historical working papers (10 boxes and files).
Downside Abbey.

[212] **DON, Alan Campbell** (1885-1966)
Dean of Westminster 1946-59.

Corresp and papers rel to CG Lang and to the Scottish episcopal church 1931-60 (79ff).
Lambeth Palace Library (MS 1469).

Diaries as chaplain to CG Lang and canon of Westminster 1931-46 (11 vols).
Lambeth Palace Library (MSS 2861-71). Presented by him 1960.

Letters of congratulation on his appointment as canon 1940 and dean 1946 of Westminster (103 items) and as KCVO 1948 (12 items); misc corresp and papers as dean 1952-3, nd (*c*26 items); diary 1947-53 (1 vol); reminiscences of Elizabeth II's coronation 1953 (3pp).
Westminster Abbey (WAM 63189, 66950-9). Partly closed to research.

[213] **DONNELLY, James** (1823-1893)
RC bishop of Clogher 1865-93.

Corresp and misc papers rel to Monaghan elections incl letters from Paul Cullen, Lord O'Hagan and others 1871, 1880 (38 items); diaries 1849-9, 1852-93 rel to fund raising tours for the Catholic University of Ireland, diocesan affairs, travels abroad, etc; accounts 1865-86 (2 vols); list of parishes 1892 (1 vol).
Bishop of Clogher. Copies in the Public Record Office of Northern Ireland (DIO (RC) 1/11 A-E). NRA 19966.

[214] **D'ORSEY, Alexander James Donald** (1812-1894)
Incumbent of St John, Anderston, Glasgow 1846-50.

Letters to him, mainly from Michael Russell and Walter Trower, bishops of Glasgow and Galloway, rel to his ordination, St John, Anderston and liturgical disputes etc 1845-59 (241ff).
National Library of Scotland (MS 19325). Purchased 1973. NRA 27276.

[215] **DOUGLAS, John Albert** (*c*1868-1956)
Rector of St Michael Paternoster Royal, London 1933-53; honorary general secretary of the Church of England Council on Foreign Relations 1933-45.

Corresp and papers *c*1876-1955 (99 vols) mainly as editor of *The Christian East* and rel to the Council on Foreign Relations.
Lambeth Palace Library.

Corresp and papers rel to London University 1922-5 (1 box).
London University Library.

C

[216] **DOUGLASS, John** (1743-1812)
Vicar apostolic of the London district 1790-1812.

Corresp and papers as vicar apostolic (5 vols, 7 boxes) incl corresp with Charles Walmesley and others rel to the Catholic committee 1791 (*c*150 items), letters from John Milner (230 items), Charles Plowden (32 items), Richard Southwark (67 items), his agents in Rome (146 items) and others, and personal and misc papers; diary 1795-1811 (2 vols).
Westminster Diocesan Archives (A43-7, 50-54a, Z1, 72). NRA 28616.

Corresp and papers 1792-1800, mainly rel to the transfer of the English College, Douai to Old Hall Green, Herts (*c*185 items); notes on logic 1762 (400pp); sermons as vicar apostolic (3 vols).
Westminster Diocesan Archives (St Edmund's College Ware, series 2, 9). NRA 16303.

[217] **DOWDEN, John** (1840-1910)
Bishop of Edinburgh 1886-1910.

Corresp and papers 1858-1940 (10 boxes) incl family corresp (5 boxes), liturgical papers (1 box) and other working papers rel to his books, etc (4 boxes).
National Library of Scotland (Dep 171). Deposited by the provost and chapter of St Mary's Cathedral, Edinburgh. NRA 27987.

Papers mainly rel to Scottish church history (9 vols).
National Library of Scotland (MSS 3555-63). Presented by his daughter, Mrs HR Pyatt 1945.

[218] **DOYLE, James Warren** (1786-1834)
RC bishop of Kildare and Leighlin 1819-34.

Account book 1817-33.
St Patrick's College, Carlow. See Manuscript sources for the history of Irish civilisation: first supplement, 1979.

[219] **DOYLE, Thomas** (1793-1879)
Provost of Southwark RC cathedral 1850-79.

Corresp and papers rel to the building of Southwark cathedral, incl letters from AW Pugin 1839-79 (5 boxes); extensive papers rel to the Talbot inheritance dispute 1840-58.
Southwark Diocesan Archives. NRA 27760.

[220] **DRANE, Augusta Theodosia [Francis Raphael]** (1823-1894)
Prioress of Stone, Staffs 1872-81; prioress provincial of the English Dominicans 1881-94.

Letters from her to nuns and churchmen 1868-94 (234 items) incl letters to WB Ullathorne 1877-87 (79 items); autobiography 1876; working papers rel to her literary and historical publications *c*1840-93 (30 bundles and vols); spiritual notebooks 1833, 1881, nd (4 vols) and

instructions *c*1855-77 (4 bundles and vols); MS summary of her corresp with Dominican Master-General Joseph Larroca 1884-5 rel to the change in government of the congregation and narrative of facts about this 1887 (1 item); misc papers of and rel to her 1881-1924 incl press cuttings (1 bundle, 11 items).
St Dominic's Convent, Stone. NRA 27580.

[221] **DRUMMOND, Henry** (1851-1897)
Professor of natural science, Free Church College, Glasgow 1884-97.

Corresp 1872-95 incl letters from JS Blackie, Marcus Dods, WL Moody and others (1 bundle); family corresp 1863-96 (1 bundle); journals and notebooks rel to African geological survey 1883-4; university notebook 1868-9 (1 vol); misc literary MSS, sermon and lecture notes 1874-99.
National Library of Scotland (Acc 5890). Presented by HJH Drummond 1973. NRA 27275.

[222] **DRUMMOND, William Abernethy** (d1809)
Bishop of Edinburgh 1787-1805, of Glasgow 1805-9.

Letters to him rel to Scottish episcopal church affairs etc 1789-1805 (1 bundle); family and personal papers 1762-1862 (1 bundle) incl the concordat between the Scottish bishops and Samuel Seabury rel to his consecration 1784; legal corresp and misc papers 1765-1802 (2 bundles).
Scottish Record Office (GD 230). NRA 10137.

Misc corresp and papers rel to diocesan affairs, relations with English congregations in Scotland, doctrinal questions and personal affairs 1782-1803 (*c* 90 items).
Scottish Record Office (CH 12).

[223] **DU BUISSON, John Clement** (1871-1938)
Dean of St Asaph 1927-38.

Diaries 1879-1938 (26 vols).
Hereford and Worcester Record Office, Hereford (K 53). NRA 27101.

[224] **DUNN, Samuel** (1798-1882)
Wesleyan methodist minister 1819-49; free methodist minister at Camborne 1855-64.

Diary as a missionary in the Shetland Islands 1822-5.
Methodist Archives, Manchester. NRA 25824.

[225] **DUNN, Thomas** (1870-1931)
Bishop of Nottingham 1916-31.

Corresp and papers 1916-31 incl reports to Rome (2 items), corresp with Westminster archdiocese 1916-22 (19 items), with other bishops 1916-23 (113 items) and general corresp 1918-31 (*c*3

boxes); financial, statistical and synodical documents 1916-31 (8 boxes).
Bishop of Nottingham. NRA 27317.

[226] EDWARDS, Ellis (1844-1915)
Calvinistic methodist; principal of Bala Theological College 1907-15.

Letters to him 1867-1915 (*c*336 items); diaries 1860-73, 1906 (3 vols); commonplace book 1864-6; misc papers incl passports, certificates, press cuttings, etc.
National Library of Wales (Presbyterian Church of Wales MSS, General Collection). NRA 28345.

Letters to him rel to the Welsh Intermediate Education Act, the establishment of a Welsh university, the Davies lecture, etc 1871-1915; diary, probably belonging to him, 1900-4; translations of hymns.
National Library of Wales. Deposited by Mrs E Yale and Miss N Lewis. See *Annual Report* 1947-8, p43, 1948-9, p61, 1963-4, pp52-3.

[227] EDWARDS, Lewis (1809-1887)
Calvinistic methodist; principal of Bala Theological College 1837-87.

Letters from Owen Thomas 1845-87 (20 items); essays (4 items).
National Library of Wales (Presbyterian Church of Wales MSS, General Collection). NRA 28345.

[228] EDWARDS, Roger (1811-1886)
Calvinistic methodist minister, Bethesda, Mold 1835-86; editor of *Y Drysorfa* 1847-86.

Letters to him, mainly rel to *Y Drysorfa* 1862-86; memorandum book 1829-30; notebook *c*1829; sermons (2 vols).
National Library of Wales. Deposited by Mrs E Yale 1934. See *Annual Report* 1947-8, p43, 1948-9, p61.

Letters to him 1828-86 (19 items); letters to him and his wife from his son Ellis 1862-82 (98 items).
National Library of Wales (Presbyterian Church of Wales MSS, General Collection). NRA 28345.

Misc corresp and papers incl minutes and papers rel to Calvinistic Methodist Association meetings 1842-53; sermon notes 1830-80; notes of sermons by other preachers.
University College of North Wales, Bangor (Belmont MSS 1-28, Yale MSS). NRA 8487.

[229] EDWARDS, Thomas Charles (1837-1900)
Calvinistic methodist; principal of the University College of Wales, Aberystwyth 1872-91.

Corresp (*c*9,000 items) incl letters from Lord Aberdare, Benjamin Jowett, Sir Hugh Owen, Mark Pattison, JF Roberts and others and corresp with his father.

National Library of Wales. NRA 11472: partial list. See *Annual Report* 1943-4, p29.

Letters to him 1872-97 (14 items); misc notes and papers.
National Library of Wales (Presbyterian Church of Wales MSS, Bala College Group). NRA 28416.

[230] EELES, Francis Carolus (1876-1954)
Secretary of the Central Council for the Care of Churches 1924-54.

Corresp and papers 1892-1958 (*c*250 bundles and volumes) incl corresp with J Wickham Legg rel to liturgical questions etc 1898-1915 (*c*250 items), corresp and papers as secretary of the archbishop's committee on the ministry of women 1916-19 (14 bundles), liturgical papers 1905-47 (82 bundles) and papers rel to the care of churches *c*1920-55 (47 bundles).
Church House, Westminster. NRA 25406.

Collections rel to liturgical history (51 vols).
Lambeth Palace Library (MSS 1501-51). Presented 1954.

[231] EGERTON, Philip Reginald (1832-1911)
Fellow of New College, Oxford 1851-63; headmaster 1860-87 and warden 1887-96 of All Saints School, Bloxham.

Letters to him and misc papers, mainly rel to the foundation of Bloxham School and its relations with the Woodard Corporation and Keble College, Oxford 1855-98 (142 items); letters of spiritual advice etc from HP Liddon 1857-90 (51 items); draft letters etc, mainly rel to the school 1840-97 (26 items); draft letters to the bishop of Oxford etc about confession 1869 (1 vol); school accounts 1859-96 (2 bundles, 7 vols, 31 items); sermons 1858-93 (*c* 66 items); commonplace book 1864-*c*1875 (1 vol) and misc papers, some printed, 1838-1934 (5 vols, 17 items).
All Saints School, Bloxham. NRA 19923.

[232] ELIAS, John (1774-1841)
Calvinistic methodist minister.

Letters to him 1801-26 (17 items); diaries 1820, 1823-7 (6 vols); memoranda books 1807-8, 1817-25 (5 vols); notebooks 1801, nd (5 vols); sermon notes 1802-36 (*c*18 bundles); misc notes, extracts and papers.
National Library of Wales (Presbyterian Church of Wales MSS, Bala College Group). NRA 28416.

Sermons 1800-35 (18 items).
National Library of Wales (Presbyterian Church of Wales MSS, General Collection). NRA 28345.

[233] ELLIS, Robert (1812-1875)
Baptist minister.

Corresp, mainly letters to him 1805-1924 (*c*114 items); letters to his son Robert 1864-7 (80

items); memoranda book 1836-40; diaries 1840-66
(8 vols); autobiography (1 vol); lecture notes (*c*10
vols); sermons, poems and notes (9 vols); literary
and other MSS.
National Library of Wales. Purchased 1935. NRA
28609.

[234] **ELRINGTON, Thomas** (1760-1835)
Provost of Trinity College Dublin 1811-20;
bishop of Limerick 1820-2, of Leighlin and Ferns
1822-35.

Corresp and misc papers, mainly as provost,
*c*1782-1831 (*c*78 items).
Trinity College, Dublin (TCD/MUN/P/I). NRA
24840.

[235] **ELVEN, Cornelius** (1797-1873)
Minister of Garland Street Baptist Church, Bury
St Edmunds 1823-73.

Diaries 1825-33 (3 vols); misc corresp and papers
*c*1836-43 (*c*14 items).
Suffolk Record Office, Bury St Edmunds.
Deposited by the officers and deacons of Garland
Street Baptist Church 1957. NRA 4938.

[236] **ENTWISLE, Joseph** (1767-1841)
Wesleyan methodist minister.

Corresp 1792-1841 incl letters from Jabez Bunting
1804-34 (10 items), Adam Clarke 1811-26 (5
items), Thomas Coke 1804-13 (11 items), French
prisoners of war and others (*c*145 items); collected
letters from him 1802-41 (146 items); diaries
1794-1841 (10 vols); Hoxton class book (1 vol);
misc notes (4 items).
Methodist Archives, Manchester.

[237] **ERRINGTON, George** (1804-1886)
Bishop of Plymouth 1851-5; titular archbishop
1855 and coadjutor to the archbishop of
Westminster 1855-62.

Coresp and papers, mainly rel to his removal as
archbishop coadjutor of Westminster, incl corresp
with Thomas Grant, HE Manning and NPS
Wiseman, an account of his audience with the
Pope and his history of the affair (*c*200 items);
account book as administrator of Clifton diocese
1855-7.
Bristol Record Office (Clifton diocesan records).
NRA 21476.

Corresp 1843-6, mainly letters from Thomas
Walsh (82 items); corresp with WB Ullathorne
1862-3 (10 items).
Archbishop's House, Birmingham. NRA 8129.

[238] **ERSKINE, Henry David** (1786-1859)
Dean of Ripon 1847-59.

Letters to him 1814-58 (3 vols); diary 1856 (1
vol); domestic accounts 1813-36 (1 vol); sermons

(2 vols); ecclesiastical papers (1 vol); family
papers 1822-40 (1 vol).
Bodleian Library, Oxford (MS Eng lett c401 and
passim). NRA 21249.

[239] **ESTCOURT, Edgar Edmund** (1816-1884)
Canon of Birmingham RC cathedral and diocesan
oeconomus 1850-84.

Letters to him, mainly financial 1862-84 (*c*3,100
items); financial papers and draft accounts (*c*50
items).
Archbishop's House, Birmingham. NRA 8129.

Misc corresp 1850-81 (1 bundle).
Gloucestershire Record Office (D 200). Presented by
EW Sotheron-Estcourt 1941. NRA 3531.

Notebook and misc papers rel to Jane Dormer,
Duchess of Feria *c*1830-50 (*c*2 bundles).
Warwick County Record Office (CR 895).
Deposited by Lord Dormer 1964. NRA 11084.

[240] **EVANS, Christmas** (1766-1838)
Baptist minister.

Notebooks etc *c*1815-26 (3 vols); sermons (9 vols).
National Library of Wales (MSS 647, 7033-41,
7829, 10259).

Account book with sermon notes 1812-14 (1 vol).
National Library of Wales (EK Jones MSS). NRA
28610.

[241] **EVANS, George Eyre** (1857-1939)
Unitarian minister and antiquary.

Family and personal corresp and papers (*c*450
vols) incl papers of the Powell family of Colyton,
Devon 1788-1901, corresp rel to his publications
1896-1904, letters by and about ministers 1775-
1904, letters rel to Welsh unitarianism 1775-1905,
diaries, journals, autobiographical papers and
notes on archaeological, historical and unitarian
matters etc.
National Library of Wales (MSS 4280-300, 7945-
84, 13271-685). NRA 28325. See *Annual Report*
1939-40, p24.

[242] **EVANS, William Hugh** (1831-1909)
Wesleyan methodist minister.

Corresp, diaries, essays, notes and accounts 1850-
1908 (*c*5 boxes).
University College of North Wales, Bangor.

[243] **EVANS, William Owen** (1864-1934)
Wesleyan methodist minister.

Corresp, family papers, diaries, sermons,
addresses, essays and hymns, scrapbooks and
notes on Wesleyan history 1882-1933 (10 boxes).
University College of North Wales, Bangor.

[244] **EVERETT, James** (1784-1872)
Founder of the United Methodist Free Churches
1857.

Corresp and papers, mainly letters to him 1802-51
(c700 items); copies of his letters 1810-29 (19
items); diaries 1804-66 (20 vols); misc MSS and
sermons (2 boxes).
Methodist Archives, Manchester.

[245] **EYRE, Charles Petre** (1817-1902)
Archbishop of Glasgow 1878-1902.

Personal corresp and papers 1853-1902 (2 boxes);
college notes, lectures and historical essays 1850-
92 (3 boxes); papers rel to the life of St Cuthbert
(1 box); travel journals 1865-85 (4 vols); diaries
1869-1902 (28 vols); papers rel to Newcastle upon
Tyne 1841-81 (1 box); memoranda 1867-99 (1
box); sermons 1840-92 (1 box); papers rel to the
Eyre inheritance case 1828-87 (1 box); family and
financial papers 1843-1901 (2 boxes); misc papers
1865-1901 (2 boxes).
Glasgow Archdiocesan Archive.

[246] **EYRE, John** (1754-1803)
Perpetual curate of Ram's episcopal chapel,
Homerton 1785-1803.

Corresp, mainly letters to him, rel to the Village
Itinerancy Association 1796-1800 (81 items).
Dr Williams's Library, London (New College 41).
NRA 13042.

[247] **EYRE, Thomas** (1748-1810)
President of Crook Hall (later Ushaw College)
1795-1810.

Letters to him 1785-1810 (3 vols); corresp and
papers rel to suppression of the English College,
Douai and its re-establishment in England 1791-
1800 (c30 items); collections for the history of
catholicism in the northern vicariate 1688-1810
(c2 vols).
Ushaw College, Durham. NRA 13674.

[248] **EYRE, William Henry** (1823-1898)
Rector of Stonyhurst College 1879-85.

Corresp (1 box); notes, corresp and papers rel to
the Eyre inheritance case 1880-92 (1 box); poems
(1 vol).
Society of Jesus, London.

[249] **FABER, Frederick William** (1814-1865)
Oratorian.

Letters to him 1838-61 (2 vols), incl those from
JH Newman (380 items) and WA Hutchison (50
iems); misc corresp 1840-65 (2 vols); collected
letters from him to JB Morris 1833-63 (1 vol), the
16th Earl of Shrewsbury and others 1841-61 (1
vol); priests at the London and Birmingham

oratories 1846-63 (4 vols), his biographer JE
Bowden 1848-63 (1 vol) and Anne, Duchess of
Argyll 1857-63 (1 vol); novice papers with
material rel to oratorian life (2 vols, 1 bundle);
drafts and MSS of published works (6 vols);
sermons and sermon notes from 1837 (1 box, 7
bundles, 3 vols); travel journals 1841 (2 vols);
unpublished devotional MSS from 1832 (4 vols).
The Oratory, London. NRA 16631.

[250] **FARQUHAR, George Taylor Shillito**
(c1857-1927)
Dean of St Andrews, Dunkeld and Dunblane
1910-27.

Diary 1879-1927 (16 vols).
Bishop of St Andrews, Dunkeld and Dunblane.
Enquiries to NRA (Scotland) (NRA (S) 2706).

Sermons (2 vols) and draft of a 'Shorter
ecclesiastical history of Perth' 1926.
National Library of Scotland (Dep 251). NRA
27272.

[251] **FARRAR, Frederic William** (1831-1903)
Headmaster of Marlborough College 1871-6;
rector of St Margaret Westminster 1876-95; dean
of Canterbury 1895-1903.

Corresp and misc papers 1859-1908 (c48 bundles
and vols) incl letters from Queen Victoria
1872-92, GG Bradley, SR Hole, JB Lightfoot, JJS
Perowne and BF Westcott, letters rel to his *Life
of Christ*, commonplace book, sermons by him
and others and MSS of lectures on schools of
painting.
Canterbury Cathedral Library.

Letters from AP Stanley 1861-81 (29ff).
Lambeth Palace Library (MS 1812).

Letters from Matthew Arnold 1868-88 (18 items).
Bodleian Library, Oxford (MS Eng misc c107).

[252] **FIELD, Frederick** (1801-1885)
Fellow of Trinity College, Cambridge 1824-43;
rector of Reepham 1842-63.

Papers incl theological, philological and classical
notes, notes on Bible revision and papers rel to
his edition of Origen's *Hexapla* etc (11 boxes).
Trinity College, Cambridge.

Collations for his edition of St John Chrysostom's
homilies on St Paul's epistles c1840-60 (5 vols).
Bodleian Library, Oxford (MS Gr th b 3-7).

[253] **FIGGIS, John Neville** (1866-1919)
Rector of Marnhull 1902-7; member of the
Community of the Resurrection, Mirfield 1907-
19.

Corresp and papers (2 boxes), incl letters mainly
to him from Lord and Lady Acton, Mandell
Creighton, WH Frere and others 1889-1919 (c60

items), sermons 1898-1917 (98 items), notebooks, misc papers etc (*c*20 items).
Borthwick Institute, York (Mirfield Deposit 9). NRA 18541.

[254] **FISHER, John** (1748-1825)
Bishop of Exeter 1803-7, of Salisbury 1807-25.

Corresp 1785-1824 incl letters from Hannah More, Lord Nelson, the Duke of Wellington and the royal family (*c*50 items).
Vice-Admiral Sir Peter Berger. NRA 5457.

[255] **FITZALAN-HOWARD, Henry** (1847-1917), 15th Duke of Norfolk 1860

Religious and educational corresp and papers 1860-1917 (40 bundles and items) incl letters from FW Faber and JH Newman, general and charitable corresp incl corresp of his private secretaries (*c*500 bundles) with other political, family and estate corresp and papers.
Duke of Norfolk. Partly closed to research.

[256] **FLETCHER, John William** (1729-1785)
Methodist; vicar of Madeley, Shropshire 1760-85.

Family and personal corresp, papers and literary MSS (44 boxes) incl corresp, journals, commonplace books, and notes and papers of his wife and their adopted daughter, Mary Tooth.
Methodist Archives, Manchester.

[257] **FLINT, Robert** (1838-1910)
Professor of divinity, Edinburgh 1876-1903.

Notebooks and papers (50 vols, 3 boxes).
Edinburgh University Library (MSS Gen 631-89).

Lecture notes, sermons and papers (3 boxes).
New College, Edinburgh.

[258] **FOLEY, Henry** (1811-1891)
Jesuit; historian.

Letters to him, incl some from John Morris, 1853-74 (2 bundles); corresp, notes and papers 1836-91 (1 box, 1 bundle); working papers for *Records of the English province of the Society of Jesus* (5 vols); notes on St Francis Xavier, Liverpool and Lancashire history (2 bundles); financial papers 1851-84 (3 bundles); legal precedents (3 vols); misc papers (3 bundles).
Society of Jesus, London.

[259] **FOLLOWS, Ruth (née Alcock)** (1717-1808)
Quaker minister, Castle Donington.

Personal and family corresp 1763-1807 (2 boxes).
Society of Friends Library, London (Temp MSS 127). Presented by GE Follows 1968.

[260] **FORBES, Alexander Penrose** (1817-1875)
Bishop of Brechin 1847-75.

Corresp and misc papers 1844-75, mainly rel to the eucharistic controversy of 1860 and other doctrinal questions (*c*900 items), incl letters from John Keble (54 items) and EB Pusey (64 items).
Dundee University Library. Deposited with the Brechin diocesan library 1977. NRA 26461.

Corresp rel to ecclesiastical and liturgical affairs 1845-75 (*c*60 items) incl letters from WE Gladstone (4 items), HP Liddon (4 items) and JH Newman (3 items); notebooks and papers rel to liturgical and devotional matters *c*1853-74 (6 items).
Bishop of Brechin. Enquiries to NRA (Scotland) (NRA (S) 2706).

Letters from AJ Beresford Hope and others rel to lay membership of church synods etc 1848, 1852 (33ff).
Lambeth Palace Library (MS 1543).

[261] **FORBES, George Hay** (1821-1875)
Episcopalian minister at Burntisland 1848-75.

Corresp 1812-95 (9 boxes) incl letters from AP Forbes and Charles Wordsworth; misc papers, mainly rel to his liturgical work and the Pitsligo press (5 boxes).
St Andrews University Library.

Corresp, literary and historical papers 1839-67 (*c*500 items).
Scottish Record Office (CH 12).

[262] **FORD, Hugh Francis [Edmund]** (1851-1930)
Abbot of Downside 1900-6; superior at Ealing 1906-16.

Corresp with Edmund Bishop, EC Butler, WJH Clifford, Paul Cullen, FA Gasquet, Lord Petre, HA Vaughan and others 1873-1930 (*c*50 bundles); papers and misc corresp rel to Downside and Benedictine affairs, incl constitutional reforms (3 boxes, 3 vols, 15 bundles); papers and sermons as missionary priest at Beccles 1889-94 (14 vols, 3 bundles); student notes at Downside 1867 and in Rome 1885, projected monastic history 1906, and theological papers incl corresp with George Tyrrell rel to Biblical inspiration 1903-5 and Martin D'Arcy rel to the eucharist 1924-5 (25 vols, 26 bundles); diaries 1872-3, 1876-7, 1895-7, 1914-15 (10 vols); travel journals and notes, mainly in Italy, *c*1912-22 (17 vols); engagement diaries *c*1888-1930 (29 vols); misc notes and music MSS (1 box, 6 bundles, 1 vol); family papers and personal accounts (*c*3 vols); photographs and press cuttings (1 box, 6 bundles, 2 vols).
Downside Abbey.

Corresp with Sebastian Cave 1902-15 (45 items) and JG Dolan 1899-1904 (184 items); misc

collected letters from him largely rel to the Ealing house 1896-1908 (234 items).
Ealing Abbey.

[263] **FOWLER, Robert** (1724-1801)
Archbishop of Dublin 1779-1801.

Accounts 1766-97 (1 vol).
National Library of Ireland (MS 14, 123). See *Manuscript sources for the history of Irish civilisation: first supplement*, 1979.

[264] **FOWLER, Robert** (1768-1841)
Bishop of Ossory 1813-35, of Ossory, Ferns and Leighlin 1835-41.

Personal and family corresp incl letters from the Duke of Wellington.
Brigadier BJ Fowler. See *Manuscript sources for the history of Irish civilisation: first supplement*, 1979.

Diary 1792-4.
Representative Church Body Library, Dublin (MS T 20).

[265] **FOX, William Johnson** (1786-1864)
Independent minister of South Place Chapel, Finsbury, London 1824-52.

Diary 1812-15.
Public Record Office of Northern Ireland.

[266] **FRASER, Alexander Campbell** (1819-1914)
Professor of logic and metaphysics, Edinburgh 1856-91.

Corresp of Fraser and his family, mainly rel to the *North British Review*, university administration etc 1830-1915 (5 boxes); personal corresp 1834-1910 (8 boxes) incl letters from Sir David Brewster, John Cairns, Sir William Kaye, Alexander Macmillan, David Masson, Bonamy Price, AS Pringle-Pattison, Isaac Taylor and Richard Whately; family corresp 1821-1931 (7 boxes); journals 1839-1908 (11 vols); diary 1850 (1 vol); lectures, sermons, business and legal corresp, etc 1815-1913 (10 boxes); notebooks, literary MSS, memoranda, notes etc 1834-1902 (26 items).
National Library of Scotland (Dep 208). NRA 27273.

Notebooks 1869-81 (3 vols).
Edinburgh University Library (Dc 5 79-81).

[267] **FREMANTLE, William Henry** (1831-1916)
Canon of Canterbury 1882-95; dean of Ripon 1895-1915.

Misc letters to him rel to the Anglo-Continental Society 1880-6, nd (c40ff).
Lambeth Palace Library (MSS 1477, 1479-81).

Sermons (7 boxes).
Bodleian Library, Oxford. Deposited by Ripon College, Cuddesdon 1984.

[268] **FREND, William** (1757-1841)
Unitarian.

Corresp and misc papers (c350 items) incl letters from Theophilus Lindsey 1788-1838 (30 items), Richard and Mary Reynolds 1793-1812 (40 items) and others (c160 items); letters from him to Augustus De Morgan 1828-36 (20 items); memoirs.
Cambridge University Library (Add 7886-7).

[269] **FRERE, Walter Howard** (1863-1938)
Superior of the Community of the Resurrection, Mirfield 1902-13, 1916-22; bishop of Truro 1923-35.

Papers rel to church history, music and liturgy (10 boxes); corresp and papers rel to church affairs (4 boxes); corresp, reports, personal notebooks, minutes etc rel to the Malines Conversations 1921-35 (5 boxes); corresp and papers rel to prayer book revision 1903-25 (7 boxes); misc corresp 1913-37 (1 box).
Borthwick Institute, York (Mirfield Deposit 1-5, 10). NRA 18541.

[270] **FROUDE, Richard Hurrell** (1803-1836)
Fellow of Oriel College, Oxford 1823-36.

Corresp with JH Newman (2 files); letters from Samuel and RI Wilberforce and Isaac Williams (1 file); corresp of Froude and his brother with their mother (1 file).
The Oratory, Birmingham. NRA 27809.

[271] **FROUDE, Robert Hurrell** (1770-1859)
Archdeacon of Totnes 1820-59.

Letters from his son RH Froude 1823-30 (4 files) and from his son's friends on the latter's death (2 files).
The Oratory, Birmingham. NRA 27809.

Journal of Scottish tour 1792 (1 vol).
Houghton Library, Harvard University, Cambridge, Massachusetts (MS Eng 1141).

[272] **FRY, Elizabeth (née Gurney)** (1780-1845)
Quaker minister; prison reformer.

Letters from royalty and other notable correspondents 1818-45 (2 vols); corresp rel to Newgate Prison c1816-45 (13 items); journals 1797-1845 (19 vols) incl journal of her husband Joseph 1833-55 (1 vol); letters to her daughter Richenda 1820-45 (85 items).
Society of Friends Library, London (Temp MSS 9/18, 61/9, 64/1-2, MS Vols s 255-73). Mainly deposited by the Fry family.

Family corresp 1812-45 (*c*145 items).
Society of Friends Library, London (Gurney MSS).
Deposited by Mr QE Gurney.

Corresp with her husband, her daughter
Katharine and between other members of her
family 1700-1872 (6 vols); copy journals and
journal extracts 1796-1845 (2 vols).
British Library (Add MSS 47456-7, Eg MSS 3672-5).

Journals 1816-18, 1821-2 (2 vols); notebook rel to
prisons etc 1828.
Norfolk Record Office.

Extracts from her early journals 1830-6 (1 vol).
Johnson Matthey plc. Microfilm in the Society of
Friends Library.

[273] **FULLER, Andrew** (1754-1815)
Baptist minister, Kettering 1782-1815; secretary
of the Baptist Missionary Society 1792-1815.

Corresp 1793-1815 (2 boxes, 1 vol); letters from
John Fawcett, JW Morris, John Ryland etc 1773-1811 (1 vol); letters to J Sutcliffe 1790-1814 (1
vol); notebook 1791-2.
Baptist Missionary Society, London. NRA 12965.

[274] **GABELL, Henry Dison** (1764-1831)
Headmaster of Winchester College 1810-23.

Letters from Lord Eldon, Edward Maltby, Sir
Walter Scott and others 1787-1830 (*c*50 items).
Winchester College. Purchased at Sotheby's 2 Mar
1965, lots 486-7. NRA 7893.

[275] **GAISFORD, Thomas** (1779-1855)
Regius professor of Greek 1812-35 and dean of
Christ Church, Oxford 1831-55.

Corresp, incl letters from the Duke of Wellington
rel to the bishopric of Oxford etc and from LH
Dindorf, Cyril Jackson and Sir Robert Peel (*c*300
items).
CS Gaisford-St Lawrence Esq.

Misc letters to him 1835, 1843-4 (4 items);
notebook, will and literary MSS etc (1 vol, 1 box,
6 bundles).
Christ Church, Oxford (MSS 349, 458, 461,
489-92a, 538).

[276] **GARBETT, Cyril Forster** (1875-1955)
Archbishop of York 1942-55.

Corresp and papers 1884-1955 (15 boxes, *c*78
vols, 1 bundle) incl corresp and papers rel to
religious broadcasting 1926-50 (1 box) and to the
Moravian church 1935-44 (1 box), memoirs to
1942, war journal and diaries *c*1939-55 (*c*17 vols)
and sermons and addresses 1913-55 (61 vols).
York Minster Library. NRA 26607.

[277] **GASQUET, Francis Neil [Aidan]** (1846-1929)
Prior of Downside 1878-85; president of the
English Benedictine Congregation 1899-1914;
cardinal 1914.

General corresp 1900-28 (20 bundles), corresp
1885-1928 selected by Sir JRS Leslie for his
biography (9 bundles, 1 vol); clerical 1884-1926
(*c*14 bundles) and scholarly and publishing
corresp 1890-1928 (*c*14 bundles); subject files and
corresp rel to the dioceses of Westminster,
Southwark, Newport and Menevia, the
Benedictine Federation, the English colleges at
Rome, Lisbon and Valladolid, international
relations, military chaplaincies, Palestine, Ireland,
the Catholic Union of Great Britain and clergy at
English universities etc (25 files); papers rel to the
Vatican Library, archives etc (2 bundles);
devotional notes and sermons (*c*3 bundles); diaries
1874-1916 (7 vols); autobiography; account books
1915, 1935; family and personal corresp and
papers 1780-1926 (*c*3 bundles); working papers,
notes and transcriptions incl some by Edmund
Bishop and JB Tolhurst (*c*20 bundles, 45 vols);
misc MSS and mementos (*c*7 bundles, 2 boxes);
printed papers and pamphlets, photographs and
press cuttings.
Downside Abbey.

[278] **GEDDES, Alexander** (1737-1802)
Biblical critic.

Misc MSS, mainly poetry (1 bundle); essay on the
situation of English catholics 1791 (1 item).
Essex Record Office (D/DP F 187-191, 257). NRA
23544.

[279] **GEDDES, John** (1735-1799)
Bishop coadjutor of the lowland district, Scotland
1779-97.

Corresp and papers incl autobiographical papers
(6 bundles), papers rel to Scotland and the
Scottish mission 16th-18th cent (15 bundles), 'On
the duties of a Catholic missionary' (2 vols or
bundles), theological complications etc (8
bundles) and accounts 1767-92 (15 bundles).
Scottish Catholic Archives (B 2; BL 3, 4; ED 1;
SM 10).

[280] **GEORGE, Alfred John** (1879-1956)
Baptist minister, Llanberis and Llanrug 1909-24,
Llithfaen and Tyddynshon 1924-56.

Corresp, mainly letters from his brother William,
his father and other relatives and letters rel to
pastoral matters etc 1897-1951 (*c*1,200 items);
sermons; misc papers.
National Library of Wales. Presented by GW
George. See *Annual Report* 1970-1, p31.

[281] **GIBSON, Matthew** (1734-1790)
Vicar apostolic of the northern district 1780-90.

Corresp and papers 1780-90 (c125 items) incl
corresp rel to students intended for the English
College, Rome, to former Jesuits and the
appointment of the London district vicar apostolic
1790 and the oath of allegiance, itinerary of visits
to his district 1782-4 and bulls of appointment,
faculties etc.
Ushaw College, Durham (Ushaw collection). NRA
13674.

Corresp and papers 1780-90 incl letters to him as
vicar apostolic, drafts of pastoral letters and
copies of reports to Rome (c70 items).
Bishop of Leeds.

[282] **GIBSON, William** (1738-1821)
President of the English College, Douai 1781-90;
vicar apostolic of the northern district 1790-1821.

Corresp and papers 1780-1821 (c900 items) incl
letters from other vicars apostolic and from
Charles and Robert Plowden rel to compensation
for the seizure of Douai, the Catholic committee,
the oath of allegiance etc.
Bishop of Leeds.

Letters to him, mainly from John Milner 1788-
1813 (30 items); proposals for the establishment
of a successor college to Douai in northern
England 1798 etc.
Ushaw College, Durham (President's archives and
Ushaw college history). NRA 13674.

Letters from bishops, clergy and others rel to
Catholic emancipation 1796-1814 (95 items), to
mission funds etc 1790-1814 (c50 items) and to
other financial matters 1790-1810 (9 items).
Northumberland Record Office (Hexham and
Newcastle diocesan archives). NRA 28236.

[283] **GILLETT, George** (1837-1893)
Quaker minister.

Corresp and papers (1 box), mainly letters from
him to his wife Hannah Rowntree c1860-70 and
earlier corresp; letters from AW Davidson of the
Friends Foreign Mission Association, Chungking,
China to Sir GM Gillett 1897-1938 (1 bundle).
Society of Friends Library, London (Temp MSS
119). Presented by the children of Sir GM Gillett
1968.

[284] **GILLIS, James** (1802-1864)
Vicar apostolic of the eastern district, Scotland
1852-64.

Corresp and papers, mainly as coadjutor bishop
and vicar apostolic, 1827-64 (81 bundles) incl
letters from JR Hope-Scott 1851-63 (1 bundle),
JF Kyle 1833-62 (5 bundles), AW Pugin and his
family 1850-6 (2 bundles) and JM Strain 1838-63
(6 bundles) and corresp and papers rel to
individual missions etc 1830-64 (26 bundles);

personal corresp, sermons and other papers 1827-
63 (c56 bundles).
Scottish Catholic Archives (B 6; ED 2).

[285] **GILMORE, Isabella** (1842-1923)
Deaconess.

Corresp and papers incl letters from bishops and
others 1885-1923, family corresp and memoir of
her work in Southwark diocese from 1886 (1
box).
Church House, Westminster. NRA 26474.

[286] **GILPIN, William** (1757-1848)
Rector of Pulverbatch 1806-48.

Drafts of his letters from Cheam School and
letters to him 1792-1830 (191ff); journal and
related notebooks 1793-1847 (176 vols).
Bodleian Library, Oxford (MSS Eng misc c 392, f
201-376). NRA 8157.

Letters to his wife 1775-1821 (c100 items) and
literary papers.
Bodleian Library, Oxford (MSS Eng lett b 36,
c 534 and *passim*).

[287] **GLEIG, George** (1753-1840)
Bishop of Brechin 1808-40 and primus of the
Scottish episcopal church 1816-37.

Corresp and misc family papers 1787-1927 (4
vols), incl copy of his memoirs 1886 (1 vol) and
corresp of his son GR Gleig, chaplain-general of
the forces.
National Library of Scotland (MSS 3869-72).
Purchased at Sotheby's 19 June 1951, lots 460,
462-3, 465-8, 470.

[288] **GOBAT, Samuel** (1799-1879)
Bishop in Jerusalem 1846-79.

Corresp and papers rel to his diocese 1844-78
(194ff) among those of the Jerusalem and the East
Mission Fund.
Lambeth Palace Library (MS 2338). Presented by
the Fund 1969.

Journals of tours in the Middle East and
Abyssinia 1827-41 (3 vols); remarks on Abyssinia
1833 (24pp).
Church Missionary Society, London (Mediterranean
missions). NRA 12770.

[289] **GOLIGHTLY, Charles Pourtales** (1807-
1885)
Anti-tractarian.

Corresp, mainly rel to his opposition to
tractarianism in the university and diocese of
Oxford, 1823-81 (8 vols).
Lambeth Palace Library (MSS 1804-11).

[290] **GORDON, Alexander** (1841-1931)
Principal of the Unitarian Home Missionary
College, Manchester 1890-1911.

Letters from James Martineau 1867-89 (25 items),
William Pierce 1906-19 (16 items) and others
1867-1928 (25 items).
John Rylands University Library of Manchester
(Unitarian College Manchester MSS).

[291] **GORDON, John** (1807-1880)
Unitarian minister.

Letters from RB Aspland 1844-69 (249 items),
Samuel Bache 1842-70 (105 items), Charles Beard
c1850-80 (184 items), James Martineau 1842-78
(46 items), William Smith 1856-80 (69 items) and
others c1839-80 (c630 items).
John Rylands University Library of Manchester
(Unitarian College Manchester MSS).

[292] **GORDON, William Thomas [Philip]**
(1827-1900)
Oratorian.

Letters from JH Newman 1849-87 (1 vol); journal
as superior of the Oratory 1869 with extracts from
his journal 1847-53 annotated by RF Kerr; diaries
1852-3, 1856 (2 vols).
The Oratory, London. NRA 16631.

[293] **GORE, Charles** (1853-1932)
Bishop of Worcester 1902-5, of Birmingham
1905-11, of Oxford 1911-19.

Corresp and papers rel to his ecclesiastical career
1876-1935 (2 bundles); corresp rel to liturgical
practices 1893-1926 (47 items); family corresp
1864-1931 (328 items); misc corresp c1895-1927
(c50 items).
Borthwick Institute, York (Mirfield Deposit 12).
NRA 18541.

[294] **GORHAM, George Cornelius** (1787-1857)
Vicar of Brampford Speke 1847-57.

Pastoral journal 1843 (9ff); misc papers c1847-60
(70ff) with letters to his daughter Jane Eulalia
1838-56 (112ff).
Bodleian Library, Oxford (MSS Eng th d 42, Eng
lett d 142).

Letters from Robert Southey and others 1835-49
(9 items).
Cowper and Newton Museum, Olney, Bucks. See
*Transactions of the Cambridge Bibliographical
Society,* iv, 2, 1965.

Sermons 1811-35 (3 boxes).
Queens' College, Cambridge (MSS 80-82). NRA
28854.

[295] **GOSS, Alexander** (1814-1872)
RC bishop of Liverpool 1856-72.

Letters to him as bishop (14 boxes *passim*) incl
some personal corresp and letters from Cornelia
Connelly; letter books 1855-72 (5 vols) and
secretary's letter books 1855-67 (2 vols); visitation
diaries 1865-8 (2 vols) and secretary's copies 1855-
68 (c900pp); collection for a history of catholicism
in northern England (1 bundle).
Lancashire Record Office (Liverpool archdiocesan
records).

Papers rel to Ushaw and higher education c1860
incl corresp with NPS Wiseman and the
Propaganda (6 boxes).
Ushaw College, Durham (Liverpool diocesan
archives).

Collections for a history of catholicism in
northern England (c4 boxes).
Upholland College, Skelmersdale.

[296] **GOULBURN, Edward Meyrick** (1818-
1897)
Headmaster of Rugby School 1849-57; dean of
Norwich 1866-89.

Letters to him 1849-88 (11 vols, 25 items) and
letter book 1868-73 (1 vol).
Norfolk Record Office (MC 47, DCN 121/1, 5).

Engagement diaries 1861-87 (14 vols) and
sermons.
Norwich Cathedral Library.

[297] **GRADWELL, Robert** (1777-1833)
Rector of the English College, Rome 1818-28;
bishop coadjutor of the London district 1828-33.

Corresp and papers as rector and agent of the
English vicars apostolic; personal and family
corresp 1806-18; memorials on the state of the
English mission 1818 (1 vol).
English College, Rome (Scritture 54-55 *passim*, 56-
62, Libri 650).

Letters to him, mainly from William Poynter,
1817-27 (1 vol); corresp with JY Bramston 1828
(1 bundle); personal corresp and papers 1828-32
(120 items); journals as rector 1817-25 (2 vols);
diary, Rome 1818 (1 vol).
Westminster Diocesan Archives (A70, 75, B30, E7,
8, Z41). NRA 28616.

Misc corresp and papers 1795-1834 (14 bundles
and vols) incl corresp at Crook Hall, Claughton
and Rome 1797-1831 (1 bundle), letters from or
rel to sisters of Sion House, Lisbon 1814-17 (3
bundles) and account books 1810-17 (2 vols).
Lancashire Record Office (RCCl/3). NRA 14963.

[298] **GRANT, Thomas** (1816-1870)
Rector of the English College, Rome 1844-51;
bishop of Southwark 1851-70.

Corresp with the Admiralty, Colonial and Foreign
Offices, and corresp and papers rel to the

Crimean War and military chaplaincies 1850-70 (4 boxes); letters from clergy 1852-70, incl John Briggs 1852-9, James Brown 1859-66 and John Morris 1866-8 (1 box); corresp and papers rel to family affairs, the Achilli case and Ireland 1856-66 (1 box); letters to him in Rome 1869-70, mainly from James Danell (1 box); letters to him 1845-70 from George Errington 1850-60, James Butt at Scutari 1852, NPS Wiseman 1852-64, WB Ullathorne and HE Manning 1853-68, Francis Searle and George Talbot *c*1860-70 and others (6 boxes *passim*); financial and executorship papers (4 boxes).
Southwark Diocesan Archives. NRA 27760.

Letters to him 1845-51 and papers as rector.
English College, Rome (Scritture 77-78 *passim*).

[299] **GRAVES, Charles** (1812-1899)
Bishop of Limerick, Ardfert and Aghadoe 1866-99.

Corresp and papers as bishop, mainly rel to the reformed episcopal churches in Spain and Portugal 1875-95 (6 files) incl corresp with RS Gregg 1889-94 (21 items), WC Plunket 1883-94 (12 items) and Charles Reichel 1889-94 (21 items).
Representative Church Body Library, Dublin (D 13). NRA 29206.

Papers rel to Irish antiquities 1850, 1866.
Royal Irish Academy, Dublin (MSS 3 A 56, 24 E 13). See *Manuscript sources for the history of Irish civilisation*, 1965.

[300] **GRAY, John** (1817-1872)
Bishop coadjutor 1862-65 and vicar apostolic 1865-69 of the western district, Scotland.

Corresp and papers as coadjutor 1862-5 (12 bundles *passim*), rel to the *Free Press* affair 1863-4 (4 bundles) and as vicar apostolic 1866-9 (4 bundles).
Scottish Catholic Archives (OL 2, 3).

Corresp as bishop coadjutor and vicar apostolic with Alessandro Barnabo, JF Kyle, James Lynch, HE Manning and others 1862-9 (8 bundles).
Glasgow Archdiocesan Archive.

[301] **GREEN, Charles Alfred Howell** (1864-1944)
Bishop of Monmouth 1921-8, of Bangor 1928-44; archbishop of Wales 1934-44.

Diaries 1889-1944; addresses 1889-1944; sermons 1930-42; visitation articles and returns 1939-42 (12 vols); misc notes and papers rel to the church in Wales and Welsh history.
National Library of Wales. Mainly deposited by his widow. See *Annual Report* 1943-4, p18.

Corresp 1894-1941 (8 vols); printed and misc official papers rel to the church in Wales 1869-1942 (52 vols and bundles).

St Deiniol's Library, Hawarden. Access through the County Archivist, Clwyd Record Office. NRA 24327.

[302] **GREEN, Sidney Faithhorn** (1841-1916)
Rector of St John the Evangelist, Miles Platting 1869-82, of Charlton, Dover 1889-1914.

Corresp and papers rel to his imprisonment in Lancaster gaol 1881-2 incl letters from the archbishops of Canterbury and York (1 box, 2 vols).
Manchester Central Library (MS f 922.3 G100).

[303] **GRESLEY, William** (1801-1876)
Perpetual curate of Boyne Hill, Berks 1857-76.

Corresp and misc papers rel to 'The Englishman's Library' etc 1835-67 (356 items) incl letters from Edward Churton 1839-60 (97 items).
Pusey House, Oxford. NRA 29543.

[304] **GRIFFITH, John Thomas** (1845-1917)
Baptist minister in the United States and Wales.

Diaries 1871-1914 (35 vols); misc letters, family papers, notes etc *c*1816-1915.
University College of North Wales, Bangor.

Papers.
National Library of Wales. Presented by North Wales Baptist College 1979.

[305] **GRIFFITHS, Evan** (1795-1873)
Independent minister.

Diaries 1848-69 (2 vols); sermons, addresses etc (2 vols, 2 bundles).
National Library of Wales (MSS 28, 176-7, 275, 2188-9).

[306] **GRIFFITHS, Peter Hughes** (1871-1937)
Minister of Charing Cross Road Welsh Presbyterian Church, London 1902-37.

Corresp and papers, mainly letters to him and his wife, rel to his *Cofiant WE Prytherch* 1932-6 (1 box); corresp and papers incl diary notes and memoranda of his visit to South Africa 1919, sermons, notes rel to preaching engagements etc (1 box).
National Library of Wales. Presented and deposited by TI Ellis. See *Annual Report* 1954-5, p25, 1963-4, p50, 1966-7, p26.

[307] **GRIFFITHS, Thomas** (1791-1847)
President of St Edmund's College, Ware 1818-34; vicar apostolic of the London district 1836-47.

Corresp and papers as coadjutor and vicar apostolic 1835-47 (25 boxes); corresp and papers, incl letters from NPS Wiseman 1829-47 (*c*60 items), and from other vicars apostolic, Thomas

Brindle and John Lingard 1833-47 (*c*827 items), corresp with Gregory XVI, papers rel to churches overseas, the *Dublin Review*, Catholic Institute, charities, confraternities etc 1830-47 (*c*108 items); copies of letters to Rome and to clergy 1836-47 (2 vols); notebook 1841-7 (1 vol); official diary 1832-47, personal diaries 1819, 1834-7.
Westminster Diocesan Archives (A77-101, W1 and 2 passim, B4, 5, E10, Z40-42, 76). NRA 28616.

Corresp and papers rel to St Edmund's College 1818-46 (*c*100 items).
Westminster Diocesan Archives (St Edmund's College Ware, series 2, 14). NRA 16303.

[308] **GRIFFITHS, William** (1788-1861)
Calvinistic methodist minister in the Gower.

Personal and family corresp incl letters from Lord and Lady Barham 1817-61; journals 1815-55 (6 vols); diaries 1837-51 (6 vols); day book 1854-61; autobiographical notebook nd; text book 1817-61; sermon notes 1817-61 (45 items); accounts rel to chapel building etc 1838-54; misc papers.
National Library of Wales. Bequeathed 1974-5.

Journal 1819-22 (1 vol).
National Library of Wales (Presbyterian Church of Wales MSS, General Collection). NRA 28345.

[309] **GRUBB, Edward** (1854-1939)
Quaker minister; secretary of the Howard Association 1901-06; editor of the *British Friend* 1901-13.

Letters, mainly to his sister Sarah 1869-75 (20 items); account of his visit to France 1919 and autobiography to 1930 (1 vol).
Society of Friends Library, London (Temp MSS 35/5, 57/14). NRA 20087.

Notebooks rel to prison visits, mainly in Britain and the United States 1903-5 (2 vols).
Warwick University Modern Records Centre (Howard League for Penal Reform MSS 16A/7/6-7). NRA 16356.

[310] **GURNEY, Joseph John** (1788-1847)
Quaker minister.

Corresp mainly with members of his family *c*1803-46 (*c*900 items) incl letters to his family from North America 1837-40 (130 items); private journals 1808-47 (5 vols) incl journal of his readings, studies and literary work 1811-37; autobiography 1837; proof copy of MS describing his travels in North America, with his corrections 1841.
Society of Friends Library, London (Gurney MSS; MS Vols 181-5, MS Vols s 32, 356-7). Partly deposited by Mr QE Gurney.

Private journals 1818-46; notebooks and journals *c*1806-18 (4 items); journals of visits to Ireland, the West Indies and Europe 1827-43 (3 items); autobiography 1837; memoranda (1 bundle); MS

of *Chalmeriana* 1830-3; letters to his children and sisters from North America 1837-40; misc papers.
Norfolk Record Office and *Mrs RQ Gurney*. NRA 15293.

[311] **GWALCHMAI, Humphrey** (1788-1847)
Calvinistic methodist minister.

Diary 1816; notebooks, mainly containing minutes of various associations 1810-28 (26 vols); misc papers rel to the Confession of Faith etc.
National Library of Wales (Presbyterian Church of Wales MSS, Bala College Group). NRA 28416.

[312] **GWATKIN, Henry Melvill** (1844-1916)
Dixie professor of ecclesiastical history, Cambridge 1891-1916.

Collected corresp and papers of and rel to him 1856-1928 (10 boxes) incl corresp with his family, churchmen and other scholars 1856-1916 (*c*550 items), journals 1855-6 (2 vols), sermons and lectures to clergy 1888-1914 (23 items), lecture notes nd (7 bundles, 1 vol) and corresp and papers rel to HD Hazeltine's unpublished memoir of him *c*1922-8.
Emmanuel College, Cambridge (COL 9.39).

[313] **HAIGH, Mervyn George** (1887-1962)
Bishop of Coventry 1931-42, of Winchester 1942-52.

Letters to him 1927-42 (18ff) rel to prayer book revision, church and state relations and the Lambeth Conference 1930; misc papers, mainly printed, 1917-64 (13ff).
Lambeth Palace Library (MSS 1468, 1773). Presented by his sister, Mrs Monica Blackman 1963.

HALIFAX, Earl of, see Wood CL.

[314] **HALL, George William** (1770-1843)
Master of Pembroke College, Oxford 1809-43; vice-chancellor of Oxford University 1820-4.

Corresp and papers *c*1784-1844 (74 bundles, 8 vols, *c*100 items), mainly rel to college and university administration, incl letters to him from Lord Grenville 1814-24 (1 bundle) and Robert Peel 1822-8 (*c*2 bundles).
Pembroke College, Oxford. Mainly presented by his grandson, LH Hall. NRA 29439.

General corresp 1799-1839 incl letters from bishops and churchmen rel to patronage, personal, university and college affairs (1 vol).
Pembroke College, Oxford. Purchased from his grandson HW Hall, 1949. NRA 29439.

[315] **HALLAHAN, Margaret Mary** (1803-1868)
Founder of the English Congregation of St
Catherine of Siena.

Collected corresp and papers of and rel to her
1800-88 (13 boxes).
St Dominic's Convent, Stone. NRA 27580.

[316] **HAMILTON, Walter Kerr** (1808-1869)
Bishop of Salisbury 1854-69.

Family, personal and diocesan corresp *c*1820-69
(10 boxes); journals, notebooks and commonplace
books (42 vols).
Pusey House, Oxford.

Personal notes on his clergy and other diocesan
and parochial affairs *c*1856-60 (1 vol).
Wiltshire Record Office. P Stewart, *Guide to the
records of the bishop ... of Salisbury*, 1973, p19.

[317] **HAMPDEN, Renn Dickson** (1793-1868)
Regius professor of divinity, Oxford 1836-48;
bishop of Hereford 1848-68.

Corresp and misc papers 1802-66 (337 items),
mainly rel to the controversies over his
appointments as professor of divinity and bishop
of Hereford, incl letters from Edward Copleston
1827-49 (13 items), Lord Melbourne 1836-41 (18
items), Lord John Russell 1847-8 (9 items), the
Duke of Wellington 1834-7 (11 items), Richard
Whately 1833-47 (15 items) and Samuel
Wilberforce 1847-63 (11 items).
Oriel College, Oxford.

[318] **HANNAH, John** (1792-1867)
Wesleyan methodist minister.

Letters from Jabez Bunting, Alexander Kilham
and others 1824-52 (51 items); sermon registers
1814-67; notebooks on baptism and schism (2
vols).
Methodist Archives, Manchester.

[319] **HARE, Julius Charles** (1795-1855)
Archdeacon of Lewes 1840-55.

Letters from William Whewell 1818-52 (109
items).
Trinity College, Cambridge (Add MS a215-16,
c53). NRA 8804.

Letters from AT Gilbert, bishop of Chichester
1842-55 (180 items).
West Sussex Record Office (Add MS 1867).
Deposited by Bishop Bell 1958.

[320] **HARRISON, Benjamin** (1808-1887)
Archdeacon of Maidstone 1845-87.

Letters to him 1854-8, 1873-81 (2 vols).
Bodleian Library, Oxford (MSS Eng lett d 317-
18). Purchased 1972.

[321] **HARTLEY, Marshall** (1846-1928)
Wesleyan methodist minister.

Letters from FW MacDonald 1905-23 (16 items),
JS Simon 1907-23 (11 items), WL Watkinson
1901-14 (18 items), Sylvester Whitehead 1904-10
(11 items), Luke Wiseman 1913 (14 items), DT
Young 1914-21 (7 items) and others 1850-1925
(*c*40 items).
Methodist Archives, Manchester.

[322] **HATCH, Edwin** (1835-1889)
Vice-principal of St Mary Hall, Oxford 1867-85;
university reader in ecclesiastical history 1884-9.

Corresp 1865-89 (96ff); hymns by him (14ff).
Lambeth Palace Library (MS 1467). Presented by
Miss EC Hatch 1951.

Corresp and photographs, incl letters to Edward
Hawkins (1 vol); biography by his wife (4 vols).
Oriel College, Oxford.

Engagement diaries 1858-86 (13 vols).
Pembroke College, Oxford (63/11). NRA 29439.

[323] **HAVERGAL, Frances Ridley** (1836-1879)
Hymn-writer.

Corresp, poems, hymns, autobiography and other
literary papers 1884-*c*1890 (*c*115 vols), with
personal and family papers incl diaries, poems,
photographs etc 1848-76 (*c*30 items).
Hereford and Worcester Record Office, Worcester.
Deposited by her great-niece, Miss CAM
Havergal, 1975-6. NRA 19451.

Notebook of poems 1869-72 (1 vol); corresp 1879
(1 bundle).
Church Missionary Society, London (Unofficial
papers Acc 95). Presented by Miss MVG
Havergal 1886. NRA 22944.

[324] **HAVERGAL, Francis Tebbs** (1829-1890)
Vicar choral of Hereford cathedral 1853-74; vicar
of Pipe with Lyde 1861-74, of Upton Bishop
1874-90.

Letters from his sister Frances 1841-79 (1 vol and
loose items); corresp and papers rel to Hereford
cathedral fabric and furnishings *c*1871-81 (1 vol)
and to the Hereford *Mappa Mundi* 1870-*c*1881 (1
vol and loose items); misc papers rel to parochial
affairs.
Hereford Cathedral Library.

Letters to him mainly on antiquarian subjects
1853-84 (4 vols).
Hereford and Worcester Record Office, Hereford
(C 71). NRA 29105.

[325] **HAWKER, Robert Stephen** (1803-1875)
Vicar of Morwenstow 1834-75 and of Welcombe
1851-75.

Corresp with his family and others, mainly letters
from him *c*1840-75 (4 vols); books of reflections

*c*1844-58 (7 vols); sermons and sermon notes
*c*1844-65 (7 vols); literary papers and verses (3
vols); accounts and misc papers 1819-72 (2 vols).
Bodleian Library, Oxford. (MSS Eng lett d 223-6
and *passim*). Purchased 1968. NRA 17021.

Corresp with WD Anderson and misc papers
1848-63, mainly letters from him rel to parochial
life and personal affairs (90 items).
Pembroke College, Oxford. NRA 29439.

Misc corresp and papers rel to him 1860-75 (1
vol).
Bodleian Library, Oxford (MS Eng misc d 16).
Purchased 1892.

Book of reflections *c*1860.
British Library (Add MS 41090).

[326] **HAWKINS, Edward** (1789-1882)
Provost of Oriel College, Oxford 1828-82.

Corresp and misc papers 1815-82 (*c*750 items) incl
letters from EB Pusey 1827-66 (*c*40 items) and
Joseph Blanco White 1828-41 (*c*40 items) and
corresp with Edward Copleston 1829-48 (*c*70
items), WE Gladstone 1845-73 (96 items), JH
Newman, mainly rel to the controversy about the
Oriel tutorial system, 1830-69 (*c*40 items),
Richard Whately 1826-63 (*c*110 items) and
William Whewell 1845-60 (*c*40 items).
Oriel College, Oxford. Mainly deposited by his
grandson Edward Hawkins.

MS lectures, with those of Richard Whately, 1847
(2 boxes).
Oriel College, Oxford.

[327] **HAWTREY, John** (1781-1853)
Rector of Kingston Seymour.

Letters to him 1798-1853 (58 items); diaries as an
army officer 1804-9 (5 vols); misc papers mainly
rel to his career as a methodist minister and
anglican clergyman 1798-1888 (15 bundles and
vols).
Buckinghamshire Record Office (D 65). NRA
11166.

[328] **HAY, George** (1729-1811)
Vicar apostolic of the lowland district, Scotland
1778-1805.

Corresp and papers as vicar apostolic; mission
accounts 1767-1807 (35 bundles); pastoral letters
from him and others, some printed, 1777-98 (22
items); trust papers 1772 (1 bundle); refutation of
Principal Gordon's *Memoire*, 1786; theological and
misc papers of or rel to him (36 bundles and
vols).
Scottish Catholic Archives (B 1; BL 3-4; PL 3; SM
passim).

[329] **HEADLAM, Arthur Cayley** (1862-1947)
Bishop of Gloucester 1923-45.

Corresp and papers 1890-1946 (36 vols) incl
corresp with archbishops of Canterbury 1909-45
(1 vol), papers rel to prayer book revision 1906-29
(3 vols) and to the archbishop's committee on
relations with the Orthodox churches 1913-25 (2
vols) and corresp and papers rel to the world
Conference (later Council) on Faith and Order
1927 and 1937 and Anglican responses to it 1922-
39 (8 vols).
Lambeth Palace Library (MSS 2615-50). Presented
by K Headlam-Morley 1960.

Corresp and papers as editor of *The Church
Quarterly Review* with those of Claude Jenkins,
1901-29 (14 vols).
Lambeth Palace Library (MSS 1616-29).

[330] **HEDLEY, John Cuthbert** (1837-1915)
Bishop of Newport and Menevia 1881-1915.

Corresp and papers of or rel to him (100 files) incl
corresp with other Benedictines (5 bundles), with
Rome, other bishops and rel to diocesan
administration, with HE Manning, Lord Bute (1
file) and others and sermons, accounts etc.
Archbishop of Cardiff.

[331] **HENDERSON, Thomas** (*c*1801-1861)
Vicar of Messing 1827-61 and prebendary of St
Paul's 1842-61.

Corresp 1838-56 (36 items) incl letters from JH
Newman 1838-43 (8 items) and EB Pusey 1842-56
(10 items); copy of lost letter from Newman to
Pusey on Newman's conversion 1845 (1 item).
Pusey House, Oxford. Presented by his descendant
David Tew 1959. NRA 28379.

[332] **HENSON, Herbert Hensley** (1863-1947)
Bishop of Durham 1920-39.

Corresp, memoirs, autobiographical notes etc (3
boxes, 16 bundles, 1 vol); letter books 1882-1944
(11 vols); journals 1885-1947 (103 vols);
commonplace books (3 vols).
Durham Dean and Chapter Library. NRA 28047.

[333] **HERVEY, Lord Arthur Charles** (1808-
1894)
Bishop of Bath and Wells 1869-94.

Letters, mainly to him, 1828-94 from WE
Gladstone (33 items), Connop Thirlwall (8 items),
Richard Chenevix Trench (8 items), Samuel
Wilberforce (8 items) and others (365ff).
Bodleian Library, Oxford (MS Eng lett c 297).
Purchased 1971.

Letters and papers rel to Hervey genealogy and
misc papers 1838-71 (1 vol, 2 bundles, 62 items).

Suffolk Record Office, Bury St Edmunds
(Ac 941/63). Deposited by the National Trust
1958-9. NRA 6892.

[334] **HEURTLEY, Charles Abel** (1806-1895)
Lady Margaret professor of divinity, Oxford
1853-95.

Misc corresp 1881-2 (6 items); travel journal
1866-7 (1 vol).
Pusey House, Oxford. NRA 28380.

Letters from EB Pusey, CR Sumner, AC Tait and
others (1 vol).
Untraced. Sold by Stride and Son 30 Apr 1986,
lot 320.

[335] **HICKS, Edward Lee** (1843-1919)
Bishop of Lincoln 1910-19.

Corresp with his clergy, incl some corresp of his
registrar.
Lincolnshire Archives Office (COR/B/7). NRA
11190.

Misc letters to him *c*1875-*c*1912 (24 items).
Honnold Library, Claremont, California.

[336] **HICKS, Frederick Cyril Nugent** (1872-
1942)
Bishop of Lincoln 1933-42.

Corresp and papers rel to the Church Assembly
1935-41 (1 bundle) and Lincoln Cathedral etc (1
bundle).
Lincolnshire Archives Office (Misc Dep 56). NRA
11190.

[337] **HINDS, Samuel** (1793-1872)
Bishop of Norwich 1849-57.

Letter book 1856-73.
Norfolk Record Office (MS 21702, 507x).

[338] **HINSLEY, Arthur** (1865-1943)
Archbishop of Westminster 1935-43; cardinal
1937.

Official papers 1935-43 (*c*350 boxes) incl papers
rel to anti-fascist and anti-communist activities
and the 'Sword of the Spirit' movement, letters,
bulls, speeches and wartime broadcasts.
Westminster Diocesan Archives.

Papers as rector of the English College, Rome.
English College, Rome (Scritture 86 *passim*).

Corresp and papers rel to the controversy about
the publication of Alfred Noyes's *Voltaire* 1938-9
(*c*70 items).
Westminster Diocesan Archives (St Edmund's
College Ware, series 20). NRA 16303.

[339] **HOCKING, Silas Kitto** (1850-1935)
United Methodist Free Church minister 1870-96;
novelist.

Diary of visit to Ireland 1874; sermons, lecture
notes, papers etc 1871-96 (*c*800 items).
Warwick University Modern Records Centre (MSS
131). Purchased 1976.

[340] **HODGKIN, John** (1800-1875)
Quaker minister.

Corresp rel to personal and Friends' affairs *c*1842-
74 (*c*1,000 items); letter books 1847-68 (11 vols);
misc family papers.
Durham County Record Office (D/Ho). Deposited
by Miss Lois Hodgkin 1966. NRA 12281.

Misc corresp 1819-68 (33 items).
Society of Friends Library, London.

[341] **HODGKIN, Jonathan Backhouse** (1843-
1926)
Quaker minister.

Letters received 1878-1900 (9 bundles); corresp
rel to Great Ayton estate 1873-1902 (17 bundles);
Australian letter books 1866-8 (3 vols); letter
books 1873-97 (5 vols); misc family corresp and
papers.
Durham County Record Office (D/Ho). Deposited
by Miss Lois Hodgkin 1966. NRA 12281.

Corresp and papers, mainly rel to quarterly
meetings and the special premises committee on
Devonshire House *c*1908-18 (*c*125 items).
Society of Friends Library, London (Temp MSS
110).

Corresp and papers mainly rel to the Friends
Foreign Mission Association board revision
committee 1905-7 and corresp rel to ministerial
visits 1892-5 (1 box).
Society of Friends Library, London (Temp MSS
374). Presented by Ronald Hodgkin 1969.

[342] **HODGSON, John** (1779-1845)
Rector of Jarrow 1803-33, vicar of Kirk
Whelpington 1823-33, of Hartburn 1833-45.

Corresp and papers 1801-44 (*c*220 bundles and
vols), incl corresp rel to the Felling mine disaster
1812 (1 bundle), clerical corresp 1802-34 (1
bundle), journals 1832-44 (3 vols), sermons (2
bundles) and extensive antiquarian collections.
Northumberland Record Office (Society of
Antiquaries of Newcastle upon Tyne M14-M15).
NRA 0701.

[343] **HOGARTH, William** (1786-1866)
Vicar apostolic of the northern district 1848-50;
bishop of Hexham (later Hexham and Newcastle)
1850-66.

Letters to him (*c*70 items); letter books 1841-56
(6 vols); pastoral letters, accounts etc 1849-64 (6
vols); misc papers 1850-66 (67 items).

Northumberland Record Office (Hexham and Newcastle diocesan archives). NRA 28236.

[344] **HOOK, James** (c1772-1828).
Dean of Worcester 1825-8.

Corresp of Hook and his wife 1794-1838 (c60 items); letters to them from their son WF Hook 1806-25 (c6 bundles); misc letters to him from political, scientific and literary figures (c20 items).
Mrs Barnaby Green. NRA 0302.

[345] **HOOK, Walter Farquhar** (1798-1875)
Vicar of Leeds 1837-59; dean of Chichester 1859-75.

Letters from bishops and clergy 1830-75 (c100 items), incl EB Pusey 1839-45 (8 items) and Samuel Wilberforce 1868-72 (8 items); letters from political, scientific and literary figures and others (c40 items).
Mrs Barnaby Green. NRA 0302.

Letters from and to Samuel Wilberforce 1836-70 (91ff).
Bodleian Library, Oxford (MS Wilberforce d 38). NRA 7132.

[346] **HOPE-SCOTT, James Robert** (1812-1873)
Ecclesiastical lawyer; RC 1851.

Letters from William Adams 1840-8 (1 vol), HE Manning and EB Pusey 1836-72 (2 vols), letters to EL Badeley 1838-68 (1 vol) and corresp with WE Gladstone 1837-71 (3 vols), NPS Wiseman and others 1840-72 (1 vol); diaries (15 vols).
National Library of Scotland (MSS 3667-94). Purchased 1937.

Letters from his family 1847-71 (3 vols *passim*).
National Library of Scotland (MSS 1556-8).

[347] **HORNE, Percy [Ethelbert]** (1858-1952)
RC parish priest of Stratton-on-the-Fosse 1891-1940.

Corresp and papers (26 boxes) incl letters from and rel to FA Gasquet (2 boxes), letters from JA Robinson (1 box), monastic papers (2 boxes), memoirs and papers as a parish priest (4 boxes), antiquarian corresp and papers rel to Glastonbury excavations 1926-51, martyrs and relics etc (c11 boxes, 2 bundles) and family and personal papers (1 box).
Downside Abbey. NRA 19936.

[348] **HORNE, Thomas Hartwell** (1780-1862)
Prebendary of St Paul's 1831-62.

Letters from peers, bishops and clergy, biblical scholars, historians and others, with misc family corresp, 1822-71 (90ff).
British Library (Add MS 46844).

[349] **HORSLEY, Samuel** (1733-1806)
Bishop of St Davids 1788-93, of Rochester 1793-1802, of St Asaph 1802-6.

Corresp and papers, with those of his son Heneage, dean of Brechin, and misc family papers 1732-1904 (233ff).
Lambeth Palace Library (MS 1767). Presented by Miss EM Jebb 1960.

Transcripts of his biblical papers and sermons made 1807-10 by WJ Palmer, his nephew and chaplain.
Lambeth Palace Library (MSS 2801-13). Presented by Lord Selborne 1975.

Papers rel to theology, Roman and biblical chronology and scientific subjects.
Royal Society (MSS 544-6).

[350] **HORT, Fenton John Anthony** (1828-1892)
Lady Margaret professor of divinity 1887-92, Cambridge.

Letters from HM Butler 1847-70 (c20 items).
Trinity College, Cambridge.

Corresp rel to the Greek NT.
Emmanuel College, Cambridge.

[351] **HOWARD, Edward Henry** (1829-1892)
Cardinal 1887.

Student notebook, Oscott 1845 with list of persons received into the RC church; personal corresp incl letters from HE Manning and HA Vaughan, papers, sermons etc.
English College, Rome (Libri 563, 842, Scritture 92).

[352] **HOWLEY, William** (1766-1848)
Bishop of London 1813-28; archbishop of Canterbury 1828-48.

Letters and papers rel to his early career 1766-1827 (214ff); letters to him as archbishop 1828-47 (250ff); letters from Lord Aberdeen 1808-46 (72ff), Cyril Jackson 1809-13 (53ff) and mainly from bishops rel to his *Letter addressed to the clergy and laity of his province* 1845 (60ff); letters to his wife [1813]-1832 and verses by him (13ff); papers concerning the royal family 1820-47 (197ff); misc papers 1805-48 (416ff and c20 items).
Lambeth Palace Library (MSS 2184-2202). Purchased from his descendant WH Kingsmill 1968.

Corresp and papers as bishop of London 1801-28 (54 vols).
Lambeth Palace Library (Fulham papers).

Corresp rel to the Church of England overseas 1813-28 (4 vols).
Lambeth Palace Library (Fulham papers: Howley 1-4). Deposited by the USPG.

Letters to him and his wife from the royal family 1819-48 (164ff).
Lambeth Palace Library (MS 1754). Purchased 1960.

[353] **HUGHES, Hugh Michael** (1858-1933)
Minister of Ebenezer Congregational Church, Cardiff 1894-1933.

Letters to him 1883-1926 (28 items); diaries 1923-32 (5 vols); papers rel to Griffith John incl letters from him 1889-94 (1 bundle); papers rel to 'Y Gronfa' 1916-23 (1 bundle); corresp, papers and addresses, mainly rel to religious and educational matters (12 bundles); sermons and sermon notes (34 bundles).
National Library of Wales. NRA 28287.

[354] **HUGHES, John** (1775-1854)
Calvinistic methodist minister, Pontrobert.

Letters to him 1808-52 (19 items); letters to his wife 1803-54 (13 items); diary 1828 (3 copies); autobiographical fragments; sermons and sermon notes (10 vols and bundles); preaching register (1 vol); metrical psalms and hymns (*c*3 vols); hymns and letters of Ann Griffiths, taken down by him 1804 (2 vols); notebooks, misc papers.
National Library of Wales (Presbyterian Church of Wales MSS, General Collection). NRA 28345.

[355] **HUGHES, Marian Rebecca** (1817-1912)
Founder of the Society of the Holy and Undivided Trinity.

Letters from JF Mackarness 1877-83, EB Pusey *c*1840-59 and Samuel Wilberforce 1854-9, journals 1841-1911 (4 vols) and other papers.
Pusey House, Oxford.

[356] **HUGHES, Thomas** (1803-1898)
Calvinistic methodist minister.

Family and personal corresp 1838-98 (*c*1,440 items) incl letters from Daniel Davies 1880-98 (46 items); sermons 1861-6 (92 items); lectures, addresses, collected sermons, misc papers.
National Library of Wales (Presbyterian Church of Wales MSS, General Collection). NRA 28345.

[357] **HUNTER, Andrew** (1743-1809)
Professor of divinity, Edinburgh 1779-1809.

Theological lectures 1779-1806 (11 vols) incl lectures on the Epistles (5 vols).
Edinburgh University Library (Dc 3 22-32).

[358] **HUNTINGFORD, George Isaac** (1748-1832)
Warden of Winchester College 1789-1832; bishop of Gloucester 1802-15, of Hereford 1815-32.

Letters to him 1785-1830 (137 items); letters from him to H Richman (37 items) and Henry

Huntingford (65 items); notebooks incl sermons (7 vols) etc.
Winchester College (Fellows Library MSS 137, 137B, 138).

[359] **HUSENBETH, Frederick Charles** (1796-1872)
Mission priest and chaplain to the Jerningham family at Costessey, Norfolk from 1820; vicar-general of Northampton 1852.

Extracts of letters from Thomas Walsh 1826-49 and William Wareing 1840-8, copy of journal of John Milner 1803-25 (1 vol); misc poems, translations etc (5 vols).
Norfolk Record Office (Colman MSS 218-9).

Letters from NPS Wiseman 1831-59 (13 items).
Ushaw College, Durham. NRA 13674.

Notes on Norfolk churches 1847 (1 vol).
Norfolk Record Office (Walter Rye Collection MS 115). NRA 23099.

[360] **HUTCHISON, William [Antony]** (1822-1863)
Oratorian.

Misc corresp and papers 1845-61 incl letters to him (20 items) and papers rel to ragged schools etc (11 items); letters from him in Rome, mainly to FW Faber, 1856 (1 vol); letters from him in the Holy Land and Egypt to priests of the Oratory 1857-8 (107 items) and papers rel to the grotto at Nazareth etc (8 items).
The Oratory, London. NRA 16631.

[361] **HUTTON, James** (1715-1795)
Founder of the Moravian Church in England.

Corresp incl letters from Benjamin Ingham 1738-64, Charles and John Wesley and others 1740-82 (*c*33 bundles).
Moravian Church House, London.

[362] **HUTTON, William Holden** (1860-1930)
Fellow of St John's College, Oxford 1884-1923; dean of Winchester 1919-30.

Letters from RT Davidson, Lord Halifax, CG Lang, Leighton Pullan and others (1 bundle); scrapbook.
Pusey House, Oxford.

Corresp and press cuttings rel to his *Letters of William Stubbs*; misc letters to him *c*1902-23; commonplace book 1876-9.
St John's College, Oxford (MSS 277-8, 331). NRA 7453.

[363] **INGE, William Ralph** (1860-1954)
Dean of St Paul's 1911-34.

Family corresp 1846-98 (1 box); diaries 1888-1951 (38 vols); press cuttings 1914-29 (4 vols).
Magdalene College, Cambridge.

D

Sermons (*c*250 items).
St Paul's Cathedral Library, London.

[364] **JACKSON, John** (1811-1885)
Bishop of Lincoln 1853-68, of London 1868-85.

Papers as bishop of London (29 boxes), incl notes
on clergy interviewed by him 1869-81 (1 vol),
corresp with clergy 1868-84 (19 boxes) and papers
on ritualism mainly rel to individual parishes (4
boxes).
Lambeth Palace Library (Fulham papers).

Letter books 1853-62 (6 vols).
Lincolnshire Archives Office. Transferred from
Lambeth Palace Library (Lambeth Palace
Library, *Annual Report* 1973-4).

Letters to him, his family, chaplains and
suffragan 1839-1903 (2 vols).
British Library (Add MSS 63114-15). Bequeathed
by TS Blakeney 1976.

[365] **JACKSON, Thomas** (1783-1873)
Wesleyan methodist minister.

Letters from Eliza Bradburn 1826-53 (31 items),
William France 1816-44 (64 items), Joseph
Sutcliffe 1823-55 (17 items), Adam Clarke, Joseph
Entwisle and others 1811-57 (*c*60 items); journals
1821, 1836.
Methodist Archives, Manchester.

[366] **JEBB, John** (1775-1833)
Bishop of Limerick 1822-33.

Corresp 1805-33, incl letters from Irish bishops,
clergy and politicians (*c*580 items).
Trinity College, Dublin (MSS 6396-7). Presented
by Miss EM Jebb. NRA 23147.

Letters from his brother Richard 1814-33 (*c*146
items).
In private possession. Copies in Trinity College,
Dublin (MS 7106). NRA 23147.

Letters from Alexander Knox 1799-1830 (2 vols)
and to Knox 1800-31 (2 vols).
British Library (Add MSS 41163-6).

[367] **JEBB, John** (1805-1886)
Canon of Hereford 1870-86.

Corresp 1827-69 (113 items).
Trinity College, Dublin (MS 6398).

Letters from John Keble, HE Manning, JH
Newman and others 1836-62 (24ff).
Lambeth Palace Library (MS 1680). Presented by
Miss EM Jebb 1961.

[368] **JENKINS, Claude** (1877-1959)
Canon of Christ Church and regius professor of
ecclesiastical history, Oxford 1934-59.

Corresp and papers, mainly as professor of
ecclesiastical history at King's College, London
and as canon of Canterbury (3 vols); general
corresp 1902-58 (1 vol); corresp and papers, with
those of AC Headlam, as editor of *The Church
Quarterly Review* 1901-29 (14 vols); corresp and
papers as secretary of the archbishop's advisory
committee on liturgical revision 1911-15 (1 vol);
sermons, lectures and misc papers (7 vols);
indexes and transcripts (37 vols); misc MSS
collected by him (26 vols).
Lambeth Palace Library (MSS 1590-1679).

Misc corresp and papers as canon of Christ
Church and regius professor 1934-58 (5 vols, 2
bundles).
Christ Church, Oxford (1xxiii, a1-5, b1-2). NRA
26895.

[369] **JENKYNS, Henry** (1796-1878)
Canon of Durham 1839-78; professor of divinity,
Durham 1841-65.

Corresp 1821-43 incl letters from Edward
Hawkins, Charles Manners-Sutton, Charles Thorp
and others, and corresp with Henry Hobhouse
1834-43 (1 box); corresp and papers rel to
Durham etc (4 boxes) incl letters from Thomas
Arnold 1819-33 (1 bundle).
Balliol College, Oxford. NRA 25537.

[370] **JENKYNS, Richard** (1782-1854)
Master of Balliol College, Oxford 1819-54 and
dean of Wells 1845-54.

Corresp and papers *c*1793-1834 (3 boxes), incl
letters from Lord Grenville 1824-33 (1 bundle),
corresp and papers rel to Wells 1842-54 (3
bundles) and to Frederick Oakeley and WG Ward
1844-5 (1 box).
Balliol College, Oxford. NRA 25537.

Corresp with his cousin Henry Hobhouse about
the Deanery 1845-6 (1 bundle); misc papers (2
bundles).
Wells Cathedral Library.

[371] **JEUNE, Francis** (1806-1868)
Master of Pembroke College, Oxford 1843-64;
bishop of Peterborough 1864-8.

Corresp and misc papers rel to university and
college administration and reform 1843-64 (175
items) incl letters from WE Gladstone 1853-5 (36
items) and Goldwin Smith 1855-7 (48 items).
Pembroke College, Oxford. NRA 29439.

Corresp, mainly as vice-chancellor, 1859-67 (98ff)
incl letters from Lord Derby 1859-63 (6 items),
WE Gladstone 1859-60 (6 items) and EB Pusey
1862-6 (26 items).
Bodleian Library, Oxford (MS Eng lett d 193).

[372] **JOBSON, Frederick James** (1812-1881)
Wesleyan methodist minister.

Letters from Jabez Bunting 1840-56 (14 items),
WM Bunting 1845-66 (16 items) and John
Hannah and others 1851-80 (c200 items); corresp
with Thomas Cooper 1874-80 (c100 items); misc
notes 1849.
Methodist Archives, Manchester.

[373] **JOHNSON, Hewlett** (1874-1966)
Dean of Manchester 1924-31, of Canterbury 1931-
63.

Corresp and papers c1895-c1966 (c15,000 items),
mainly as dean of Canterbury, incl personal and
family corresp and papers, corresp with GF
Fisher, Victor Gollancz, CG Lang, FJ Shirley and
others rel to ecclesiastical, social and political
affairs, diary 1891 (1 vol) and sermons from c1914
(c300 items).
University of Kent Library. Deposited by his
widow.

[374] **JOLLY, Alexander** (1756-1838)
Bishop of Moray 1798-1838.

Corresp and papers c1771-1838 (c535 items) incl
letters to him on diocesan and general church
affairs 1777-1838 (208 items), corresp with Arthur
Petrie 1778-86 (c20 items) and rel to the
consecration of MHT Luscombe to a continental
bishopric 1825-5 (c35 items), American church
papers, sermons and working papers.
Scottish Record Office (CH 12).

Corresp, sermons and other papers 1781-1827, nd
(c28 items).
Bishop of Aberdeen and Orkney. Enquiries to NRA
(Scotland) (NRA(S) 2698).

[375] **JONES, Evan** (1820-1852)
Minister of Saron Independent Chapel, Tredegar
1845-8; poet and journalist.

Literary MSS, notes, sermons and biographical
collections rel to him made by RO Rees (c30
vols).
National Library of Wales (MSS 1025-36, 2694-5,
2755-69, 2877).

[376] **JONES, Hugh** (1800-1872)
Congregational minister.

Letters to him rel to church and family matters
1832-71 (220 items); diaries 1833-53 (5 vols);
draft letters, sermons, articles and notes (2
bundles); sermon notes (11 bundles and vols);
misc papers (4 bundles and vols).
National Library of Wales (MSS 10275-94).

[377] **JONES, Hugh Chambres** (1783-1869)
Treasurer of St Paul's 1816-69 and archdeacon of
Essex 1823-61.

Personal and official corresp and papers 1708-
1869 (c150 bundles and vols) incl official and
other ecclesiastical corresp 1829-67 (c33 bundles);
further personal corresp 1800-64 (11 bundles);
papers rel to St Paul's (2 bundles, 1 vol); sermons
1798-1850 (64 vols, 3 bundles); misc papers 1746-
1868 (4 bundles, 1 vol and loose items).
Lt-Colonel HMC Jones-Mortimer (Hartsheath MSS
914-1004, 1231-54). Enquiries to Clwyd Record
Office, Hawarden. NRA 16179.

[378] **JONES, Hugh William** (1802-1873)
Minister of Tabernacle Baptist Church,
Carmarthen 1835-72.

Diaries 1835-73 (4 vols).
National Library of Wales (MSS 18996-9). See
Annual Report 1964-5, p28.

[379] **JONES, Michael** (1787-1853)
Principal of the Independent College, Bala 1842-
53

Letters to him 1841-53 (1 vol).
National Library of Wales (MS 6416). Presented
by Goronwy Owen 1929.

Corresp and papers.
National Library of Wales. Presented by AL
Davies. See *Annual Report* 1940-1, p18.

[380] **JONES, Michael Daniel** (1822-1898)
Principal of the Independent College, Bala 1853-
92.

Corresp, diaries, commonplace book, notebooks,
essays, sermons and sermon notes, family papers
and papers rel to the Welsh settlement in
Patagonia 1634-1897 (11 boxes).
University College of North Wales, Bangor.

[381] **JONES, Morgan Hugh** (1873-1930)
Calvinistic methodist historian.

Letters from Richard Bennett 1909-30 (36 items),
EE Morgan 1906-27 (107 items) and others 1888-
1930 (381 items); diary 1911; sermons 1903-28;
corresp, articles, lectures, notes, extracts etc rel to
the Calvinistic Methodist Historical Society;
papers rel to Howel Harris, Griffith Jones,
William Williams and the Trevecca MSS.
National Library of Wales (Presbyterian Church of
Wales MSS, General Collection). NRA 28345.

[382] **JONES, Owen** (1833-1899)
Calvinistic methodist minister, Blaenau Ffestiniog
1864-72, Chatham Street, Liverpool 1872-92.

Letters from Griffith Davies, Robert Roberts and
others 1854-72 (4 vols); diaries 1841-98 (c30

items); literary, topographical and misc papers
(*c*27 vols).
National Library of Wales (MSS 2641-79, 9437-
42).

[383] JONES, Rees Jenkin (1835-1924)
Unitarian minister.

Corresp and papers incl letters from Welsh
emigrants to the United States and rel to
Carmarthen Presbyterian College etc (*c*12 vols);
diaries 1858-1920 (*c*68 vols); commonplace books;
account books; biographical notes rel to Welsh
unitarians, sermon and other notes; materials for
a projected Welsh unitarian hymnal (7 vols);
literary MSS, extracts, transcripts, collected MSS
and misc papers.
National Library of Wales (MSS 4361-70, 14147-
14213). See *Annual Report* 1966-7, p32.

[384] JONES, Robert (1806-1896)
Baptist minister of Llanllyfni, Caerns.

Letters, diaries, sermon notes, legal papers 1842-
91 (1 box).
University College of North Wales, Bangor.

Sermons 1866-82 (3 vols); lectures 1872-9 (1 vol);
'historical record' by him (1 vol).
National Library of Wales (MSS 19571-5).

[385] JONES, William (1726-1800)
Perpetual curate of Nayland 1777-1800.

Sermons 1773-96 (2 vols, 12 items).
Pusey House, Oxford. Presented 1884.

[386] JONES, William (1760-1838)
Quaker minister, Charlbury.

Journals 1784-1838 (11 vols); notebooks 1790-4,
nd (5 vols).
Society of Friends Library, London (MS Box I).

[387] JONES, William Arthur (1818-1873)
Unitarian minister of Mary Street Chapel,
Taunton 1852-66.

Corresp, notes, extracts and papers 1836-73 (7
bundles, 1 vol) incl corresp rel to Taunton
College 1855-73 (1 bundle) and letters from EA
Freeman and others rel to antiquarian and
genealogical matters; diaries 1837-40 (2 vols).
Somerset Record Office. Deposited by Miss A
Farewell Jones 1983. NRA 28386.

[388] JONES, William Owen (1861-1937)
Minister of Free Welsh Chapel, Canning Street,
Liverpool.

Diaries 1898, 1901-8, 1929-31 (7 vols); sermons
and sermon notes (105 vols); addresses (6 vols);
press cuttings 1899-1901 (1 vol).

National Library of Wales. See *Annual Report*
1946-7, p27.

[389] JOWETT, Benjamin (1817-1893)
Master of Balliol College, Oxford 1870-93.

Letters from AP Stanley 1841-58 (*c*150 items).
Balliol College, Oxford (MS 410).

Letters from Sir RBD Morier *c*1873-93 among
other Morier papers (1 bundle, 3 boxes *passim*).
Balliol College, Oxford. Presented by Morier's
granddaughter, Mrs FH Cunnack 1965, 1973.
NRA 26599.

[390] JULIAN, John (1839-1913)
Canon of York 1901-13 and vicar of Topcliffe
1905-13.

Letters and notes to him concerning his
Dictionary of Hymnology 1892 (14 vols); letters to
Daniel Sedgwick, hymnologist, collected by
Julian (11 vols).
British Library (Add MSS 57496-57520).

[391] KAYE, John (1783-1853)
Bishop of Bristol 1820-7, of Lincoln 1827-53.

Corresp as bishop of Lincoln (*c*350 bundles) incl
corresp rel to individual parishes (*c*260 bundles).
Lincolnshire Archives Office (COR/B/5).

[392] KEATING, Frederick William (1859-1928)
Bishop of Northampton 1908-21; archbishop of
Liverpool 1921-8.

Corresp as bishop incl personal letters to him
1909-14 (*c*2 boxes).
Bishop of Northampton.

Papers as archbishop.
Archbishop of Liverpool.

[393] KEATING, Joseph Ignatius (1865-1939)
Editor of *The Month* 1912-39.

Letters to him 1925-39 (1 bundle); copies of
letters from Edward Carroll 1925 (1 bundle);
retreat notes etc 1885-1930 (2 vols, 2 bundles);
literary papers (2 vols); misc personal papers (1
bundle).
Society of Jesus, London.

[394] KEBLE, John (1792-1866)
Professor of poetry, Oxford 1831-41; vicar of
Hursley 1836-66.

Letters from JT Coleridge 1820-60 (60 items),
RH Froude and his family 1823-64 (44 items),
WE Gladstone (23 items), FD Maurice (14
items), Henry Phillpotts (17 items), EB Pusey (2
vols, 134 items) and others 1820-66 (*c*295 items);
family corresp 1806-62 (*c*928 items) incl corresp

with his father 1806-29 (44 items), his brother Thomas 1806-66 (689 items) and letters from his sister Elizabeth 1806-41 (163 items); corresp with members of the Cornish family 1820-66 (1 vol, *c*350 items); corresp and papers for his *Life* of Thomas Wilson (*c*30 bundles, *c*14 vols) and rel to Richard Hooker 1810-47 (6 bundles); legal papers rel to his ordination etc (7 items); sermons 1825-38 (7 items); patristic, biblical and literary MSS (*c*50 vols).
Keble College, Oxford. Presented by his brother Thomas Keble. NRA 21028.

Letters from EB Pusey 1843-4 (10 items); misc family corresp 1814-20; diaries 1825, 1829 (2 items).
Pusey House, Oxford. NRA 19807.

Letters from JT Coleridge 1850-65 (1 vol).
Bodleian Library, Oxford (MS Eng lett d 132).

Collected corresp 1811-66 (101 items) incl letters to him from JH Newman, EB Pusey and others 1840-66 (11 items).
Lambeth Palace Library. Deposited by the Revd Edward Keble 1966.

[395] **KEBLE, Thomas** (1793-1875)
Vicar of Bisley, Glos 1827-73.

Corresp 1806-66 (*c*450 items), mainly letters from his brother John 1806-62 (422 items), EB Pusey 1859 (6 items) and HP Liddon 1866 (7 items).
Keble College, Oxford. NRA 21028.

Letters from Isaac Williams 1832-41, nd (77 items) and others 1835-68 (41 items); letter books 1829-63 (5 vols); papers rel to JC Patteson 1857-63, nd (12 items); list of admissions to Corpus Christi College, Oxford 1517-1843 (1 vol); collected letters from him 1837-69 (34 items).
Lambeth Palace Library. Deposited by the Revd Edward Keble 1966.

Corresp mainly rel to Bisley parish church and choir *c*1845-63 (17 items) and corresp and papers rel to a committee for the relief of distressed weavers 1837-43 (32 items).
Gloucestershire Record Office (P47).

[396] **KEELING, Isaac** (1789-1869)
Wesleyan methodist minister.

Letters from John Beaumont 1811-35 (13 items) and others (15 items); sermon notes.
Methodist Archives, Manchester.

[397] **KELLY, Charles** (1833-1911)
Wesleyan methodist minister.

Corresp, mainly letters from William Arthur and others, 1884-1902 (68 items); preaching registers 1853-68 (2 vols); sermon and lecture notes (5 vols); misc personal papers (4 items).
Methodist Archives, Manchester.

[398] **KELLY, Herbert Hamilton** (1860-1950)
Director of the Society of the Sacred Mission 1893-1910.

General corresp 1890-1950 (30 files); Society letter books 1892-*c*1909 (8 vols); newsletters to members of the Society 1907-10 (1 vol) and to his family 1910-37 (7 items); letters and papers, Japan 1913-17 (3 vols); diary 1906, 1913 (1 vol); autobiography 1919 (1 vol); papers, mainly theological and controversial, 1897-1950 (44 files); subject files (45); papers rel to Society affairs 1891-1912, 1929 (5 vols); retreat addresses 1891-1905 (8 vols); theological and philosophical notes etc 1909-19 (12 vols).
Society of the Sacred Mission, Willen Priory. NRA 26270.

[399] **KENRICK, John** (1788-1877)
Unitarian.

Misc letters to him 1804-64 (*c*18 items); notes of lectures, addresses etc (27 vols and bundles).
Dr Williams's Library, London (24.81, 24.107). NRA 13168.

Letters from him to his wife 1830-60 (7 items); 'memorandum of my life' 1872 and misc biographical material; lectures on English literature (2 vols).
University College London. NRA 20377.

European travel journal 1819.
Borthwick Institute, York. Deposited by St Saviourgate Chapel, York 1968. NRA 13264.

[400] **KENRICK, Timothy** (1759-1804)
Unitarian commentator.

Letters to him and papers rel to him 1773-1804 (1 vol); corresp with his first wife Mary 1785-92 (27 items); letters to his father 1786-99 (10 items).
University College London. NRA 20377.

[401] **KIERAN, Michael** (1807-1869)
RC archbishop of Armagh 1866-9.

Corresp and papers as archbishop (12 files).
Archbishop of Armagh. Microfilm in the Public Record Office of Northern Ireland (MIC 451).

[402] **KILHAM, Alexander** (1762-1798)
Founder of the Methodist New Connexion.

Corresp and papers (4 boxes) mainly letters from Samuel Eversfield 1796-8 (19 items), James Hannam 1796-9 (17 items), William Thom 1796-8 (23 items) and others 1794-8 (*c*350 items); misc papers rel to founding of the Methodist New Connexion 1790-8 (*c*80 items).
Methodist Archives, Manchester. NRA 25770.

[403] **KILVERT, Robert Francis** (1840-1879)
Curate of Clyro 1865-72.

Diaries Apr-July 1870 (2 vols).
National Library of Wales (MSS 21666, 22090).
One volume for Apr-June purchased at Sotheby's
23 July 1979, lot 242; the other for June-July
purchased from Charles Harvey 1985.

Diary July-Aug 1870 (1 vol).
Durham University Library (William Plomer
collection). Purchased *c*1973.

The other nineteen volumes of the original diary
have been destroyed.

[404] **KING, Edward** (1829-1910)
Regius professor of pastoral theology, Oxford
1873-85; bishop of Lincoln 1885-1910.

Corresp with his secretary WW Smith 1885-1909
(312 items).
Lincolnshire Archives Office (COR/B/7/2 People).
From the bishop's registry. NRA 11190.

Sermons, drafts of pastoral letters, visitation
charges and addresses to diocesan conferences etc
1889-96 (18 items); misc letters and papers 1884-
99 (24 items); letters to HR Bramley 1863-1902
(126 items).
Lincolnshire Archives Office (Larken). Deposited
1967. NRA 12435.

Misc papers *c*1863-1910, incl some rel to his trial
1889-90, among those of his domestic chaplain
GF Wilgress.
Lincolnshire Archives Office. See *Archivists' Report*
1953-4, p56.

[405] **KINGSLEY, Charles** (1819-1875)
Rector of Eversley, Hants 1844-75; canon of
Westminster 1873-5.

Corresp of him and his wife with FD Maurice
1851-72 (1 vol); letters to his parents and others
1825-73 (1 vol); letters mainly to him and
members of his family 1839-1910 (1 vol); MS of
'Elizabeth of Hungary' (1 vol).
British Library (Add MSS 41296-9).

Letters to him and his wife (*c*250 items), with
sermons and misc papers.
Princeton University Library, New Jersey (Parish
collection).

Letters from him to his wife and family 1840-74
(*c*650 items).
British Library (Add MSS 62552-7).

Sermons *c*1842-5 (7 vols).
Magdalene College, Cambridge.

[406] **KIRK, John** (1760-1851)
RC priest and antiquary.

Letters from Joseph Berington and others 1783-
1829 (*c*550 items); corresp with Charles Butler

and John Milner 1803-25 (51 items); literary,
theological and historical working papers and
collections *c*1780-1830 (125 items) incl his
annotations of Charles Dodd's notes; collected
papers rel to the Cisalpine committee and
Catholic relief acts 1789-95, incl letters to Thomas
Southwark, (*c*300 items); family papers (20
items); misc papers rel to district finances.
Archbishop's House, Birmingham (St Mary's
College, Oscott). NRA 8129.

Corresp rel to Dodd's *Church history*, to Joseph
Berington's *The faith of Catholics*, with misc
official corresp 1800-26 (26 items); letters to him
1830-51 (*c*50 items) mainly from Thomas Walsh
(31 items) with some draft replies; misc family
letters and financial notes.
Archbishop's House, Birmingham. NRA 8129.

Papers rel to Catholic emancipation 1817-35 (2
boxes), incl corresp 1816-27 (155 items), collected
corresp of the British Catholic Association 1824-
35 (70 items) and copies of Robert Gradwell's
corresp with William Poynter and Charles Butler
1820-1 (2 folders).
Westminster Diocesan Archives (Bramston and
Poynter papers). NRA 28616.

Transcripts of MSS for *Church history* (6 boxes),
biographical collections 1685-8 (4 bundles).
Westminster Diocesan Archives (MSS B8-13, Z6).
NRA 28616.

Diary as a student in Rome 1773-9.
English College, Rome (Libri 816).

[407] **KIRK, Kenneth Escott** (1886-1954)
Bishop of Oxford 1937-54.

Corresp rel to personal affairs 1931-3, Woodard
schools etc 1932-4 and misc papers 1922-34, nd (1
box, 1 bundle).
Oxford University Archives. NRA 27776.

Misc corresp and papers (1 box); sermon notes
and other misc papers.
Rt Revd EW Kemp.

[408] **KNIGHT, Edmund** (1827-1905)
RC bishop of Shrewsbury 1882-95.

Letter books as bishop 1882-1901, with letters of
John Carroll and Hugh Singleton (6 vols).
Bishop of Shrewsbury.

[409] **KNOX, Alexander** (1757-1831)
Theological writer.

Letters from John Jebb 1800-31 (2 vols) and to
Jebb 1799-1830 (2 vols).
British Library (Add MSS 41163-6).

[410] **KNOX, Edmund Arbuthnott** (1847-1937)
Bishop of Manchester 1903-21.

Family corresp incl letters from his sons Ronald
and Wilfred (1 box, 2 bundles).
Earl of Oxford and Asquith.

Corresp and misc papers, mainly rel to his
appointment as bishop of Manchester, incl letters
from FJ Chavasse and other evangelical
churchmen, 1865-1933 (*c*125 items).
Taylor Garrett, solicitors, London.

[411] **KNOX, Ronald Arbuthnott** (1888-1957)
RC chaplain, Oxford University, 1926-39;
monsignor 1936.

Letters to him about his conversion and last
illness (1 file); corresp rel to his translation of the
Bible (1 file); business corresp with Douglas
Woodruff (1 file); copies of letters to enquirers on
matters of faith and doctrine *c*1940-57 (1 file);
sermons, talks and lectures (7 files, 3 boxes, 1
bundle, 1 vol); travel diaries 1904, *c*1955 (2 vols);
Oxford diary 1906 (1 vol) and undergraduate
essays (1 vol); reasons for and against his
conversion (1 item), notes for his successor at the
chaplaincy, Oxford (1 item) and other literary,
devotional and misc papers; papers collected by
Evelyn Waugh for his *Life* (1 file).
Earl of Oxford and Asquith.

[412] **KNOX, Thomas Francis** (1822-1882)
Oratorian.

Letters to him 1841-70, biographical and misc
papers (88 items); letters from JH Newman 1845-
69 (29 items); diaries 1840-64 (2 vols).
The Oratory, London. NRA 16631.

[413] **KNOX, Wilfred Lawrence** (1886-1950)
Warden of the Oratory House, Cambridge 1924-
40; biblical scholar.

Corresp and misc papers as chaplain and fellow of
Pembroke College, Cambridge, mainly letters
from his pupils and family, 1940-50 (9 bundles,
18 items).
Mrs Mary E Knox.

Scholarly papers published as *Sources of the
Synoptic Gospels.*
Revd Professor Henry Chadwick.

[414] **KYLE, James Francis** (1788-1869)
Vicar apostolic of the northern district, Scotland
1827-69.

Northern district corresp, mainly letters to him
and his clergy, 1827-68 (*c*23,000 items); collected
corresp, mainly letters from him, 1799-1868
(*c*1,700 items); family corresp 1744-1884 (*c*9,500
items); letters from AP Forbes (1 bundle); letter
book 1842-4; mission accounts 1840-68 (22
bundles); papers rel to the Scottish mission and

early Scottish church (5 bundles); diary 1817;
autobiographical notes 1829 (1 bundle);
theological papers and sermons (5 bundles);
business and financial papers (8 bundles); misc
papers (2 bundles).
Scottish Catholic Archives (B 5: BL 6, 9; PL 2, 3;
SM 10). Among the historical collections
assembled by Kyle and noted in HMC, *First R,
App,* 1870, p120.

[415] **LACEY, Thomas Alexander** (1853-1931)
Canon of Worcester 1918-31; ecclesiologist.

Letters, mainly concerning the recognition of
anglican orders, from Lord Halifax 1894-8
(157ff), Fernand Portal 1895-1923 (303ff), FW
Puller 1895-1921 (89ff) and others 1893-1929
(166ff).
Lambeth Palace Library (MSS 1974-6).

[416] **LAFFAN, Robert** (d 1833)
RC archbishop of Cashel 1823-33.

Papers 1793-4, 1822-33.
Archbishop of Cashel. See *Manuscript sources for the
history of Irish civilisation: first supplement,* 1979.

[417] **LANG, Cosmo Gordon** (1864-1945)
Archbishop of York 1909-28, of Canterbury
1928-42.

Corresp, mainly as archbishop of Canterbury,
1920-42 (186 vols) incl corresp rel to general
reunion 1920-6 (1 vol), reunion with the Free
churches 1920-41 (3 vols), Prayer Book revision
1925-9 (2 vols), church and state 1929-39 (1 vol),
the Orthodox churches 1930-2 (2 vols), Old
Catholics 1930-40 (1 vol), the ministry of women
1930-42 (2 vols), peace 1933-9 (3 vols), the
Coronation 1936-7 (3 vols) and the second world
war 1939-42 (12 vols); royal corresp 1923-45 (1
vol); family corresp and papers 1864-1947 (6
vols); papers rel to the reservation of the
sacrament 1929-38 (1 vol); autobiography 1864-
1942 (5 vols); notebooks, journals and pocket
diaries 1910-45 (61 vols); financial papers 1933-42
(14 vols); sermons and addresses 1894-1945 (10
vols); misc papers 1864-1945 (32 vols).
Lambeth Palace Library.

Corresp and papers as archbishop of York (2
boxes).
Borthwick Institute, York (Bp C & P XII).

[418] **LATROBE, Christopher Ignatius** (1758-
1836)
Moravian minister.

Letters to him and associated papers rel to West
Indian missions 1768-1823 (217 items) and
missions to North American Indians 1770-1817
(11 items); copies of letters to missionaries in

Labrador 1789-98 (1 vol); diary 1800; 'Trauer
Cantate' (1 vol).
Moravian Church House, London.

Journal 1788-9, 1792 (1 vol).
John Rylands University Library of Manchester (MS
1244).

[419] **LEAHY, Patrick** (1806-1875)
RC archbishop of Cashel 1857-75.

Corresp and papers 1833-74 (*c*700 items) incl
letters from Rome and from bishops, clergy and
British politicians, misc copies of letters sent, and
diaries and sermons.
Archbishop of Cashel. Copies in National Library
of Ireland.

[420] **LEE, Frederick George** (1832-1902)
Vicar of All Saints, Lambeth 1867-99; RC 1901.

Corresp and papers mainly rel to Christian unity
1857-77 (155ff); letters to him about *The repeal of
the Public Worship Regulation Act* 1877 (65ff).
Lambeth Palace Library (MSS 2074-5).

Letters to him 1856-87 (12 items).
Pusey House, Oxford.

Letters from JR Bloxam (1 vol).
Magdalen College, Oxford (Old Library MS 315).

Buckinghamshire and Oxfordshire antiquarian
papers 1850-84 (4 vols and bundles).
Bodleian Library, Oxford (MS Top Bucks c 1, MS
Top Oxon c 3-4, 6).

[421] **LEE, John** (1779-1859)
Principal of Edinburgh University 1840-59.

Corresp, mainly rel to church and university
affairs, 1797-1859 (20 vols); corresp of the
General Assembly of the Church of Scotland from
1638 (2 vols); extracts made by him, chiefly from
kirk session records 17th-19th cent (42 vols);
notebooks, addresses and literary MSS (9 vols);
collected MSS incl papers of and rel to Alexander
Carlyle (15 vols).
National Library of Scotland (MSS 3430-518).
Presented by his grand-daughter 1942.

Papers, chiefly lectures and notes on theology,
philosophy and rhetoric *c*1812-52 (2 boxes);
student notebooks 1794-1801 (27 items).
Edinburgh University Library (Dk 8 7-8, Dc 8 140-
165).

Collections rel to St Andrews university 1412-
1823, compiled *c*1830 (*c*400ff).
St Andrews University Library.

[422] **LEE, Robert** (1804-1868)
Professor of biblical criticism, Edinburgh
1847-68.

Papers (1 box); lectures on the canon of the OT
1847-8 (2 vols).
New College, Edinburgh.

[423] **LEFROY, William** (1836-1909)
Dean of Norwich 1889-1909.

Letters to him rel to cathedral affairs (30 items).
Norfolk Record Office (DCN 122/1). Deposited by
Norwich dean and chapter 1975.

[424] **LESSEY, Theophilus** (1787-1841)
Wesleyan methodist minister.

Corresp incl letters to him 1821-40 (*c*45 items).
Methodist Archives, Manchester.

[425] **LEVI, Thomas** (1825-1916)
Calvinistic methodist minister; author.

Corresp (3 vols); diaries 1843-1914 (72 vols);
accounts of foreign travel 1867-78 (2 vols);
autobiographical notes etc 1855-1912; sermons
1846-1907 (26 vols); lectures, essays, addresses
1856-1907 (3 vols); publications book 1865-1906;
misc notebooks, family and other papers.
National Library of Wales (MSS 17531-17652,
21808).

[426] **LIDDELL, Henry George** (1811-1898)
Headmaster of Westminster School 1846-55; dean
of Christ Church, Oxford 1855-91.

Family corresp and papers 1833-*c*1933 (9 bundles,
1 file) incl corresp with AP Stanley rel to
ecclesiastical reform and patronage, Christ Church
affairs, controversies etc 1856-81 (*c*80 items) and
letters to his daughter Alice Hargreaves *c*1872-98
(*c*50 items).
Mrs MJ St Clair. On loan to Christ Church,
Oxford 1984.

Scholarly notes and corresp 1838-90 (11 items);
copy of HG Liddell and R Scott *A Greek-English
Lexicon*, 7th edn, 1882 with corresp and notes rel
to it (1 bundle).
Christ Church, Oxford (MSS 348, 393).

[427] **LIDDON, Henry Parry** (1829-1890)
Vice-principal of St Edmund Hall, Oxford 1859-
62; canon of St Paul's 1870-90.

Corresp and misc papers, mainly as canon of St
Paul's, 1851-89 (*c*39 boxes).
Keble College, Oxford. NRA 21029.

Letters to him (11 bundles); corresp and misc
papers (*c*40 bundles); corresp and press cuttings
rel to the case of Edward King, the St Paul's

reredos etc (14 vols); papers for his life of EB Pusey (*c*20 vols, 7 bundles); sermons (2 bundles). *Pusey House, Oxford.*

Letters from Samuel Wilberforce 1854-72 (1 vol) and WK Hamilton 1858-69 (1 vol); diaries 1858-90 (33 vols) with misc letters to him etc; account book 1851-3 (1 vol); travel journals 1852, 1855, 1885-6, nd (4 vols); book of meditations (1 vol). *Liddon House, London.* NRA 26974.

Letters, mainly to his sisters, 1857-90 (244ff); letters rel to the case of Edward King 1889 (56ff); corresp and papers 1848-90 (*c*12 items); letters to him rel to his life of Pusey (10 items); diary 1850; misc notes and papers (*c*90 items); sermons 1859-62 (7 items). *Bodleian Library, Oxford* (MSS St Edmund Hall 63-65, 69). Deposited 1954, 1964. NRA 7418.

Misc corresp *c*1853-9 (24 items); diaries 1854-8 (2 vols). *Ripon College, Cuddesdon.*

[428] **LIGHTFOOT, Joseph Barber** (1828-1889) Bishop of Durham 1879-89.

Corresp 1845-89 (*c*6,000 items) incl letters from EH Browne 1861-83 (37 items), RW Church 1867-89 (37 items), FW Farrar 1857-86 (33 items), FJ Hort 1856-89 (40 items), HP Liddon 1870-89 (62 items), AP Stanley 1856-81 (68 items), AC Tait 1862-81 (35 items) and BF Westcott 1850-89 (227 items); papers (9 boxes, 4 vols); Coptic and patristic papers (5 boxes); appointment books 1873, 1879-89 (12 vols); sermons 1854-89 (236 items); lectures, misc and printed papers 1865-89 (43 bundles, 10 items); Lightfoot Fund accounts 1889-1931 (13 vols). *Durham Dean and Chapter Library.* Deposited by the Lightfoot Trustees. NRA 28624.

[429] **LIGHTFOOT, Robert Henry** (1883-1953) Professor of the exegesis of Holy Scripture, Oxford 1934-49.

Letters from churchmen and scholars, lectures, sermons and other corresp and papers (11 boxes). *Bodleian Library, Oxford* (Lightfoot papers).

[430] **LILLEY, Alfred Leslie** (1860-1948) Canon of Hereford 1911-36.

Corresp and misc papers rel to modernism etc 1903-49 (*c*450 items, 4 vols) incl letters from Friedrich von Hügel 1903-25 (71 items), Alfred Loisy 1903-10 (10 items), Maude Petre 1905-42 (43 items), Hastings Rashdall 1905-21 (12 items) and George Tyrell 1903-09 (120 items). *St Andrews University Library* (MSS 30513-890). Presented by his daughter Miss Barbara Lilley 1969. NRA 16115.

[431] **LINDSEY, Robert** (1801-1863) Quaker minister from 1843.

Journals of him and his wife Sarah, incl accounts of his travels in America and Australia 1801-63 (19 vols); notebooks and loose papers (1 box). *Society of Friends Library, London* (MS Vols s 228-47).

[432] **LINDSEY, Theophilus** (1723-1808) Unitarian minister of Essex Street Chapel, London 1778-93.

Corresp incl letters from Francis Blackburne 1756-75 (105 items) and Joseph Priestley 1766-1803 (2 vols); sermons and prayers 1763-87 (7 vols). *Dr Williams's Library, London* (12.12-13, 52). NRA 13168. See *Transactions of the Unitarian Historical Society*, 14, p134.

Corresp with William Tayleur of Shrewsbury 1773-1800 (3 vols, 2 bundles). *John Rylands University Library of Manchester* (Unitarian College Manchester MSS).

[433] **LINGARD, John** (1771-1851) RC mission priest at Hornby, Lancs 1811-51.

Letters from John Butler, George Oliver, John Walker and others 1821-51 (76 items); collected letters from him 1815-51 (988 items) with copies (22 vols); journals 1800, 1817 (2 vols); drafts and misc papers rel to his *History of England* and history of the Anglo-Saxon church; notebooks, commonplace books and accounts (*c*9 vols). *Ushaw College, Durham* (Lingard papers). NRA 13674.

Letters to him (*c*40 items); personal accounts etc (*c*20 vols); sermons (*c*50 items). *Lancashire Record Office* (Liverpool archdiocesan records).

Corresp, mainly with MA Tierney, 1818-60 (1 vol); copies of corresp with Robert Gradwell, Tierney and others 1818-21 (2 vols). *Society of Jesus, London.*

[434] **LLOYD, Daniel Lewis** (1843-1899) Headmaster of Christ College, Brecon 1878-90; bishop of Bangor 1890-9.

Corresp and papers 1867-98 (*c*600 items, 2 vols, 2 bundles) incl letters etc mainly of congratulation on his appointment as bishop (389 items), letters from WBT Jones and others 1891-7 (104 items), corresp and papers rel to Christ College, Brecon 1881-90 (44 items), to Dolgellau National School finances 1887-95 (1 bundle) and to his Welsh hymnal 1895-8 (1 bundle) and diaries 1888, 1898 (2 vols). *National Library of Wales.* Deposited 1969.

[435] **LOFTUS, Lord Robert Ponsonby Tottenham** (1773-1850)
Bishop of Killaloe 1804-20, of Ferns 1820-2, of Clogher 1822-50.

Corresp 1804-49 (1 vol), visitation notebooks for Killaloe 1811-14 (2 vols) and Clogher 1825-45 (11 vols), diaries 1826, 1843 (2 vols) and account books 1819-48 (4 vols), with other family papers.
National Library of Ireland. See *Manuscript sources for the history of Irish civilisation*, 1965.

[436] **LONGLEY, Charles Thomas** (1794-1868)
Archbishop of Canterbury 1862-8.

Corresp and papers 1811-56 (8 vols) incl those rel to ritualistic controversies 1848-68 (1 vol), Father Ignatius, prayers etc 1860-8 (1 vol), colonial bishoprics (1 vol) and the Lambeth Conference 1867 (1 vol).
Lambeth Palace Library (Longley 1-8). Vols 1-2 and 7-8 deposited by his grandson, Bishop Wilfred Parker 1956; vols 3-6 presented by his son, Sir Henry Longley 1888. See JE Sayers and EGW Bill, *Calendar of the papers of Charles Thomas Longley, archbishop of Canterbury 1862-1868*, 1976.

Family corresp, misc letters to him and other papers 1812-68 (155ff).
Lambeth Palace Library (MS 1841). Presented by Gregory Rowcliffe & Co 1964.

Corresp and papers as headmaster of Harrow School 1829-36 (2 vols, *c*20 items).
Harrow School. NRA 27630.

Engagement books 1862, 1864-6 (4 vols).
Lambeth Palace Library (MSS 2323-6). Presented by Viscount Bridgeman 1969.

'Archives of the See of Ripon 1836' (1 vol), compiled by Longley in 1856 (continued up to 1898) incl original documents, memoranda etc.
Leeds District Archives (RDB 1). NRA 25809.

Notebooks rel to the state of parishes in the diocese of Ripon compiled from his visitation returns 1837-56 (3 vols).
Brotherton Library, University of Leeds (Holden Library MS 2). Presented by JA Longley 1900. NRA 25809.

[437] **LOTHIAN, Andrew** (1763-1831)
Secession minister, Portsburgh, Edinburgh 1796-1831.

Personal and family corresp, sermons, papers etc *c*1781-1831 (4 boxes).
National Library of Scotland (Acc 7617).

[438] **LOWDER, Charles Fuge** (1820-1880)
Vicar of St Peter, London Docks 1866-80.

Corresp with bishops; corresp with others (1 vol); scrapbook rel to his life; printed papers and press cuttings (3 vols etc).

St Peter's Church, London Docks. See LE Ellsworth, *Charles Lowder and the ritualist movement*, 1982.

[439] **LOWE, Edward Clarke** (1823-1912)
Canon of Ely 1873-1912; provost of Denstone College 1873-91, of Lancing College 1891-8.

Letters from Nathaniel Woodard rel to the Woodard schools 1848-89 (40 bundles) incl some rel to clerical celibacy and the age of confirmation; misc corresp incl letters from AT Lyttelton and George Ridding 1892-1902 (1 bundle) and JG Lonsdale (1 bundle).
Lancing College. NRA 26582.

Corresp with Woodard rel to Denstone statutes 1889-91 (1 bundle), with the archbishops of Canterbury and York 1891 (1 bundle) and misc administrative corresp and papers 1891-6, nd (5 bundles).
Denstone College. NRA 27387.

[440] **LUNDIE, Robert** (1774-1832)
Minister of Kelso 1807-32.

Personal and family corresp incl letters from Thomas Chalmers, AM Thomson and others 1703-1874 (2 vols).
National Library of Scotland (MSS 9847-8).

[441] **LUNDIE, Robert Henry** (1824-1895)
Presbyterian minister of St Andrew's Church, Birkenhead 1850-66, of Fairfield, Liverpool 1866-95.

Letters to him and his family from JW Bardsley, RS Candlish, HE Manning and others 1851-1909 (60 items).
National Library of Scotland (Acc 8673).

[442] **LYNE, Joseph Leycester** (1837-1908)
'Father Ignatius'; founder of Llanthony Abbey 1869.

Papers incl autobiography (1 vol) and personal log of his voyage on the *Arizona* 1891 (1 vol) etc.
Norfolk Record Office (MSS R 152C, 21436, 293x6).

[443] **McCABE, Edward** (1816-1885)
Archbishop of Dublin 1879-85; cardinal 1882.

Corresp with bishops, clergy, religious orders and others 1863-85 and papers rel to diocesan administration, the Land League, home rule, education, personal affairs etc (20 boxes).
Dublin Diocesan Archives.

[444] **McCHEYNE, Robert Murray** (1813-1843)
Minister of St Peter's Church, Dundee 1836-43.

Family and personal corresp 1827-46 (*c*330 items)
incl letters from WC Burns 1839-42 (28 items);
diaries, letters and sketches during a journey to
Palestine 1839-42 (4 vols); visitation, travel and
convocation notes 1835-43 (4 vols); sermon,
lecture and other notes 1827-43 (9 vols); poetry
scrapbooks 1820-36 (2 vols); sermons (5 bundles).
New College, Edinburgh. NRA 27817.

[445] **McCRIE, Thomas** (1772-1835)
Secession minister and ecclesiastical historian.

Extracts rel to historical and ecclesiastical matters
(2 vols).
Edinburgh University Library (La III 533).

[446] **MACDONALD, Angus** (1844-1900)
Bishop of Argyll and the Isles 1878-92;
archbishop of St Andrews and Edinburgh 1892-
1900.

Letters from Scottish bishops 1879-1900 (47
bundles), from other bishops 1892-9 (4 bundles)
and from the Propaganda 1878-1900 (4 bundles);
letter books 1878-1900 (7 vols); corresp with
Blairs and Scots colleges abroad 1878-1900 (24
bundles); general corresp 1879-1900 (14 bundles);
corresp and papers rel to diocesan administration
1892-9 (*c*15 bundles), missions and pilgrimages
1892-1900 (15 bundles), the Catholic Truth
Society 1894-9 (7 bundles) and religious orders
1895-9 (5 bundles); papers rel to diocesan synods
1881-98 (6 bundles) and the liturgy 1896, nd (3
bundles); personal accounts and misc papers
1879-99 (8 bundles); diary 1892-7 (1 vol);
sermons 1874-98 (1 bundle).
Scottish Catholic Archives (ED 5).

[447] **MACDONALD, John** (1779-1849)
Free Church of Scotland minister.

Report and journals of visits to St Kilda 1822,
1824.
Scottish Record Office (GD 95/11/12).

[448] **MACDONALD, Ranald** (1756-1832)
Vicar apostolic of the western district, Scotland
1827-32.

Corresp and misc papers rel to district affairs
*c*1764-1829 (2 bundles).
Scottish Catholic Archives (OL 1).

[449] **McDONNELL, Charles Francis** (1774-
1843)
President of Baddesley College, Warwicks 1801-7,
1820-4; provincial of the Friars Minor in
England.

Corresp 1815-43 (*c*125 items); account books as
procurator 1822-43 (2 vols); notebook 1815-38 (1

vol); notes on a visit to Rome 1840 (5pp); misc
personal and testamentary papers (1 bundle).
*Archives of the English Province of Friars Minor,
London.*

[450] **MACEWEN, Alexander Robertson** (1851-
1916)
Professor of church history, New College,
Edinburgh 1901-16.

Corresp and papers rel to the union of the Free
and United Presbyterian churches 1900 (2 boxes).
New College, Edinburgh.

[451] **MACFARLAN, Duncan** (1771-1857)
Principal of Glasgow University 1823-57.

Corresp and misc papers mainly rel to university
and church affairs incl corresp with the 3rd and
4th Dukes of Montrose, Sir JRG Graham and
others, 1746-1877 (*c*830 items); journal notes
1820, 1825-57 (*c*30 items); sermons (41 bundles,
43 items); misc papers (*c*50 items).
Glasgow University Archives. NRA 17695.

[452] **McGETTIGAN, Daniel** (1815-1887)
RC archbishop of Armagh 1870-87.

Corresp and papers as archbishop (100 files).
Archbishop of Armagh. Microfilm in the Public
Record Office of Northern Ireland (MIC 451).

[453] **MACGREGOR, James** (1832-1910)
Minister of St Cuthbert, Edinburgh 1873-1910.

Corresp mainly from or rel to Queen Victoria and
the royal family 1875-1909 (34 items).
National Library of Scotland (Acc 4177).

Diaries of him and his wife 1892-1903 (10 vols).
National Library of Scotland (MSS 557-66).

[454] **MACKINTOSH, Donald** (1877-1943)
Archbishop of Glasgow 1922-43.

General corresp as archbishop 1922-43 (22 boxes)
and misc personal papers 1924-30 (1 box).
Glasgow Archdiocesan Archive.

[455] **MACKONOCHIE, Alexander Heriot**
(1825-1887)
Perpetual curate of St Alban, Holborn 1862-82.

Letter book 1868-76; scrapbook of letters and
papers rel to him 1848-1940; journal of his work
at St George's Mission, Stepney.
Greater London Record Office (P 82/ALB/4, 27,
133). Deposited 1951.

[456] **MACLAGAN, William Dalrymple** (1826-
1910)
Bishop of Lichfield 1878-91; archbishop of York
1891-1908.

Letters from John Wordsworth and others rel to
the *Responsio* of the English archbishops to the
papal bull *Apostolicae curae* 1896-7 (57ff).
Lambeth Palace Library (MS 2797). Presented by
ERD Maclagan 1920.

Corresp rel to his retirement 1908 and misc
corresp (1 vol and loose items).
Michael Maclagan Esq.

[457] **MACLEAN, Arthur John** (1858-1943)
Bishop of Moray, Ross and Caithness 1904-43 and
primus of the Scottish episcopal church 1935-43.

Corresp and papers rel to provincial and diocesan
affairs 1906-42 (*c*200 items).
Bishop of Moray, Ross and Caithness. Enquiries to
NRA (Scotland) (NRA (S) 2705).

[458] **MACLEOD, Donald** (1831-1916)
Minister of the Park, Glasgow 1869-1909; editor
of *Good Words* 1892-1905.

Corresp, mainly letters from contributors to *Good
Words,* 1869-1914 (1 vol); editorial corresp (54ff);
letters from his brother Norman 1856, nd (25ff);
letter book *c*1877-80 (1 vol); European travel
journal 1855-6 (1 vol); autobiography 1831-69 and
related papers (2 vols); sermons 1876-1909 (1
vol).
National Library of Scotland (MSS 9827-33).
Presented by the Revd KO Macleod 1960. NRA
27986.

[459] **MACLEOD, Norman** (1812-1872)
Minister of the Barony, Glasgow 1851-72.

Journal 1851-74; journal extracts 1840-6.
Glasgow University Archives (UGD/109/12/1-2).
NRA 21082.

[460] **McMILLAN, Samuel** (d 1864)
Minister of St Paul's Street Relief Church,
Aberdeen 1807-41.

Diary 1816-63 (1 vol).
Glasgow University Library (MS Gen 1264).

[461] **MCNALLY, Charles** (1787-1864)
RC bishop of Clogher 1844-64.

Letters from students at Maynooth and clergy of
Clogher diocese 1815-43 (36 items); letters mainly
to him from Paul Cullen, John McHale and
others rel to a dispute about the Irish educational
system etc 1843-71 (77 items); pastorals, sermons
and misc papers 1851-65 (43 items).

Bishop of Clogher. Copies in the Public Record
Office of Northern Ireland (DIO (RC) 1/10 A-C).
NRA 19966.

[462] **MACNICOL, Donald** (1735-1802)
Minister of Lismore, Argyllshire 1766-1802.

Papers, mainly sermons, in Gaelic (*c*95 items).
Glasgow University Library. NRA 20977.

[463] **MACPHERSON, Paul** (1756-1846)
Rector of the Scots College, Rome 1820-6, 1834-
46.

Autobiography to 1783 (1 vol); memoirs 1792-3 (1
item); account of the Catholic Relief Act 1793 (1
item); notes and MSS rel to his historical studies
of the Catholic church in Scotland (*c*16 bundles
and vols) incl history of the Scots College, Rome,
to 1795 (3 vols) etc.
Scottish Catholic Archives.

Corresp 1811-35.
Scots College, Rome. See L Macfarlane, 'The
Vatican Archives', *Archives*, iv, 22, p100.

[464] **MAGILL, Robert** (1788-1839)
Minister of First Antrim Presbyterian Church
1820-39.

Papers incl diaries 1821-4, 1831-7, preaching and
pastoral engagement diary 1834, sermons,
probably by him, *c*1816 (1 vol), papers rel to his
congregation 1819-36 and genealogical notes 1741-
1833.
Public Record Office of Northern Ireland (D 2194,
D 2930).

[465] **MACGUIRE, John Aloysius** (1851-1920)
Archbishop of Glasgow 1902-20.

General corresp as archbishop 1903-20 (18 boxes);
papers rel to bishops' meetings 1901-9 (3 boxes);
misc personal papers 1875-1920 (1 box).
Glasgow Archdiocesan Archive.

[466] **MAJOR, Henry Dewsbury Alves** (1871-
1961)
Principal of Ripon Hall, Oxford 1919-48.

Corresp (55 boxes) and misc sermons and press
cuttings.
Bodleian Library, Oxford. Deposited by Ripon
College, Cuddesdon 1984.

[467] **MALLALIEU, William** (1798-1871)
Treasurer of missions of the Moravian Church
1835-57.

General corresp 1812-57 (1 vol); letters from his
father and stepmother 1818-32 (2 vols); letter
book 1833-5 (1 vol); diaries 1818-20, 1825 (2

vols); memoranda and account books 1817-35 (6 vols); family corresp and papers (2 vols).
British Library (Add MSS 58835-48). Purchased from AG Thomas 1975.

[468] MALTBY, Edward (1770-1859)
Bishop of Chichester 1831-6, of Durham 1836-56.

Letters to Samuel Parr rel to the *Lexicon Graeco-prosodiacum* 1812-15 (31 items); corresp with his family and friends, draft sermons and notes on Latin and Greek to 1800 (1 bundle); misc notebooks and papers rel to his early university career 1785-1807 (1 bundle, 15 items).
West Sussex Record Office. Deposited 1980. NRA 27226.

[469] MANNERS-SUTTON, Charles (1755-1828)
Archbishop of Canterbury 1805-28.

Letters to him 1794-1828 (*c*50 items).
Lambeth Palace Library. Purchased at Phillips, 7 June 1984, lot 763.

Corresp (2 vols) and papers (31 vols) as a member of the Queen's Council on George III's malady 1811-20.
Lambeth Palace Library (MSS 2107-39).

Letters from bishops about attendance at George IV's coronation 1821 (20ff).
Lambeth Palace Library (MS 1751).

Papers rel to his estate 1805-37 (148ff); bank book 1823-8 (45ff).
Lambeth Palace Library (MSS 1916-17). Deposited by the British Records Association 1931.

[470] MANNING, Henry Edward (1808-1892)
Archbishop of Westminster 1865-92; cardinal 1875.

Corresp with RI Wilberforce and the Wilberforce family 1826-51 (2 boxes), with William Dodsworth 1837-51 (1 box), with John Keble, JH Newman, EB Pusey and other tractarians 1836-50 (1 box), with bishops and churchmen, mainly rel to Chichester diocesan affairs, 1838-58 (1 box) and misc corresp 1831-51 (1 box); corresp with or letters from RC converts and others incl TW Allies, Lord and Lady Herbert of Lea and JR Hope-Scott 1842-52 (1 box); letters to Miss Maurice, Miss Stanley and others 1836-56 (3 boxes); letter book 1829-30; papers rel to Woolavington church and the archdeaconry of Chichester 1806-50 (6 boxes and vols); notebooks, commonplace books and misc papers (7 boxes and vols).
Bodleian Library, Oxford. Presented 1982. NRA 25566.

Corresp and papers, mainly as a Roman Catholic, to *c*1891, incl corresp with Paul Cullen, JH

Newman, Frederick Oakeley, WB Ullathorne and HA Vaughan, and diaries 1844-90.
Abbé Chapeau.

[471] MARKHAM, William (1719-1807)
Archbishop of York 1777-1807.

Corresp mainly letters to him from the Prince of Wales and the royal family 1771-*c*1807 (12 items). *Untraced.* Withdrawn from the Borthwick Institute, York in 1974 and sold. Copies available at the Borthwick Institute. NRA 12168.

[472] MARRIOTT, Charles (1811-1858)
Principal of Chichester Theological College 1839-41; vicar of St Mary the Virgin, Oxford 1850-8.

Diaries (5 vols); memoir and transcripts of his letters (39 items); sermons and devotional papers. *Pusey House, Oxford.*

Letters from WE Gladstone rel to university reform 1851-5 (24 items); letters to him and his brother John from JH Newman 1830-53 (40 items), and from John Keble, EB Pusey and other churchmen 1824-58 (*c*60 items); copies of letters from him to JT Coleridge and others 1854-5, nd (*c*40 items).
Untraced. Sold at Christie's 29 May 1986, lots 50, 70, 82.

[473] MARSDEN, George (1773-1858)
Wesleyan methodist minister.

Letters from Jabez Bunting, Adam Clarke and others 1795-1856 (*c*120 items); diaries 1801-38 (5 vols).
Methodist Archives, Manchester.

[474] MARTIN, Alexander (1857-1946)
Principal of New College, Edinburgh 1918-35.

Personal corresp (2 boxes); papers rel to the inter-church relations committee (6 boxes) and associated corresp (2 boxes); papers rel to Scottish church re-union 1908-29 (19 boxes); lectures on apologetics 1897-8 (1 vol).
New College, Edinburgh.

[475] MARTINEAU, James (1805-1900)
Unitarian; principal of Manchester New College 1869-85.

Letters from Francis Darbishire 1824-7 (37 items), FW Newman 1846-93 (58 items) and others 1828-49 (43 items) and rel to the Dublin settlement 1828-32 (24 items); corresp with RH Hutton and family 1846-54 (27 items) and rel to hymns and hymn-writers (1 bundle); letters to RL Carpenter 1839-93 (83 items) and JE Carpenter 1860-98 (74 items); letters incl copies to William Knight 1869-97 (200 items) and rel to college affairs 1874-95 (25 items); family corresp

incl letters and abstracts of letters from Harriet
Martineau 1819-49 and letters to James and Helen
Martineau in Germany 1848-9 (1 bundle); lectures
and addresses (1 vol); speeches rel to removal of
the college to Oxford and its opening (1 vol);
biographical memoranda and early reminiscences
(1 vol); poems, prayers etc (1 bundle).
Manchester College, Oxford.

Letters from JH Thom 1847-94 (64 items).
Dr Williams's Library, London (24.153). NRA
13168.

Lectures on moral philosophy etc 1853-4 (162ff).
St Hilda's College, Oxford. NRA 12359.

[476] **MASON, Arthur James** (1851-1928)
Canon of Canterbury 1895-1928 and master of
Pembroke College, Cambridge 1903-12.

Letters from EW Benson (1 box); diaries mainly
as Truro diocesan missioner *c*1876-84.
Revd Canon Lancelot Mason.

Corresp and papers rel to proposed reunion with
the Moravian church 1906-25 (1 vol).
Lambeth Palace Library (MS 2785).

[477] **MASSINGBERD, Francis Charles** (1800-
1872)
Chancellor of Lincoln Cathedral 1862-72.

Letters from bishops and clergy 1841-72 (1 vol)
and from his family, Sir Charles Anderson and
others 1817-73 (*c*260 items); diaries and
notebooks 1826-66 (6 vols); literary notes etc
1833-70 (82 items).
Lincolnshire Archives Office. Deposited by Miss
Dorothy Massingberd 1954, 1957. NRA 6239.

Letters mainly from the Massingberd and Mundy
families 1831-47 (25 items).
Lincolnshire Archives Office (2MM). Deposited by
the Society of Genealogists 1980. NRA 5989.

[478] **MATTHEWS, Walter Robert** (1881-1973)
Dean of Exeter 1931-4, of St Paul's 1934-67.

Draft lectures rel to systematic theology etc 1918-
19 and sermons 1949-60 (1 box).
King's College London.

[479] **MAURICE, Frederick Denison** (1805-
1872)
Christian socialist.

Letters from JMF Ludlow 1852-71 (1 folder).
Cambridge University Library (Add 7348). NRA
10589.

Papers 1841-73 incl letters to Sara Coleridge (1
box).
King's College London.

[480] **MEANS, Joseph Calrow** (1801-1879)
General Baptist minister, Chatham, Kent 1843-55
and Worship Street, London 1855-74.

Diary of his ministerial duties 1838-77 (1 vol.)
National Library of Wales (MS 13623).

[481] **MELVILLE, David** (1813-1904)
Canon of Worcester 1880-1902.

Letters from politicians and clergy about religious
education 1861-94 (62ff); Oxford papers 1830-6
(45ff); misc papers, mainly printed (59ff).
Lambeth Palace Library (MS 1995).

[482] **MEYNELL, Henry** (*c*1828-1903)
Provost of Denstone College 1891-6, of King's
College, Taunton 1897-1902.

Oxford diary 1849-51.
Godfrey Meynell Esq. NRA 4101.

Letter book mainly rel to the establishment of
Denstone College 1866-98 (1 vol); letters to him
1885 (1 bundle) and misc corresp (1 bundle);
diaries 1885-92; scrapbook 1867 (2 vols); sermons
by him and others 1869-95 (1 bundle).
Denstone College. NRA 27387.

Letter books 1886-98 (2 vols) and letters and
papers rel to the foundation of Worksop College
1885-97 (1 vol).
Worksop College. NRA 27579.

[483] **MEYRICK, Frederick** (1827-1906)
Secretary of the Anglo-Continental Society 1853-
98.

Letters from Lord Acton, Mandell Creighton, RT
Davidson, JJI von Döllinger, WE Gladstone,
John Keble, HE Manning, JH Newman, EB
Pusey, AP Stanley and others (89 items).
Pusey House, Oxford.

[484] **MILEY, John** (*c*1805-1861)
Private chaplain to Daniel O'Connell 1847; rector
of the Irish College, Paris 1849-59.

Letters from Paul Cullen 1849-59.
Diocesan Archives, Archbishop's House, Dublin.

Corresp with RR Madden rel to Daniel O'Connell
1846.
British Library (Add MS 43684).

[485] **MILL, William Hodge** (1792-1853)
Principal of Bishop's College, Calcutta 1820-38;
rector of Brasted 1843-53 and regius professor of
Hebrew, Cambridge 1848-53.

Corresp and papers mainly rel to the Gorham
controversy and anti-tractarian and anti-papal
disturbances at Brasted 1846-53 (184ff).
Lambeth Palace Library (MS 1491).

Collections made for a history of the Syrian Christian community of St Thomas in Malabar 1815-40 (6 vols); travel journals 1820-38 (10 vols); misc papers written or collected by him 1753, 1815-45 (4 vols).
Bodleian Library, Oxford (Mill MSS 191-5, 202-16).

[486] **MILMAN, Henry Hart** (1791-1868)
Professor of poetry, Oxford 1821-31; rector of St Margaret Westminster 1835-49; dean of St Paul's 1849-68.

Corresp, mainly letters to him 1841-1904 (163ff).
Bodleian Library, Oxford (MS Eng lett d 166). Purchased 1955.

[487] **MILNER, John** (1752-1826)
Vicar apostolic of the midland district 1803-26.

Corresp 1791-5, 1803-26 with members of the Cisalpine Club, JC Hippisley, John Kirk, Charles Plowden, William Poynter and others (c67 items); diary 1803-25 (1 vol); doctrinal notes 1803-26 (c12 items); appointments, faculties, passports 1776, 1803-25 (12 items); financial papers etc (c18 items); executorship papers 1826-7 (55 items).
Archbishop's House, Birmingham (St Mary's College, Oscott). NRA 8129.

Corresp 1798-1826 incl letters from the Propaganda and English and Irish bishops' agents in Rome (c110 items); misc lists and notes 1795-1826 (13 items); appointments and faculties 1803-8 (c10 items).
Archbishop's House, Birmingham. NRA 8129.

[488] **MILNER-WHITE, Eric** (1884-1963)
Dean of King's College, Cambridge 1918-41; dean of York 1941-63.

Corresp rel to the Liturgical Commission; notebooks rel to personal affairs, administrative matters etc (c52 vols); sermons and addresses (c15 vols, c480 items); notebooks incl drafts of collects, prayers etc (c53 vols and bundles); misc MSS of his works, notes on stained glass, memoranda etc.
King's College, Cambridge.

Corresp, sermons and papers, mainly administrative and financial papers as dean of York, 1909-66 (15 boxes, 4 bundles).
York Minster Library. NRA 28331.

[489] **MOBERLY, George** (1803-1885)
Headmaster of Winchester College 1835-66; bishop of Salisbury 1869-85.

Letter book of his and John Wordsworth's letters to clergy 1875-87 (1 vol).
Wiltshire Record Office. P Stewart, *Guide to the records of the bishop . . . of Salisbury*, 1973, p 19.

[490] **MONCREIFF, Sir Henry Wellwood** (1750-1827), 8th Bt 1767
Minister of St Cuthbert, Edinburgh 1775-1827.

Corresp and papers c1731-1827 (5 boxes), mainly corresp rel to church affairs, Indian missions and presbyterian churches in the United States and West Indies incl letters from Thomas Chalmers, George Jardine, Stevenson Macgill and others; family corresp 1773-1826 (5 files); sermons (3 bundles).
Lord Moncreiff. NRA 10980.

Prayers (1 vol).
Edinburgh University Library (La III 79).

[491] **MONK, James Henry** (1784-1856)
Regius professor of Greek, Cambridge 1809-23; bishop of Gloucester 1830-6, of Gloucester and Bristol 1836-56.

Corresp and papers (9 bundles, c60 items), incl letters from CJ Blomfield 1812-13, 1843-6, Sir Robert Peel, Lords Melbourne and Shaftesbury and other politicians 1816-56, the Duke of Gloucester, scholars and churchmen c1818-55, his family 1820-56 and his predecessor as bishop of Gloucester, Christopher Bethell, 1830.
Dr Henry Sanford. NRA 26344.

Financial and other papers rel to his Small Livings Fund 1832-72 (5 vols, 150 items); personal accounts and financial corresp and papers 1847-56 (1 vol, c300 items); letters and papers rel to his Stapleton, Leics, estate (40 items).
Gloucestershire Record Office (Gloucester diocese A 14/4, G5). IM Kirby, *Diocese of Gloucester: a catalogue of the records of the bishop and archdeacons*, 1968.

[492] **MOORE, Henry** (1751-1844)
Wesleyan methodist minister.

Letters from John Wesley and others 1780-1841 (c25 items); sermon notes and register (2 vols).
Methodist Archives, Manchester.

Letters from John Wesley 1787-90 (10 items) and others 1791-1818 (6 items); shorthand diary 1799-1800.
Wesley College, Bristol. From the collections of George Morley and Adam Clarke. NRA 27694.

[493] **MORGAN, John** (1840-1924)
Archdeacon of Bangor 1902-20.

Corresp and misc papers incl letters from WH Williams 1903-10 (1 bundle); diary 1869-70 (1 vol); address to him 1902 and misc papers (2 vols, 1 bundle, 4 items).
National Library of Wales. Deposited by Ronald Wingrove 1975.

[494] **MORGAN, Thomas** (1720-1799)
Independent minister

Letters to him 1750-74 (2 vols); letter book 1762-
94 (1 vol); diary 1741-4 (1 vol); notebooks 1740-
94, nd (2 vols); sermon notes c1746-60, 1775-94
(2 vols); misc papers (3 vols).
National Library of Wales (MSS 5453-63).

Commonplace book 1743-94 (1 vol).
National Library of Wales (MS 15603).

[495] **MORISON, James** (1816-1893)
Founder of the Evangelical Union 1843.

Letters to him 1833-92 (1 vol).
Mitchell Library, Glasgow.

[496] **MORLEY, George** (d 1843)
Wesleyan methodist minister.

Letters from Jabez Bunting 1803-18 (13 items),
Joseph Entwisle 1804-27 (7 items) and others
1792-1839 (64 items).
Wesley College, Bristol. Presented to Wesley
College, Headingley, by his son's widow 1880.
NRA 27694.

[497] **MORRALL, John [Alphonsus]** (1825-1911)
Prior of Downside 1866-8.

Personal and collected papers (62 vols, 1 box)
mainly rel to the Benedictine constitutional
controversy 1880-1900 and to antiquarian and
genealogical studies, incl notebook as prior
1866-8, diaries 1874-1910 and reports to the
general chapter 1883.
Downside Abbey.

[498] **MORRIS, John** (1826-1893)
Private secretary to NPS Wiseman and HE
Manning 1856-67; rector of the Jesuit houses at
Roehampton 1880-6 and Farm Street, London
1891-3.

Corresp 1866-92 (c12 bundles) incl letters from
Jesuit provincials 1866, 1892-3, from HE
Manning and JH Newman 1874-5, corresp rel to
Mary Queen of Scots and letters to JH Pollen and
Henry Foley; historical, instructional and spiritual
notes (2 bundles, 1 vol); autobiographical notes
and papers rel to his death (3 bundles).
Society of Jesus, London.

Letters to him about his biography of NPS
Wiseman 1892-3 (c30 items).
Westminster Diocesan Archives (W2/1/1).

[499] **MORRIS, John Brande** (1812-1880)
RC priest and writer.

Letters mainly from FW Faber 1833-63 (1 vol, 25
items).
The Oratory, London. NRA 16631.

[500] **MORRIS, Joseph** (1806-1891)
Independent minister, Madryn.

Family and other corresp and papers (228 items),
incl diaries 1841-91, autobiography to 1876,
sermon notes and record of preaching
engagements.
University College of North Wales, Bangor (Morfa
MSS). NRA 8487.

[501] **MORTON, James** (1783-1865)
Vicar of Holbeach 1831-65.

Personal and family corresp 1762-1819 (207
items); journals and diaries 1805, 1824-64 (10
vols); literary papers c1794-1819 (8 items); misc
corresp and papers 1802-77 (7 bundles).
Lincolnshire Archives Office (Misc Dep 306).
Deposited by Dr and Mrs Cecil Northcott on
behalf of the Morton family 1975. NRA 19643.

Corresp and papers collected by Morton for his
biography of John Leyden, with Morton's
corresp, 1794-1875 (5 vols).
National Library of Scotland (MSS 3380-4).
Presented by Dr John Leyden Morton 1945.

[502] **MOSES, Evan** (1726-1805)
Calvinistic methodist minister.

Corresp 1751-97 (c76 items); diaries 1781-98 (7
vols); accounts of the 'family' at Trevecca 1752-
1804 (3 vols).
National Library of Wales (Presbyterian Church of
Wales MSS, Trevecca Group). NRA 15301.

[503] **MOSS, Charles** (1763-1811)
Bishop of Oxford 1807-11.

Letters from Lord Grenville, William Wickham
and others 1792-1810 (35 items).
*William R Perkins Library, Duke University,
Durham, N Carolina.*

[504] **MOSTYN, Francis** (1860-1939)
Bishop of Menevia 1898-1921; archbishop of
Cardiff 1921-39.

Corresp and papers (2 files) incl corresp with
Rome and other bishops (2 bundles), corresp rel
to diocesan affairs (5 bundles) and sermons (2
bundles).
Archbishop of Cardiff.

[505] **MOULE, Handley Carr Glyn** (1841-1920)
Principal of Ridley Hall, Cambridge 1881-99;
Norrisian professor of divinity, Cambridge 1899-
1901; bishop of Durham 1901-20.

Letters from his family (2 bundles); diary 1916-19
(1 vol).
Tyndale House, Cambridge.

'Exposition of the [Epistle to the] Romans' (2 vols); biblical commentaries, lectures and sermons (1 box); diaries and misc papers (1 box). *Cambridge University Library* (Add 7925-7). Presented by Mrs AWH Moule 1973.

[506] **MOULTON, William Fiddian** (1835-1898) Methodist biblical scholar; headmaster of the Leys School, Cambridge 1874-98.

Letters from CJ Ellicott, FJA Hort and others (*c*47 items). *Methodist Archives, Manchester.* NRA 25811.

[507] **MOZLEY, Thomas** (1806-1893) Rector of Plymtree 1868-80; correspondent of *The Times*.

Letters from JF Christie, CP Golightly, CA Heurtley, HW Wilberforce and others (3 files) and corresp with JH Newman (3 files). *The Oratory, Birmingham.* NRA 27809.

[508] **MURDOCH, John** (1796-1865) Vicar apostolic of the western district, Scotland 1845-65.

Corresp and papers rel to the western district 1806-65, incl letters from Alessandro Barnabo, JF Kyle and Alexander Smith, (*c*47 bundles). *Scottish Catholic Archives* (OL 1-4).

Letters from Kyle and others 1848-65 (5 bundles); diaries 1854-65 (3 vols); notebook of memoranda rel to bishops of the western district 1853-9 (1 vol). *Glasgow Archdiocesan Archive.*

[509] **MURRAY, Daniel** (1768-1852) RC archbishop of Dublin 1823-52.

Corresp and papers as archbishop, incl general corresp, memoranda, sermons and accounts rel to diocesan administration, relations with government, education policy, Catholic emancipation and social conditions, (25 boxes). *Diocesan Archives, Archbishop's House, Dublin.*

[510] **MUSGRAVE, Thomas** (1788-1860) Bishop of Hereford 1837-47; archbishop of York 1847-60.

Corresp and papers 1726-1865 mainly letters from bishops and politicians rel to doctrinal and disciplinary questions, patronage etc (7 bundles). *Nottinghamshire Record Office* (Edge of Strelley 212-218). NRA 6870.

Misc family corresp and papers 1815-1932 (*c*34 items); grand tour journal 1815 (2 vols). *Borthwick Institute, York.* Deposited by the Archbishop of York 1968. NRA 13270.

[511] **NEALE, John Mason** (1818-1866) Warden of Sackville College, East Grinstead 1842-66 and founder of the Sisterhood of St Margaret 1855.

Letters to him mainly concerning the Cambridge Camden Society and St Margaret's Sisterhood with related papers 1841-1931 (124ff); papers rel to the Cambridge Camden Society, incl surveys by him, 1840-1 (132ff) and to Sackville College 1847-72 (84ff, 2 vols); minutes of a committee to protest against the consecration of Samuel Gobat 1853 (1 vol); personal papers 1832-1906 (210ff, 13 vols); copies of diaries 1838-40, 1842-4 (2 vols). *Lambeth Palace Library* (MSS 2677-84, 3107-18). Presented by St Margaret's Convent, East Grinstead 1972, 1979.

Reports on 518 churches in England, Wales and Europe for the Cambridge Camden Society 1839-42, 1851-3 (17 vols). *Lambeth Palace Library* (MSS 1977-93). Presented 1953.

[512] **NEWELL, Richard** (1785-1852) Calvinistic methodist.

Diaries, incl notes rel to associations, monthly meetings, schools, sermons etc 1813-50 (22 vols); travel journal 1838-40; notebook rel to methodist revival 1814-25; Sunday school statistics 1820-34 (11 items); misc letters to him, accounts, notes, sermons etc. *National Library of Wales* (Presbyterian Church of Wales MSS, General Collection). NRA 28345.

Papers incl diaries 1815-39, notes on associations, monthly meetings and Sunday schools, sermon notes, farm and other accounts etc (75 vols and items). *University College of North Wales, Bangor.* NRA 8487.

[513] **NEWMAN, Henry Stanley** (1837-1912) Quaker minister, Leominster; editor of *The Friend* 1892-1912.

Letters to him kept for autographs 1794-1911 (1 vol); corresp rel to Zanzibar and Pemba 1896-1900 (2 vols); narrative of visit to east Africa 1897 (1 vol); literary drafts and MSS (3 vols); press cuttings (2 vols). *Society of Friends Library, London* (Temp MSS 19-20, MS Vols s 203-6, 212-3, 352).

[514] **NEWMAN, John Henry** (1801-1890) Cardinal 1879.

Collected corresp arranged as corresp with notable individuals (171 files) incl corresp with RH Froude (2 files), JR Hope-Scott (3 files), HE Manning (1 file), Thomas Mozley (3 files), EB Pusey (14 files), WB Ullathorne (6 files) and HW Wilberforce (3 files); corresp with Oratorians (*c*81 files); corresp on specific issues (*c*81 files) incl

E

Tract XC (2 files), the Achilli trial (4 files), the *Rambler* (7 files), his *Apologia* (4 files), the *Letter to Pusey* (3 files), the Vatican Council (4 files) and his cardinalate (4 files); misc corresp, mainly letters to him, (68 files); copies of his letters (22 files); diaries and journals 1824-79; papers 1816-88, incl theological and philosophical papers 1816-86, (137 items and bundles), devotional papers 1817-88 (12 bundles etc), Oratorian papers 1847-58 (17 bundles etc), juvenilia and undergraduate papers 1818-20 (17 bundles etc), papers of biographical relevance 1832-88 (23 bundles etc), MSS of his published works and related papers (43 bundles etc), educational papers, mainly rel to the Catholic University in Ireland, 1826-63 (58 bundles etc), financial and administrative papers (c30 bundles etc); sermons to 1843 (244 items); sermons 1848-73 (42 items) and outlines of sermons 1849-78 (214 items).
The Oratory, Birmingham. NRA 27809.

Letters from John Keble 1829-63 (107 items).
Keble College, Oxford. NRA 21028.

Letters from RW Church (85 items) and papers rel to the editorship of the *British Critic* 1836-41 (1 file).
Pusey House, Oxford.

Letters from HA Woodgate 1837-44 (c40 items).
The Oratory, Birmingham. Purchased at Christie's 28 Mar 1984, lot 194.

Diary while at Munich and in Italy 1857 (1 vol).
Cambridge University Library (Add 5751).

[515] **NEWMAN, Thomas Fox** (1800-1868)
Minister of Shortwood Baptist Church, Nailsworth 1832-67.

Corresp rel to ministerial appointments, missionary work and other church matters 1826-66 (1 bundle, 71 items); memoranda and copies of letters 1822-9 (1 vol); letters to his wife and son c1847-68 (1 bundle); commonplace book 1823-c1837; memoranda book rel to visits to local Baptists 1833-4; journal 1834-5 (1 vol); notebooks 1823-30 (2 vols); sermons, sermon notes (9 bundles, 1 vol); lecture notes (4 vols, 20 items); draft pamphlet 1853, misc papers etc.
Gloucestershire Record Office (D2698). Deposited by Mrs E Newman 1972. NRA 18862.

[516] **NEWMAN, William** (1773-1835)
Minister of Old Ford Baptist Church, London 1794-1835; president of the Baptist Academical Institution, Stepney 1811-26.

Diaries 1803-34 (4 vols); sermon notes 1819-20; lecture notes.
Regent's Park College, Oxford.

[517] **NEWSHAM, Charles** (1791-1863)
President of Ushaw College 1837-63.

Official corresp as president 1838-60 (c400 items) incl letters from NPS Wiseman 1838-60 (c75 items); corresp 1835-62 (c450 items) incl letters from John Briggs 1837-58 (21 items) and Robert Cornthwaite 1851-7 (27 items).
Ushaw College, Durham (President's archives and Newsham correspondence). NRA 13674.

[518] **NEWTH, Samuel** (1821-1898)
Principal of New College, London 1872-89.

Rough minutes (5 vols) and fair copy (3 vols) of the proceedings of the New Testament Revision Company 1870-80; printed parts of the authorised version of the NT with marginal notes for the revised version (4 vols).
British Library (Add MSS 36279-90). Presented by Miss Emily Newth 1899.

Notebooks rel to NT revision (34 vols); lecture and sermon notes (c140 items); MS history of Coward's academies (1 vol).
Dr Williams's Library, London (New College L8-9, CT 12/1). NRA 13042.

[519] **NEWTON, Benjamin Wills** (1807-1899)
Founder of the Christian Brethren.

Letters from SP Tregelles and his wife 1856-82 (123 items); corresp, mainly with Lord Ashburnham, rel to financial aid for Tregelles 1862-71 (19 items); lecture and other notes mainly by Newton, incl copies of letters and records of conversations with FW Wyatt c1815-99 (81 vols).
John Rylands University Library of Manchester (Christian Brethren Archive). NRA 27063.

[520] **NEWTON, John** (1725-1807)
Curate of Olney 1764-80; rector of St Mary Woolnoth, London 1780-1807.

Letters to his wife Mary 1745-87 (218ff); general corresp 1748-1802 (55ff); letters to his wife's family and others c1749-80 and letters to him c1756-98 (181ff); misc papers (16ff); MS of *Letters to a wife* 1793 (1 vol); sermons, meditations etc from 1758 (4 vols); transcriptions of sermons by John Laton 1760-1 (1 vol); diaries 1767, 1791-1803 (3 vols).
Lambeth Palace Library (MSS 2935-43, 3096, 3098). Presented 1976, 1979.

Notebooks etc c1765-95 (64 items); interleaved copy of *Letters to a wife* 1793 (2 vols) with diary-type entries etc; misc corresp and papers 1752-1800 (c33 items).
Cowper and Newton Museum, Olney, Bucks.
K Povey, 'Hand-list of manuscripts of the Cowper and Newton Museum . . .', *Transactions of the Cambridge Bibliographical Society*, iv, 2, 1965.

Letters from his wife 1774-6 (53 items); sermon notes c1775 (2 items).
Church Missionary Society, London (Venn MSS 65, 67). NRA 2694.

Letters and sermon notes as rector of St Mary Woolnoth 1779-1807.
Guildhall Library, London (MS 8100).

Log as master of the slave vessels *Duke of Argyle* and *African* 1750-4.
National Maritime Museum.

Memoir of William Cowper 1800.
McMaster University, Hamilton, Ontario.

[521] **NICHOLAS, Thomas** (1816-1879)
Congregational minister; tutor at the Presbyterian College, Carmarthen 1856-63.

Letters to him (1 vol); journal 1838 (1 vol); antiquarian and other notes (*c*6 vols); pedigrees of Welsh families (2 vols); sermons, lectures and poems (3 vols); papers rel to Pike *v* Nicholas 1868-9 (1 vol); legal papers and letters rel to Lonsdale House School 1876-7 (1 vol).
National Library of Wales (MSS 3091-3106).

[522] **NOEL, Conrad Le Despencer Roden** (1869-1942)
Vicar of Thaxted 1910-42.

Copies of corresp rel to the bishop of Exeter's refusal to ordain him 1893-4 (1 vol); corresp, working papers and typescripts of his books *c*1916-*c*1941 (2 boxes, 9 bundles); papers rel to social theology, life after death, imperialism etc 1908-42 (12 files); Venetian travel journal 1898 (1 vol) and misc notebooks nd (5 vols); accounts 1912-14 (2 vols); misc papers 1909-38 (4 bundles, 4 items) incl papers rel to his debate with Hilaire Belloc 1909 (1 bundle); press cuttings 1894-1942 (6 vols); printed papers 1922-45 (41 items).
Brynmor Jones Library, University of Hull (DNO). NRA 17259.

NORFOLK, Duke of, see Fitzalan-Howard.

NORMANTON, Earl of, see Agar.

[523] **NORRIS, Henry Handley** (1771-1850)
Perpetual curate of St John, South Hackney 1806-31, rector 1831-50.

Letters from Christopher Wordsworth, senior 1807-38 (101ff).
British Library (Add MS 46136).

Account books 1815-50 (8 vols).
St John's College, Oxford (MSS 349-55). Purchased 1981. NRA 7453.

Collections rel to William Cartwright and the non-jurors 1784-96, 1837-8 (1 vol).
Bodleian Library, Oxford (MS 30291).

[524] **NORRIS, John Pilkington** (1823-1891)
Vicar of St Mary Redcliffe, Bristol 1877-82; archdeacon of Bristol 1881-91.

Misc corresp and papers, mainly rel to Bristol bishopric and city affairs 1862, 1884-93 (5 bundles).
Bristol Record Office (Acc 12153). NRA 7842.

'Memoranda of Chapter' comprising detailed minutes of chapter meetings, with enclosures, 1865-91 (1 vol).
Bristol Record Office (DCA/8/16).

[525] **NORRIS, William Foxley** (1859-1937)
Dean of York 1917-25, of Westminster 1925-37.

Corresp and misc papers rel to Westminster abbey affairs and royal weddings, incl letters from CG Lang, 1926-35 (*c*340 items).
Westminster Abbey (WAM 58732-59107, 61883-61944).

[526] **NORTHCOTE, James Spencer** (1821-1907)
President of St Mary's College, Oscott 1861-76.

Corresp with JH Newman (*c*60 items); personal notes, sermons, memoranda 1860-77 (*c*100 items).
Oscott College, Sutton Coldfield.

[527] **OAKELEY, Frederick** (1802-1890)
RC canon of Westminster 1852-90.

Commonplace book as an undergraduate; drafts of autobiography *c*1827, nd.
Balliol College, Oxford (MSS 407-9). Presented by Major EF Oakeley 1946.

[528] **O'BRIEN, James Thomas** (1792-1874)
Bishop of Ossory, Ferns and Leighlin 1842-74.

Sermons 1826-72 (*c*200 vols); episcopal charges 1842-66 (6 items); misc papers 1835-71 (*c*10 items); printed works 1833-73 (*c*24 items).
Brynmor Jones Library, University of Hull (DDLG/53). NRA 15284.

[529] **O'BRYAN, William** (1778-1868)
Founder of the Bible Christians.

Diaries 1825-64 (15 vols).
Methodist Archives, Manchester. NRA 25824.

[530] **O'CONOR, Charles** (1764-1828)
Chaplain to the Marchioness of Buckingham.

Corresp and papers 1747-1827 (1,439 items), incl corresp with the Grenville family (282 items), Charles Butler (24 items), Sir WH Fremantle (16 items), Sir JC Hippisley (9 items), Hugh McDermot (51 items) and JT Troy (27 items), notebooks and papers rel to the royal veto on

Catholic episcopal appointments in Ireland 1810-13 and to Irish history and manuscripts and drafts of *Rerum Hibernicarum scriptores veteres.*
Huntington Library, San Marino, California (Stowe papers).

[531] **OGILVIE, Charles Atmore** (1793-1873)
Rector of Ross, Herefs 1839-73 and regius professor of pastoral theology, Oxford 1842-73.

Corresp 1813-47 mainly letters from John Keble, Hannah More and others (2 vols).
Bodleian Library, Oxford (MSS Eng lett d 123-4).
Presented by his great-granddaughter, Mrs AC Stonehill 1951.

[532] **OLIVER, George** (1781-1861)
Priest of the Jesuit mission, St Nicholas, Exeter 1807-51; antiquary.

Corresp 1824-54 (1 box); letters to him among collected letters of John Milner, Nicholas Sewell and Marmaduke Stone (3 vols); memoirs illustrating the history of the Cliffords and Arundelliana 1817 (1 vol).
Society of Jesus, London.

Corresp with John Lingard 1827-50 (66 items).
Ushaw College, Durham (Lingard papers).

Collections towards Jesuit biography (1 bundle) and the history of the Catholic religion in Devon and Cornwall (1 vol).
Stonyhurst College (C.3.2, A.3.10). HMC, *Third R, App*, 1872, p341.

Collections on the history of the Catholic religion in Devon, Cornwall, Dorset and Somerset (1 vol).
Cambridge University Library (Mm.vi.40).

[533] **OLLARD, Sidney Leslie** (1875-1949)
Canon of Windsor 1936-48.

Corresp, incl letters from WH Hutton 1893-1930 and VSS Coles and letters to him rel to the Oxford movement and his research subjects, with other churchmen's collected papers (1 chest).
Pusey House, Oxford.

Misc corresp as canon of Windsor with WH Frere, A Hamilton Thompson and others, and MS lecture on the Aerary.
St George's Chapel, Windsor Castle. NRA 18513.

[534] **OLLIVANT, Alfred** (1798-1882)
Bishop of Llandaff 1849-82.

Corresp and papers c1849-1882 (1 box) incl letters to him 1850-69 (1 bundle) some rel to an attack on him in the House of Commons 1850, corresp with AJ Beresford Hope rel to the Bonn Conference 1876 (4 items and enclosures), misc corresp and papers rel to diocesan affairs and sermon notes etc from 1849.

National Library of Wales. Deposited by Ronald Wingrove 1975.

[535] **OMAN, John Wood** (1860-1939)
Professor of systematic theology and apologetics, Westminster College, Cambridge 1907-35; principal 1922-35.

Lectures and papers (4 bundles); sermons 1890-1905 (10 bundles); prayers (1 vol).
Westminster College, Cambridge.

[536] **OMOND, John Reid** (1804-1892)
Minister of Monzie 1836-43, of Monzie Free Church 1843-92.

Letters from Thomas Chalmers, Alexander Dunlop and others rel to church politics 1834-47 (24 items); corresp with his wife c1801-45 (6 bundles); travel journals 1823, 1826-7 (4 vols); notebooks (3 vols).
Orkney Archives. Presented by Brigadier JS Omond 1954. NRA 19068.

[537] **O'REGAN, John** (c1818-1898)
Archdeacon 1862-79 and precentor 1873-98 of Kildare.

Letters to him 1841-98 (c500 items); diaries and misc papers 1839-84 (c40 items).
Trinity College, Dublin (MSS 5123-33, 7243-6).
Purchased from John O'Regan c1977. NRA 20076.

[538] **O'REILLY, Bernard** (1824-1894)
RC bishop of Liverpool 1873-94.

Letters to him as bishop from HO Callaghan 1873-83 (1 bundle), Cornelia Connelly 1873-4, HE Manning 1875-90 (1 bundle), EJ Purbrick 1880-c1887 (1 bundle), EW Pugin c1855-c1875 (1 bundle) and others (13 boxes *passim*); corresp with clergy 1879-92 (c300 items); corresp and papers rel to his case against Canon John Holden 1882-92 (1 box); personal corresp and papers (1 box, with misc personal corresp of Alexander Goss); his secretary's letter books 1877-92 (3 vols).
Lancashire Record Office (Liverpool archdiocesan records).

[539] **OSBORN, George** (1808-1891)
Wesleyan methodist minister.

Corresp 1826-88 incl letters from Richard Treffry 1825-38 (18 items), FA West 1834-55 (35 items) and others (c170 items).
Methodist Archives, Manchester.

[540] **OWEN, John** (1854-1926)
Bishop of St Davids 1897-1926.

Corresp, memoranda, diaries and other papers 1897-1926 incl papers rel to church schools, the Welsh Church Commission and disestablishment (30 boxes).
National Library of Wales. Deposited by his daughter Miss AE Owen. Closed to research until 2002. See *Annual Report* 1971-2, p77.

[541] **PALMER, Edwin** (1824-1895)
Archdeacon of Oxford 1878-95.

Letters mainly from his brother William 1849-95, with misc papers and letters to his wife 1879-96 (3 vols).
Bodleian Library, Oxford (MSS Eng lett d 432-3, e 152). Presented by the Earl of Selborne 1973, 1979. NRA 22802.

Misc letters to him 1865-87 (34 items).
Honnold Library, Claremont, California. Presented by WW Clary 1962.

Letters to him rel to his son EJ Palmer's education and election to a Balliol fellowship etc 1879-94 (5 bundles).
Balliol College, Oxford.

Letters from Cuthbert Shields c1880-7 (4 bundles).
Queen's College, Oxford (MS 417). NRA 1097.

Journal, Greece, the Middle East and Alexandria [1850] (1 vol); sermons 1857-95 (5 vols).
Lambeth Palace Library (MSS 2852-7). Presented by the Earl of Selborne 1975. NRA 11918.

Papers as executor of his brother William 1879-82 incl letters from HE Manning, JH Newman and WB Ullathorne (1 vol).
Bodleian Library, Oxford (MS Selbornc 225). Presented by the Earl of Selborne (as Viscount Wolmer) 1970. NRA 17810.

[542] **PALMER, Edwin James** (1869-1954)
Bishop of Bombay 1908-29.

Papers as examining chaplain to the bishops of Southwark and Rochester 1903-8 (1 vol); corresp and papers rel to Indian church union etc, mainly as bishop of Bombay, 1909-45 (22 vols), to church union in India, Africa, Asia and at home etc (8 vols), and to the archbishop's commissions on dispensations 1935-43 (2 vols) and impediments to marriage 1939-48 (1 vol); family and misc corresp and papers 1837-1949 (18 vols).
Lambeth Palace Library (MSS 2965-3015).

Corresp, diary 1898 and misc papers as fellow of Balliol College c1890-1908 (2 boxes).
Balliol College, Oxford. Deposited by Lady Laura Eastaugh 1978.

[543] **PALMER, Henry** (1835-1931)
Rector of Sullington 1859-1928.

Diaries 1854-1921 (c32 vols), sermon notes and papers rel to parochial affairs c1859-1926 (3 vols, 1 bundle).
West Sussex Record Office (Add MSS 13213-15, 13450-3). NRA 21176.

[544] **PALMER, John [Bernard]** (1782-1852)
Superior 1841-8 and abbot 1848-52 of Mount St Bernard.

Corresp and papers as superior and abbot 1841-52 (9 boxes) incl papers rel to the Oxford movement (1 box), JH Newman, HE Manning and NPS Wiseman (1 box) and AW Pugin and the building of the abbey (1 box).
Mount St Bernard Abbey, Coalville.

[545] **PALMER, William** (1811-1879)
Fellow of Magdalen College, Oxford 1832-55; RC 1855.

Corresp and papers, originals and copies, incl letters mainly from churchmen 1831-55 (1 vol), family corresp 18[24]-57 (4 vols), misc corresp and papers 1840-78 (1 vol, 79ff), collections rel to the history and liturgy of the Russian Orthodox Church (5 vols), diaries, travel journals etc 1831-79 (59 vols), autobiographical notes 1823-40 (1 vol) and antiquarian drawings etc (4 vols).
Lambeth Palace Library (MSS 1894-1901, 2457-97, 2814-40). Presented by the 3rd Earl of Selborne 1962 and the 4th Earl 1970, 1975.

Corresp with his father; diaries 1831-79; notes and journals of his visits to Russia and Greece and dealings with the Russian Orthodox Church; notes on Russian history, the Church of England etc.
The Oratory, Birmingham.

[546] **PARKER, Wilfrid** (1883-1966)
Bishop of Pretoria 1933-50.

Letters from CG Lang 1908-45 (4 vols).
Lambeth Palace Library (MSS 2881-4). Presented by him 1950.

[547] **PARKINSON, Henry** (1852-1924)
Rector of St Mary's College, Oscott 1897-1924.

Corresp and papers, incl notes and lectures rel to the Society of St Cecilia and the Catholic Social Guild (6 boxes).
Oscott College, Sutton Coldfield.

[548] **PARRY, William** (1754-1819)
Congregational minister, Little Baddow; tutor of Coward Trust academy, Wymondley.

Letters, accounts and reports, mainly rel to Wymondley House Academy, 1799-1819 (c86 items); lecture notes (18 vols).

Dr Williams's Library, London (New College 411, 431, 474, L17). NRA 13042.

[549] **PATERSON, Alexander** (1766-1831)
Vicar apostolic of the lowland district 1825-7, of the eastern district, Scotland 1827-31.

Corresp and papers as vicar apostolic; accounts 1808-31 (2 vols); letterbooks concerning attempts to recover French colleges 1823-6 (4 vols); sermons, theological and misc papers (6 vols, 1 bundle).
Scottish Catholic Archives (B 4; BL 5-6, 10; SM 10).

[550] **PATTISON, Mark** (1813-1884)
Rector of Lincoln College, Oxford 1861-84.

Letters to him 1830-83 (21 vols); corresp and papers rel to the election of James Thompson as rector of Lincoln College 1851 (1 vol); diaries and engagement books 1831-79 (32 vols); account books 1841-67 (10 vols); misc notebooks, papers etc 1809-66 (14 vols).
Bodleian Library, Oxford (MSS Pattison 1-78). Presented by him 1884.

Family corresp, mainly letters to his sister Eleanor, 1839-51 (83 items).
Lincoln College, Oxford. Presented by his niece, Lady de Saumarez 1934.

[551] **PAYNE SMITH, Robert** (1819-1895)
Regius professor of divinity, Oxford 1865-70; dean of Canterbury 1870-95.

Letters to him rel to the attendance of students at his theological lectures etc and letters collected by him (3 vols).
Bodleian Library, Oxford (MSS Eng lett d 171, e 46-7). Purchased 1957.

Family and genealogical papers *c*1621-1901 (1 box) incl papers rel to Pembroke College and Christ Church, Oxford affairs (1 bundle).
Canterbury Cathedral Library.

[552] **PEACOCK, George** (1790-1858)
Dean of Ely 1839-58.

Letters from churchmen and scientists etc mainly to him *c*1802-54 (*c*530 items).
Trinity College, Cambridge (Peacock MSS 1-2, Add Ms b 49).

See also HMC, *The manuscript papers of British scientists 1600-1940*, 1982.

[553] **PEAKE, Arthur Samuel** (1865-1929)
Theologian and biblical scholar.

Corresp and papers (*c*4,000 items) incl corresp rel to his appointment to Hartley College 1892 and work as a tutor, the foundation of the Manchester

university theology faculty etc, letters from CH Dodd, JR Harris, Henry Meecham, JH Moulton and other scholars, family corresp, working papers and sermon notes.
Methodist Archives, Manchester. Presented by Canon Alan Wilkinson 1981.

Notebooks rel to OT history (3 vols).
John Rylands University Library of Manchester (MS 1270).

[554] **PEASE, John** (1797-1868)
Quaker minister.

Letters to him rel to family, business and Quaker affairs 1810-68 (352 items); to him and his wife Sophia, mainly from his father, 1823-58 (92 items); corresp, journals etc rel to journeys to Ireland, France, Germany and America 1833-64 (3 bundles, 1 item); corresp rel to the Stockton-Darlington railway 1835-67 (1 bundle); corresp rel to the Derwent Iron Co 1857-9 (1 bundle); diaries and notebooks 1817-45 (11 vols); misc corresp, notes, papers etc 1823-67 (1 vol, 6 bundles).
Durham County Record Office (D/Ho). NRA 12281.

[555] **PELLEW, George** (1793-1866)
Dean of Norwich 1828-66.

Letters to him rel to Norwich chapter affairs, patronage, cathedral services and works etc 1828-66 (*c*1,000 items); diary and notebooks rel to chapter business 1829-32, 1845-66.
Norfolk Record Office (DCN 120/1-2). Deposited by the dean and chapter 1975.

[556] **PENSWICK, Thomas** (1772-1836)
Vicar apostolic of the northern district 1831-6.

Corresp 1823-36 (237 items) incl letters from PA Baines (16 items), JY Bramston, Robert Gradwell, Thomas Griffiths and NPS Wiseman (12 items).
Bishop of Leeds.

Corresp 1798-1840 (9 items); his executorship papers (1 bundle).
Lancashire Record Office (Liverpool archdiocesan records).

[557] **PEROWNE, John James Stewart** (1823-1904)
Bishop of Worcester 1891-1901.

Cambridge diary 1841-2 (1 vol).
Corpus Christi College, Cambridge (MS 560). Presented by Canon Christopher Perowne 1954.

Press cuttings and misc corresp 1864-1904 (5 vols).
Lambeth Palace Library (MSS 1961-5). Presented by Canon Christopher Perowne 1965.

[558] **PERRONET, Vincent** (1693-1785)
Vicar of Shoreham, Kent 1728-85; methodist.

Family corresp and papers incl letters from early
methodist leaders 1725-1855 (3 vols, 9 items).
*William R Perkins Library, Duke University,
Durham, N Carolina.*

[559] **PETRE, William Joseph** (1847-1893), 13th
Baron Petre 1884
RC priest; benefactor of Downside.

Misc corresp and papers 1872-82 incl theses at
Downside 1876-8, lectures on culture and
education, corresp with Bernard Murphy, letters
to Placid de Paiva 1872-3 and Woburn Park
School timetables and prospectuses 1881-2 (1
box).
Downside Abbey. NRA 19936.

Personal accounts 1884-92 (4 vols); Woburn Park
School examination results, lists of pupils 1877-82
and account books 1877-84; Northwood Park
account books 1884-5 (9 vols).
Essex Record Office (Petre papers). NRA 23544.

[560] **PHILIP, Alexander** (1813-1861)
Minister of Portobello Free Church, Edinburgh
1849-61.

Corresp 1829-56 (8 vols); sermons (2 vols).
New College, Edinburgh.

[561] **PHILLIPS, John** (1810-1867)
Calvinistic methodist minister; principal of the
Normal College, Bangor 1863-7.

Corresp and misc papers 1833-65 (2 vols); diaries
1833-36, 1851-64 (2 vols); college subscription
books 1856-62 (2 vols); sermons, papers,
biographical notes etc (c6 vols).
National Library of Wales (MSS 4254-6, 5479-82,
7824-7).

[562] **PHILLPOTTS, Henry** (1778-1869)
Bishop of Exeter 1830-69.

Letters from CJ Blomfield, GA Denison, WE
Gladstone, William Howley, HE Manning and
others, with copies of replies, 1807-62 (72
bundles); speeches, memoranda, appointments,
printed sermons etc 1802-69 (11 bundles); diary
1831 rel to livings, his visitation of the Scilly Isles
etc (1 vol); corresp of RN Shutte, rel to his *Life*
of Phillpotts (1 bundle).
Exeter Cathedral Library (ED/11: Spencer Gift).
NRA 25909.

Letter book 1832-7 (1 vol).
Devon Record Office (Exeter diocese).

[563] **PLATER, Charles Dominic** (1875-1921)
Jesuit.

Letters to him; corresp about the Pope's peace
note 1917; papers rel to the Catholic Social Guild;
diaries and spiritual notebooks.
Society of Jesus, London. Partly closed to research.

[564] **PLOWDEN, Charles** (1743-1821)
Provincial of the Society of Jesus in England and
rector of Stonyhurst College, Lancs 1817-21.

Corresp with bishops and cardinals, with Jesuit
colleges and residences 1776-1821, with foreign
correspondents 1776-1820 and with Charles
Butler, Lord Clifford, George Oliver and others
from 1776 (c3 vols *passim*); papers rel to Catholic
emancipation 1785-1815 (3 bundles); collected
letters from him (1 vol); literary MSS incl the
Destruction of the English College at Bruges 1773,
1807 and 'General account of the origin, progress
and present state of the Jesuit mission in
England' nd; spirituals, sermons etc (8 bundles).
Society of Jesus, London.

Collected letters and misc literary MSS rel to the
Jesuits (4 vols *passim*).
Stonyhurst College (A.2.26, 29; A.3.21; A.4.6).
HMC, *Third R, App*, 1872, p341.

[565] **PLUMMER, Alfred** (1841-1926)
Master of University College, Durham 1874-1902.

Letters from JH Newman 1870-88 (42 items) and
JJI von Döllinger 1870-89 (20 items);
'conversations with Dr Döllinger' 1870-90 (4
vols).
Pusey House, Oxford.

Letters, mainly from WC Allen, rel to his edition
of St Matthew's gospel 1903-8 (10 items).
Dr Williams's Library, London (24.161). NRA
13168.

[566] **PLUMPTRE, James** (c1771-1832)
Vicar of Great Gransden 1812-32.

Personal and literary corresp, diaries and
memoranda 1804-29, accounts 1801-15, literary
MSS, collections and notes 1790-1831.
Cambridge University Library (Add 5785-5866).

[567] **POLE, Thomas** (1753-1829)
Quaker minister.

Letter books 1774-83 (2 vols); journals 1775-99 (6
vols); reflections (1 vol).
Society of Friends Library, London (MS Vols s
53–61).

[568] **POLLEN, John Hungerford** (1858-1902)
RC artist and author.

General corresp 1885-1925 incl letters from
Hilaire Belloc, Andrew Lang, TG Law, John

Morris and EI Purbrick (*c*9 boxes); corresp with his family and the Jesuits, and personal and biographical papers (2 boxes); travel journals 1895-1911 (10 vols); pocket diaries 1898-1913, 1918-19.
Society of Jesus, London.

[569] **POLLOCK, Bertram** (1863-1943)
Headmaster of Wellington College 1893-1910; bishop of Norwich 1910-42.

Misc corresp rel to prayer book revision etc 1910-42 (39ff).
Lambeth Palace Library (MS 2888). Presented by his widow 1975.

[570] **PORTEUS, Beilby** (1731-1808)
Bishop of Chester 1776-87, of London 1787-1808.

Corresp and papers as bishop of London (*c*42 vols) incl letters from clergy, mainly rel to parochial matters 1803-9, visitation returns etc.
Lambeth Palace Library (Fulham papers).

Letters to him as bishop of London rel to colonial affairs 1788-1805 (*c*40 items) and misc papers.
Lambeth Palace Library (Fulham papers, American colonial section). See WW Manross, *The Fulham papers in the Lambeth Palace Library,* 1965.

Notebooks containing his 'Occasional memorandums and reflexions' 1777-1809 (9 vols).
Lambeth Palace Library (MSS 2098-2106). Presented 1967.

[571] **POYNTER, William** (1762-1827)
Vicar apostolic of the London district 1812-27.

Corresp and papers as vicar apostolic (16 boxes) incl corresp with Rome (*c*3 boxes), with other vicars apostolic (*c*4 boxes), with London district clergy (2 boxes), with other clergy in England and abroad (5 boxes) and with John Kirk (*c*80 items) and corresp and papers rel to Peter Gandolphy (64 items); letters from Robert Gradwell in Rome 1817-28 (1 vol); draft letters 1806-14 (1 vol); letter books 1812-27 (1 box); 'The origin, distinction and mutual independence of the civil and ecclesiastical power' (1 item).
Westminster Diocesan Archives (A55-68c, B3, 20, 48, F21). NRA 28616.

Corresp and papers mainly as vice-president and president of St Edmund's College 1795-1820 (*c*200 items) incl corresp and drafts rel to Catholic emancipation 1810-20 (*c*10 items), diaries 1815-19, 1821-4 and notes on meetings of vicars apostolic 1803-10.
Westminster Diocesan Archives (St Edmund's College, Ware series 2, 12, 14, 15). NRA 16303.

[572] **PREST, Charles** (1806-1875)
Wesleyan methodist minister.

Letters to him 1835-70 (*c*135 items), mainly from WH Rule rel to methodist work among soldiers 1857-65 (100 items); sermons and circuit plans (2 vols).
Methodist Archives, Manchester.

PRETYMAN, see Tomline.

[573] **PREVOST, Sir George** (1804-1893), 2nd Bt 1816
Perpetual curate of Stinchcombe 1834-93 and archdeacon of Gloucester 1865-81.

Letters from John Keble 1824-42 and other corresp and misc papers 1824-93 (41 items).
Gloucestershire Record Office (D 2962). Deposited by Miss C Prevost 1974. NRA 18593.

[574] **PRICE, Richard** (1723-1791)
Nonconformist minister; moral and political philosopher.

Corresp and papers 1767-90 (90 items).
American Philosophical Society Library, Philadelphia. See *National union catalog* MS 61-933.

Letters to him 1766-91 from Lord Lansdowne 1775-86, Joseph Priestley and others (40 items).
Bodleian Library, Oxford (MS Eng misc c 132).

Journal, mainly in shorthand, 1787-91.
National Library of Wales. Purchased. See *Annual Report* 1971-2, p61.

[575] **PRIESTLEY, Joseph** (1733-1804)
Presbyterian minister and scientist.

Collected corresp and papers from 1762 (5 boxes).
Dickinson College, Carlisle, Pennsylvania. See *Archives and manuscript collections of Dickinson College,* 1972, p34.

Corresp and papers of and rel to him 1777-1948 (125 items) incl an account book, sermon, will etc; autobiography (2 copies).
University of Pennsylvania Library, Philadelphia. See *National union catalog* MS 62-4316.

Shorthand notes on the Scriptures (1 vol), notebook explaining Annet's shorthand system 1790, shorthand lecture notes on history and poetry (1 vol); sermons 1760-83 (52 items); communion addresses and prayers (1 vol), prayers (11 items), hymn *c*1790.
Manchester College, Oxford.

Corresp, mainly letters to his brother-in-law, John Wilkinson 1790-1802 (63 items).
Warrington Public Library.

See also HMC, *The manuscript papers of British scientists 1600-1940,* 1982.

[576] **PROSSER, David Lewis** (1868-1950)
Bishop of St Davids 1927-50; archbishop of Wales
1944-9.

Corresp and papers incl diaries 1912-50, visitation
charges, lectures on the history of St Davids
diocese, sermons, addresses etc.
National Library of Wales. Deposited by Mrs MF
Prosser and Mrs WWT Prosser. See *Annual
Report* 1954-5, p35, 1955-6, p41, 1956-7, p32.

[577] **PRYS, Owen** (1857-1934)
Calvinistic methodist minister; principal of
Trevecca College 1891-1906, of Aberystwyth
Theological College 1906-27.

Letters, mainly to him, 1901-34 (*c*200 items) incl
those from chaplains and theological students
serving in the first world war 1915-19 (138 items);
letters to his parents 1876-96 and to his brother
Rowland 1883-1903 (133 items).
National Library of Wales (Presbyterian Church of
Wales MSS, General Collection). NRA 28345.

[578] **PULLAN, Leighton** (1865-1940)
Fellow of St John's College, Oxford 1890-1930.

Notebooks, lectures and sermons (1 box).
Pusey House, Oxford.

[579] **PUNSHON, William Morley** (1824-1881)
Wesleyan methodist minister.

Corresp incl letters to him 1845-79 (*c*80 items).
Methodist Archives, Manchester.

European and Canadian travel journals 1865-71.
Queen's University Archives, Kingston, Ontario.

[580] **PURBRICK, Edward Ignatius** (d 1914)
Provincial of the Society of Jesus in England
1880-8.

Corresp as provincial; diary 1870-1 (1 vol); notes
on retreats, spiritual exercises etc (4 bundles).
Society of Jesus, London.

Diaries and notebooks.
Stonyhurst College.

[581] **PUSEY, Edward Bouverie** (1800-1882)
Regius professor of Hebrew, Oxford and canon of
Christ Church 1828-82.

Corresp (43 vols, *c*150 bundles), sermons (6 vols)
and other papers, incl transcripts of his corresp
(83 vols, 2 bundles) collected by HP Liddon for
his *Life.*
Pusey House, Oxford.

Letters from HE Manning 1845-50 (35ff).
Bodleian Library, Oxford (MS Eng lett c 654).
Presented 1982. NRA 25566.

Letters from his brother Philip 1821-45 (*c*30ff).
Bodleian Library, Oxford (MS Eng lett d 58).
Presented by Mrs Bouverie Pusey 1933.

Corresp with his wife and children 1828–78
(26ff).
Bodleian Library, Oxford (MS Eng lett c 130).

[582] **RAIKES, Henry** (1782-1854)
Chancellor of Chester diocese 1830-54.

Letters to him (180 items).
John Rylands University Library of Manchester
(Eng MS 1121).

[583] **RAINY, Robert** (1826-1906)
Principal of New College, Edinburgh 1874-1906.

Corresp, papers and notes for a speech at a
convocation of the United Free Church of
Scotland 1904 (1 bundle); lecture notes (3 vols);
collections for a projected life of St Augustine (3
boxes); album of press cuttings and obituaries
1906.
New College, Edinburgh.

[584] **RAMSAY, Henry Havelock [Leander]**
(1863-1929)
Headmaster of Downside School 1902-18; abbot
of Downside 1922-9.

Working papers, transcriptions etc rel to his
studies of the Apocalypse (*c*44 bundles, boxes and
vols); papers as headmaster and abbot.
Downside Abbey, Somerset.

[585] **RANDALL, Richard William** (1824-1906)
Dean of Chichester 1892-1902.

Corresp rel to religious controversies etc 1851-
1904 (4 vols); journals 1851-61 (5 vols); records of
parish work incl sermons, officiants at services
and sick visiting 1851-4 (3 vols).
Pusey House, Oxford.

[586] **RANDOLPH, John** (1749-1813)
Bishop of London 1809-13.

Corresp and papers as bishop of London, mainly
rel to non-residence (16 vols) incl letters from
clergy, visitation returns 1810, 1812 and return of
places of worship 1810.
Lambeth Palace Library (Fulham papers).

Letters to his brother-in-law Thomas Lambard,
rector of Ash, and other family papers 1748-1810.
Bodleian Library, Oxford (MSS Top Oxon b 170,
d 353-6).

[587] **RASHDALL, Hastings** (1858-1924)
Fellow of New College, Oxford 1895-1917 and
canon of Hereford 1909-17; dean of Carlisle 1917-
24.

Letters to him 1871-1924 (20 vols); letters from
HM Butler 1875-1917 (1 vol); family corresp
1869-1907 (1 vol); draft lectures on medieval
universities (1 vol); misc papers 1883-1923 (2
vols).
Bodleian Library, Oxford (MSS Eng lett c 342-51
and *passim*). Presented by his widow 1953. NRA
27380.

Papers (17 boxes).
Bodleian Library, Oxford. Deposited by Ripon
College, Cuddesdon 1984.

Letters to his mother 1889-1923 (3 boxes) and
copies of his letters to his family and others 1866-
1923 (6 bundles, 1 box); newspaper cuttings
1896-1919 (3 vols); printed articles, sermons etc
(1 box).
New College, Oxford.

Letters and press cuttings 1888-1936 (1 vol).
New College, Oxford (5599). See FW Steer,
Archives of New College, Oxford, 1974.

Sermons 1884-1923 (12 boxes); theological
lectures and papers etc (6 boxes).
Pusey House, Oxford (HRa). NRA 25888.

[588] **RATTENBURY, John** (1806-1879)
Wesleyan methodist minister.

Corresp, mainly letters to him, 1840-66 (*c*185
items).
Methodist Archives, Manchester.

[589] **REECE, Richard** (1765-1850)
Wesleyan methodist minister.

Letters from Jabez Bunting and others 1802-45
(*c*25 items); diaries 1788-1836 (26 vols).
Methodist Archives, Manchester.

[590] **REES, Henry** (1798-1869)
Calvinistic methodist minister, Liverpool 1836-69.

Letters from him 1835-68 (39 items); diaries
1843, 1850-69 (16 vols); sermon notes (*c*3
bundles).
National Library of Wales (Presbyterian Church of
Wales MSS, Bala College Group). NRA 28416.

Letters to his family 1839-67 (94 items) and to
Hugh Griffiths 1829-64 (9 items); letters to him
1823, 1866 (3 items); journal of visit to Ireland
1852 (2 copies); sermons 1836-51 (4 vols); misc
papers.
National Library of Wales (Presbyterian Church of
Wales MSS, General Collection). NRA 28345.

[591] **REES, Thomas** (1815-1885)
Independent minister; historian.

Letters received (*c*135ff); diaries 1862-76 (13
vols); notes for a *History of protestant nonconformity
in Wales* (11 vols); account books (7 vols);
collection books (12 vols); sermons, addresses,
notes etc (11 vols, 2 bundles).
National Library of Wales (MSS 176, 271, 362-97
passim).

[592] **REES, Thomas** (1869-1926)
Principal of Bala-Bangor Independent College
1909-26.

Letters to him 1887-1923; sermons 1899-1925;
addresses, articles etc 1913-23.
National Library of Wales. Presented by the Revd
Dr Elfan Rees. See *Annual Report* 1959-60, p35.

Letters to him 1895, 1899 (2 bundles); notebooks
(27 items); notes and essays (1 bundle).
University College of North Wales, Bangor. NRA
25182.

[593] **REEVES, William** (1815-1892)
Dean of Armagh 1875-86; bishop of Down,
Connor and Dromore 1886-92.

Corresp 1845-91 (1 bundle); papers on the Book
of Armagh and William King (4 vols, 5 bundles).
Trinity College, Dublin (MSS 2903-11, 3760).

Collections for Irish ecclesiastical history (84
vols).
Trinity College, Dublin (MSS 1059-1142).

Letters to him mainly rel to the Royal Irish
Academy (*c*70 items).
Archbishop Marsh's Library, Dublin (MS Z/1/1/18).

Corresp and papers rel to archaeological and
antiquarian subjects 1850-77 (1 vol).
National Library of Ireland (MS 8262). See
*Manuscript sources for the history of Irish
civilisation*, 1965.

Working papers rel to the history of Down,
Connor and Dromore diocese (29 items and vols).
*Down, Connor and Dromore Diocesan Library,
Belfast.* See JR Garstin, *Descriptive catalogue of a
collection of manuscripts ... of W Reeves ...*, 1899.

[594] **REID, James Seaton** (1798-1851)
Professor of church history, Glasgow University
1841-51.

MSS of his *History of the Presbyterian church in
Ireland* and *History of congregations of the
Presbyterian church in Ireland;* MS 'Life of Francis
Lambert'; transcription of the Adair MS; lecture
notes, sermons and misc MSS.
Presbyterian Historical Society of Ireland, Belfast.
See Robert Allen, *James Seaton Reid*, 1951.

[595] **RENOUF, Sir Peter Le Page** (1822-1897
RC theologian and egyptologist.

Corresp and misc papers 1837-1902 (*c*850 items)
incl letters from JH Newman 1846-84 (19 items),
corresp rel to the British Museum, Egyptian and
oriental studies 1842-96 (*c*270 items), with Lord
Acton about proposals for a RC university college
in England, and rel to JJI von Döllinger, the
Vatican Council's decrees etc 1862-97 (116 items)
and with his family rel to foreign travel, his
conversion etc 1837-78 (258 items), notes,
working papers and misc printed pamphlets etc
(*c*10 items).
Pembroke College, Oxford (63/9). Presented by his
daughter Edith Renouf 1948. NRA 29439.

Corresp and misc papers of and rel to him,
mainly from egyptologists and orientalists, 1860-
1922 (*c*300 items).
Griffith Institute, Ashmolean Museum, Oxford.
Collected by Edith Renouf and presented by WR
Dawson 1956. NRA 28749.

[596] **RICHARDS, Edward Ignatius** (1789-1828)
Provincial of the Friars Minor in England 1824-8.

Diary in Welsh 1816-17; diary at Rome 1827-8;
corresp 1827-8 (5 items).
*Archives of the English Province of Friars Minor,
London.*

[597] **RICHARDSON, George** (1773-1862)
Quaker minister.

Letters from ministers 1811-50, from elders incl
Alexander Cruickshank and Josiah Forster 1807-
56 and from others 1802-57 (3 vols); letters to
him rel to Friends in Norway 1855-9 (1 bundle);
record of visits paid by 'public' Friends to
Newcastle and neighbouring meetings 1800-50 (1
vol); accounts of the London Yearly Meeting
1833-45 (1 vol); articles, obituaries, letters etc
copied by him (4 vols).
Society of Friends Library, London (MS Boxes H3,
R4).

[598] **RIDDELL, Arthur** (1836-1907)
Bishop of Northampton 1880-1907.

Corresp with clergy, missions etc and rel to
universities (*c*2 boxes); notebooks on diocesan
affairs (8 vols); college notes (1 vol).
Bishop of Northampton.

[599] **RIDDING, George** (1828-1904)
Headmaster of Winchester College 1866-84;
bishop of Southwell 1884-1904.

Official corresp and papers as headmaster,
accounts, sermons etc 1867-84, with some papers
as bishop of Southwell (1 box).
Winchester College. Deposited 1935.

Misc corresp and papers, mainly bills, receipts
and administrative letters from him as
headmaster, 1863-1904 (*c*500 items).
Winchester College. (H/GR). Deposited by his
widow 1928. NRA 26994.

Misc personal papers 1884-1904, incl papers rel to
the reconstitution of the Southwell chapter and
the history of the minster and its locality.
Southwell Minster Library. NRA 7879.

Corresp rel to ecclesiastical controversies 1886-
1904 (138ff).
Bodleian Library, Oxford (MS Eng lett c 31).
Presented by his widow 1935.

Corresp rel to the Association for the Furtherance
of Christianity in Egypt 1898-9 (34ff).
Lambeth Palace Library (MS 1812). Presented by
his widow.

[600] **RIGBY, John** (1753-1818)
Mission priest, St Peter's RC church, Lancaster
1784-1818.

Papers and notes rel to the establishment of a
chapel, presbytery and school at Lancaster etc
1784-1811 (3 vols, 15 items); register of corresp
from 1804 (1 vol); catechism 1793 (1 vol);
commonplace book *c*1800 (1 vol).
Lancashire Record Office (RCLn). NRA 19475.

[601] **RIGG, James Harrison** (1821-1909)
Wesleyan methodist minister; principal of
Westminster training college 1868-1903.

Letters from William Arthur and others 1845-
1909 (*c*160 items).
Methodist Archives, Manchester.

[602] **RILEY, John Athelstan Laurie** (1858-1945)
Chairman of the Anglican and Eastern Church
Association; vice-president of the Church Union.

General corresp 1879-1940 (6 vols); corresp with
archbishops of Canterbury and their chaplains
1884-1939 (1 vol); letters from Lord Quickswood
1897-1940 (1 vol); corresp with Lord Halifax
1902-*c*1928, WH Frere 1895-1932 and others
1892-1940 (2 vols); notebooks, travel journals,
engagement books and misc papers 1882-1941 (59
vols).
Lambeth Palace Library (MSS 2343-2411).
Presented by Major JRC Riley 1969.

[603] **RIPPON, John** (1751-1836)
Minister of Carter Lane, later New Park Street
Baptist Church, London 1773-1836.

Letters to him 1769-1830 (4 vols); biographical
and other collections mainly rel to the dissenters'
burial-ground at Bunhill Fields (18 vols).
British Library (Add MSS 25386-9, 28513-23,
56412-18).

[604] **ROBERTS, John** (1767-1834)
Independent minister, Llanbrynmair 1798-1834.

Family and personal corresp and papers 1794-
1834.
National Library of Wales. See *Annual Report*
1937-8, p40, 1939-40, pp26, 29, 1942-3, p25,
1945-6, p28.

[605] **ROBERTS, John** (1804-1884)
Independent minister; editor of *Y Cronicl*
1857-84.

Family and personal corresp c1801-84, sermons
(c26 vols), papers rel to *Y Cronicl*; press cuttings
and notes.
National Library of Wales (MSS 590, 3266, 9511-
96 *passim*). See *Annual Report* 1937-8, p40, 1939-
40, p29, 1942-3, p25, 1945-6, p28.

[606] **ROBERTS, Richard** (1823-1909)
Wesleyan methodist minister.

Corresp 1848-1908 (c150 items).
Methodist Archives, Manchester.

[607] **ROBERTS, Samuel** (1800-1885)
Independent minister; reformer.

Family and personal corresp and papers incl
letters to him rel to social reforms, politics and
education 1808-85, and from relatives and
acquaintances in the United States 1825-82,
corresp and papers rel to a libel case instituted by
him 1869-71 and to the Bala Independent College
controversy 1873-9; letter book 1850-1; diaries
1843-85; notebooks and papers rel to *Y Cronicl*
and to other publications, American claims etc
1868-85; collecting books for Welsh
Congregational Churches Appeal Fund 1835 (2
vols) and for Bala Independent College 1870 and
letter book rel to same 1873; sermon notes etc;
reminiscences, essays, estate accounts etc 1803-85.
National Library of Wales (MSS 528-9, 589-90,
3265-6, 3268, 9511-98). See *Annual Report* 1937-
8, p40, 1939-40, pp26, 29, 1942-3, p25, 1945-6,
p28.

[608] **ROBERTS, Thomas** (1735-1804)
Member of the Trevecca 'family'.

Diaries 1773-89 (4 vols); autobiographical notes
1771-4; account book 1758-94; misc papers.
National Library of Wales (Presbyterian Church of
Wales MSS, Trevecca Group). NRA 15301.

[609] **ROBERTS, Thomas** (1816-1887)
Independent minister, Llanrwst 1858-81.

Personal and family corresp, papers, lectures,
sermons etc 1839-c1883 (3 boxes).
University College of North Wales, Bangor.

[610] **ROBERTS, William** (1813-1872)
Minister of Salem Baptist Church, Blaenau Gwent
1845-72; author.

Corresp, mainly letters to him but incl letters to
Daniel Jones and other Baptist ministers 1787-
1930 (7 vols); diaries 1835-71 (8 vols); journal
1853-65; account books 1841-69 (22 vols) incl
some rel to *Seren Gomer* 1841-65 (3 vols);
sermons, notes, essays, poems, literary and
collected MSS mainly rel to Baptist history,
churches etc (c160 vols, bundles and items).
National Library of Wales (MSS 7011-7189, 7768-
79, 9367-9, 14856, 14859-60). See *Annual Report*
1954-5, p32.

[611] **ROBERTSON, Archibald** (1853-1931)
Bishop of Exeter 1903-16.

Corresp as chairman of the archbishop's advisory
committee on liturgical revision 1911-15 (37ff).
Lambeth Palace Library (MS 1642).

[612] **ROBINSON, Arthur William** (1856-1928)
Canon of Canterbury 1916-28.

Corresp and papers mainly rel to the
establishment of the National Mission of 1916,
incl letters from RT Davidson, William Temple
and other members of the organising committee,
1893-1920 (1 vol).
Lambeth Palace Library (MS 3356).

[613] **ROBINSON, Joseph Armitage** (1858-1933)
Dean of Westminster 1902-11, of Wells 1911-33.

Corresp and papers, mainly at Cambridge and
Westminster, 1875-1938 (10 boxes) incl scholarly,
personal and family corresp 1877-1938 (c10
folders etc), diaries and devotional papers 1875-
1902 (6 vols etc) and sermons and addresses 1875-
1932 (4 boxes etc).
Westminster Abbey. Deposited by his family. NRA
28859.

Corresp and papers 1901-2 rel to the coronation
of Edward VII (190 items) and other misc papers.
Westminster Abbey (WAM 58300-489 and *passim*).

Corresp and papers 1921-7 rel to the Malines
conversations (3 vols).
Lambeth Palace Library (MSS 2222-4).

Corresp with Edmund Bishop 1900-16 (1 box);
transcripts and working papers (3 vols).
Downside Abbey (Edmund Bishop papers).

Sermons and notes on his pupils at Christ's
College, Cambridge 1887-90 (2 vols).
Lambeth Palace Library (MSS 3357-8).

[614] **ROBSON, Elizabeth** (1771-1843)
Quaker minister.

Letters from her 1811-42 (140 items); journals
1813-44 (26 vols) incl those of her husband 1820-
34 (4 vols); descriptions of her North American
journeys edited by her son Henry.
Society of Friends Library, London (MS Vols 32-7,
121; MS Vols s 129-54).

Family corresp of Elizabeth and Thomas Robson
1823-45 (29 items).
*Friends Historical Library, Swarthmore College,
Pennsylvania.*

[615] **ROBSON, Isaac** (1800-1885)
Quaker minister.

Letters from Thomas Evans and others in North
America 1828-87 (14 items) and from TMS Jones
and others on religious and educational work in
Italy *c*1861-84 (53 items).
Society of Friends Library, London (Temp MSS
1/10, 1/21). NRA 20087.

Travel journals, Ireland and the west of England,
1847, 1850.
Brotherton Library, Leeds University (MS [Deposit]
1979/1/PA85). NRA 17118.

[616] **ROBY, William** (1766-1830)
Independent Minister, Manchester 1795-1830.

Personal and family corresp and papers (1 box)
incl letters from him to his wife and father 1787-
90 and to James Turner and S Sheldon 1821-30
and corresp with Robert Haldane 1801-2; diaries
1817, 1829; addresses, sermons.
John Rylands University Library of Manchester
(Northern Congregational College MSS).

[617] **ROCK, Daniel** (1799-1871)
Chaplain to Lord Shrewsbury 1827-40; RC
mission priest at Buckland, Berks 1840-54; canon
of Southwark cathedral 1852-71.

Corresp, research papers and collected MSS, incl
letters from Thomas Griffiths, AW Pugin, Lord
and Lady Shrewsbury, Ann Talbot, Thomas
Walsh and NPS Wiseman 1839-44 and personal
papers and engagement diary 1871 (2 boxes, 1
bundle), autobiography (1 vol), sermons, misc
notes and notebooks on history, liturgy etc (*c*36
vols, 1 bundle) and MS and annotated copy of
The church of our fathers (3 vols, 1 bundle).
Southwark Diocesan Archives. NRA 27760.

Letters from Lord Shrewsbury 1838-52 (22
items).
Archbishop's House, Birmingham. NRA 8129.

[618] **RODDA, Richard** (1743-1815)
Methodist.

Corresp incl letters from Samuel Bradburn, John
Wesley and others 1779-1812 (*c*48 items); journals
(3 vols); notebooks (5 vols).
Methodist Archives, Manchester.

[619] **RODWELL, John Medows** (1808-1900)
Rector of St Ethelburga Bishopsgate, London
1843-1900.

Autobiography to 1864, with letters etc mainly rel
to ritualistic practices at St Ethelburga's, in the
register of baptisms and burials of the parish
1792-1812.
Guildhall Library, London (MS 4238).

[620] **ROSE, Hugh James** (1795-1838)
Principal of King's College, London 1836-8.

Letters from William Whewell 1817-36 (42
items).
Trinity College, Cambridge (R.2.99). NRA 8804.

Sermon notes (1 box).
Cambridge University Library (Add 5870).

[621] **ROUTH, Martha** (1743-1817)
Quaker minister.

Letters to her 1777-1816 (5 items); North
American travel journal 1794-1801 (1 vol).
Society of Friends Library, London (Gibson MSS,
Box Q).

[622] **ROUTH, Martin Joseph** (1755-1854)
President of Magdalen College, Oxford 1791-
1854.

Corresp (*c*27 vols) incl letters from Granville Penn
from 1785 and JH Newman 1835-43 (1 vol) and
corresp with Richard Chandler 1784-90 (1 vol)
and Samuel Parr (2 vols); papers rel to his MS
collection, *Reliquiae Sacrae* and Gilbert Burnet's
History etc (8 vols).
Magdalen College, Oxford (Old Library MSS 308-
981 *passim*).

[623] **ROWNTREE, John Stephenson** (1834-
1907)
Quaker minister.

Corresp and papers *c*1850-1906 rel to Friends
affairs incl registration of births, marriages and
deaths, marriage regulations, the ministry and his
lecture on George Fox 1894 (10 bundles).
Society of Friends Library, London. NRA 7629.

[624] **RULE, William Harris** (1802-1890)
Wesleyan methodist minister.

Letters to him mainly rel to army affairs 1857-71
(*c*40 items).
Methodist Archives, Manchester.

[625] **RUSSELL, Charles William** (1812-1880)
President of St Patrick's College, Maynooth 1857-
80.

General corresp (38 items) incl letters from WE
Gladstone 1859-74 (20 items); family corresp,
mainly letters from him, 1826-73 (85 items);
corresp and transcripts rel to *The life of cardinal
Mezzofanti* 1855-7 (153 items); calendar of the
Carte papers 1865-9 (5 vols).
St Patrick's College, Maynooth. NRA 28335.

[626] **RUSSELL, John Fuller** (1814-1884)
Perpetual curate of St James, Enfield 1841-54;
rector of Greenhithe 1856-84.

Commonplace book (1 vol) incl letters to him (7
items); transcripts of letters to him 1828-43.
Pusey House, Oxford.

Notes on parishioners at Enfield, verses, sermon
notes etc (1 vol).
Enfield Local History Library.

[627] **RYDER, Henry** (1777-1836)
Bishop of Gloucester 1815-24, of Coventry and
Lichfield 1824-36.

Letters and papers, with those of his family, to
1896 (4 vols).
Harrowby MSS Trust (Harrowby MSS, 3rd series,
vols 102–5). Enquiries to the Earl of Harrowby,
Sandon Hall, Stafford ST18 0BZ. NRA 1561.

[628] **RYDER, Henry Ignatius Dudley** (1837-
1907)
Oratorian.

Corresp, mainly letters to him (7 files); theological
essays and notes.
The Oratory, Birmingham. NRA 27809.

[629] **RYLAND, John** (1753-1825)
President of Bristol Baptist College 1793-1825;
secretary of the Baptist Missionary Society 1815-
25.

Letters from William Carey 1793-1825 (52 items)
and William Rhodes 1816-24; diary extracts
1794-5; Hebrew and Greek notebooks 1789-92 (4
vols); sermon notebooks 1790-1 (3 vols); literary
MSS, texts, lecture notes etc.
Northamptonshire Record Office and *College Street
Baptist Church, Northampton.* NRA 8563.

[630] **RYLE, Herbert Edward** (1856-1925)
Bishop of Exeter 1901-3, of Winchester 1903-11;
dean of Westminster 1911-25.

Corresp and misc papers as dean 1911-25 incl
letters to him about the burial of the unknown
warrior and the Westminster Abbey Fund (*c*90
items).
Westminster Abbey (WAM 58657-58731, 61870-
83).

[631] **ST JOHN, Ambrose** (1815-1875)
Oratorian.

Corresp, journals, notebooks and sermons.
Birmingham Oratory.

[632] **SALMON, George** (1819-1904)
Provost of Trinity College Dublin 1888-1904.

Papers, incl sermons and lectures, with those of
his family, 1870-1936 (9 vols, 2 bundles).
Trinity College, Dublin (MSS 2385, 2385a, 4738-
46).

[633] **SANDAY, William** (1843-1920)
Lady Margaret professor of divinity and canon of
Christ Church, Oxford 1895-1919.

Corresp, mainly letters to him 1867-1920 (8 vols).
Bodleian Library, Oxford (MSS Eng misc d 122-
28, 140).

[634] **SAVAGE, Henry Edwin** (1854-1939)
Vicar of Halifax 1904-9; dean of Lichfield
1909-39.

General corresp from 1909 (132 files); corresp and
papers 1909-39, incl lectures and papers rel to
Lichfield cathedral (*c*550 items); corresp rel to the
chapter (*c*250 items); papers rel to Lichfield
diocesan affairs (*c*500 items) and schools (2
bundles) and to his research (*c*80 bundles);
antiquarian notes, sermons, lectures etc.
Lichfield Cathedral Library. NRA 20445.

[635] **SCOTT, Andrew** (1772-1846)
Vicar apostolic of the western district, Scotland
1832-45.

Corresp rel to western district affairs, incl corresp
with Andrew Carruthers, James Gillis, JF Kyle,
John Murdoch, with other bishops and with
agents in Rome, *c*1824-46 (110 bundles); account
book, Glasgow 1805-7 (1 vol).
Scottish Catholic Archives (OL 1-4).

Corresp and papers rel to the building of Paisley
Catholic chapel, western district affairs etc 1808-
34 (2 boxes).
Glasgow Archdiocesan Archive.

[636] **SCOTT, James** (1768-1827)
Minister of Netherend Unitarian Chapel, Cradley, Worcs.

Shorthand journals 1781-90 (10 vols), travel journal 1802-27 (1 vol) and lecture notes as a student at Daventry Academy (13 vols); lectures, addresses, prayers, misc papers etc (7 vols).
Dr Williams's Library, London (28.75-91, 93-105, 111). NRA 13168.

Diary 1789-1826 (1 vol).
Harwood & Evers, solicitors, Stourbridge. NRA 3488.

[637] **SCOTT, Robert** (1811-1887)
Master of Balliol College, Oxford 1854-70; dean of Rochester 1870-87.

Corresp and misc papers 1836-97 (3 bundles) incl letters from Henry Phillpotts 1840-66 (18 items) and EB Pusey 1837-80 (42 items) and corresp with WE Gladstone 1845-85 (39 items).
Pusey House, Oxford. NRA 29545.

Letters to him 1854-70 and misc papers (*c*150 items); copies of letters from him mainly rel to college affairs 1854-73 (3 bundles).
Balliol College, Oxford.

Corresp and papers rel to the Revised Version of the Bible 1870-81 (7 vols, 2 boxes).
National Library of Scotland (Dep 172). NRA 27988.

Letters to him as dean of Rochester 1874-87 (45 items).
Kent Archives Office (AZc 11). NRA 22242.

[638] **SCOTT, William** (1813-1872)
Perpetual curate of Christ Church, Hoxton 1839-60; vicar of St Olave Jewry, London 1860-72.

Letters to him and his family, with misc papers, 1840-73 (*c*203 items) incl corresp and papers rel to ritualistic controversies at Hoxton 1840-*c*1844 (1 bundle), letters from Henry Phillpotts and his daughter 1847-69 (1 bundle), memorandum of proceedings in convocation 3 Feb 1852 entrusted by Phillpotts to him (1 item), and letters and notes mainly to him from the 3rd Marquess of Salisbury rel to the *Saturday Review* and other journals 1856-73 (3 bundles).
Sion College, London. NRA 26478.

[639] **SEEBOHM, Benjamin** (1798-1871)
Quaker minister.

Letters to him 1814-20 (85 items); misc letters to him and his wife 1850-70 (17 items); corresp with his wife 1834-64 (27 bundles) and children 1848-62 (24 items); letters to Josiah Forster 1843-70 (317 items); travel journal, Germany 1819 (1 vol); accounts 1819 (1 vol).
Hertfordshire Record Office (D/ESe). Deposited by D Seebohm 1954. NRA 4447.

[640] **SELLON, Priscilla Lydia** (*c*1821-1876)
Founder of the Society of the Holy Trinity.

Misc corresp and papers incl letters from Sidney Herbert, Florence Nightingale and sisters of the order during the Crimean war.
Ascot Priory. Copies at Pusey House, Oxford.

[641] **SELWYN, George Augustus** (1809-1878)
Bishop of New Zealand 1841-68, of Lichfield 1868-78.

Letters to him etc 1839-77 (2 folders, *c*50 items); letters from him to his wife Sarah 1850-76 (1 folder); letters to him and his wife from JR Selwyn *c*1857-77 (1 folder); register as bishop of New Zealand 1841-52 (1 vol); accounts and papers 1868-72.
Revd H Selwyn Fry. See P Mander-Jones, *Manuscripts in the British Isles relating to Australia, New Zealand, and the Pacific*, 1972, pp380-1.

Corresp and papers (3 boxes), mainly letters from him, but incl sermons, journal 1843-4 and letter book of corresp between Selwyn and others and the Church Missionary Society 1840-60.
Selwyn College, Cambridge. NRA 24352.

Letters to him in Maori and English 1842-72 (185 items) and misc papers 1827-58 (*c*30 items).
University of Waihato Library, Hamilton, New Zealand. NRA 28511.

Letter book 1841-5; diary 1848-9.
Alexander Turnbull Library, Wellington, New Zealand. Purchased from Mr KA Webster 1962, 1966. *Union Catalogue of New Zealand and Pacific Manuscripts ...*, ii, 1969.

Journals 1843-8.
Rhodes House, Oxford (USPG).

[642] **SEWELL, William** (1804-1879)
Fellow of Exeter College, Oxford, 1827-74 and warden of St Peter's College, Radley 1852-62.

Corresp with Samuel Wilberforce, other bishops and churchmen rel to Radley and St Columba's College, Rathfarnham 1845-8, nd (63 items); letters to Baroness Burdett-Coutts rel to the foundation of Radley 1845-8 (20 items); 'reminiscences' 1866-74 (typescript copy of lost original in 3 vols); sermons *c*1854-9 (1 vol).
Radley College, Abingdon.

Letters to him and his family 1838-94 (3 vols) with other misc corresp.
Bodleian Library, Oxford (MSS Autogr d 32-4). Purchased 1963.

Corresp and papers rel to the foundation of St Columba's College in 1843 incl coresp with Lord Dunraven following the publication of Tract XC (5 vols).
St Columba's College, Rathfarnham.

Journal rel to the foundation of St Columba's
College 1844-5 (1 vol).
Pusey House, Oxford.

[643] **SHARP, Samuel** (*c*1773-1855)
Vicar of Wakefield 1810-55.

Corresp, accounts and papers rel to his family and
Wakefield parish (4 boxes).
West Yorkshire County Record Office (C 281).

[644] **SHARROCK, William [Gregory]** (1742-
1809)
Vicar apostolic of the western district 1797-1809.

Letters from Rome 1780-1809 (1 vol *passim*);
corresp and papers 1780-1809 (12 vols *passim*).
Bristol Record Office (Clifton diocesan records).

[645] **SHEPHERD, William** (1768-1847)
Unitarian minister, Gateacre, Liverpool 1791-
1847.

Personal and family corresp and papers 1632-1883
(26 vols etc) incl letters from Samuel Duckworth,
Lord Holland, Edward Maltby, William Roscoe,
Gilbert Wakefield and others (*c*500 items); travel
journals 1793, 1800 (2 vols); engagement diary
1832, diary of visits to Brougham Hall 1835, 1838
(1 vol); autobiographical fragment 1833;
memoranda rel to catholic emancipation and
verses (4 vols); notes, prayers etc incl printed
material 1760-1866 (*c*9 vols, 1 box).
Manchester College, Oxford.

Lake District travel journal *c*1798.
Barrow in Furness Public Library and Museum.
MW Barley *Guide to British topographical
collections*, 1974, p41.

[646] **SHEPPARD, Hugh Richard Lawrie** (1880-
1937)
Vicar of St Martin-in-the-Fields 1914-27; dean of
Canterbury 1929-31; canon of St Paul's 1934-7.

Corresp and papers 1892-1937 (*c*50 files, 1 vol)
incl letters from the royal family (1 file), RT
Davidson 1912-29 (23 items), CG Lang from
1905, William Temple *c*1907-37 (24 items) and
other churchmen, statesmen and public figures,
corresp rel to Oxford House, Bethnal Green 1905-
37 (1 file) and St Martin-in-the-Fields 1917-*c*1934
(*c*130 items), corresp and papers as canon of St
Paul's 1934-7 (*c*125 items), copies of letters from
him collected by his biographer and sermons
1932-4 (1 vol).
Lady Richardson of Duntisbourne.

[647] **SHIPLEY, William Davies** (1745-1826)
Dean of St Asaph 1774-1826.

Letters from his father Jonathan Shipley, Edward
Edwards, Thomas Erskine, AB Madan, John
Morgan and JC Williams.

*National Library of Wales. See Annual Report
1938-9, p44.*

[648] **SHORT, Thomas Vowler** (1790-1872)
Bishop of Sodor and Man 1841-6, of St Asaph
1846-70.

Letter book 1868-9.
National Library of Wales (SA/MB/50). NRA
26745.

Commonplace book 1829 mainly rel to church
history.
National Library of Wales (MS 487).

[649] **SHUTTLEWORTH, Philip Nicholas**
(1782-1842)
Warden of New College, Oxford 1822-40; bishop
of Chichester 1840-2.

Corresp 1825-42 with that of his wife Emma
1825-48 (233ff).
Bodleian Library, Oxford (MS Eng hist c 1033).
Purchased 1981. NRA 27379.

[650] **SIMEON, Charles** (1759-1836)
Vicar of Holy Trinity, Cambridge 1783-1836.

Corresp and papers, incl letters to him collected
by William Carus; sermons, lectures etc (1
bundle, *c*50 items); papers about the disturbances
at Holy Trinity church (1 bundle); misc
autobiographical papers.
Ridley Hall, Cambridge. FWB Bullock, *The history
of Ridley Hall ...,* ii, appendix 2, 1953.

Diary 1829-32; letters from him to his nephew,
Sir Richard Simeon and his wife 1833-6 (36ff);
misc letters and papers (8ff).
Lambeth Palace Library (MS 3170). Purchased
1981.

[651] **SIMPSON, Alexander Lockhart** (1785-
1861)
Minister of Kirknewton, Midlothian 1812-61.

Letters from Thomas Chalmers 1835-41 (23
items), Sir George Sinclair (12 items) and others
*c*1830-50 (*c*25 items).
New College, Edinburgh.

[652] **SIMPSON, Richard** (1820-1876)
RC writer.

Corresp 1858-79, mainly letters to him from Lord
Acton, Augustus Jessop, WG Ward, Charles
Weld and others, with some drafts and copies of
his letters (4 boxes); family corresp; notebooks
and papers on literary, spiritual and theological
subjects (54 vols, 3 boxes); notes on Shakespeare
(1 bundle).
Downside Abbey.

Autograph songs 1860-6, 1875 (5 vols).
British Library (Add MSS 52663-7).

[653] **SINGLETON, Hugh** (1851-1934)
RC bishop of Shrewsbury 1908-34.

Letter books as bishop 1901-39, with letters of
SW Allen and AJ Moriarty (10 vols).
Bishop of Shrewsbury.

[654] **SINGLETON, Robert Corbet** (1810-1881)
Warden of St Columba's College, Rathfarnham
1843-7, of St Peter's College, Radley 1847-51.

Corresp 1847-53 (1 bundle, 28 items) some rel to
his breach with William Sewell over the
administration of Radley 1849-53 (20 items);
journal rel to the foundation of Radley 1847-8,
with conclusion 1874 (3 vols).
Radley College, Abingdon.

[655] **SKINNER, John** (1744-1816)
Bishop of Aberdeen 1786-1816 and primus of the
Scottish episcopal church 1788-1816.

Corresp and misc papers 1775-1815 incl corresp
rel to the consecration of Samuel Seabury, the
repeal of penal statutes and union with English
congregations (*c*340 items).
Scottish Record Office (CH 12).

Letters to him *c*1790-1810 (1 bundle); treatise on
the use of the English liturgy in Scotland 1810.
Bishop of Aberdeen and Orkney. Enquiries to the
National Register of Archives (Scotland) (NRA(S)
1829). NRA 22244.

Copies of his corresp rel to the union of English
and Scottish episcopalians 1804-6 (21ff).
Lambeth Palace Library (MS 1542).

[656] **SKINNER, John** (1772-1839)
Rector of Camerton, Somerset 1800-39.

Journals rel to parish life, antiquarian studies and
travels in England, Wales and abroad 1788-1832
(98 vols).
British Library (Add MSS 33633-730). Bequeathed
by him.

Journals mainly rel to personal and parochial
matters 1832-6 (21 vols); papers rel to Camerton
and misc corresp and sermons etc from 1800 (4
vols).
British Library (Eg MSS 3099-3123).

Journals, notes and copies of his corresp, mainly
rel to antiquities at Camerton 1797-1829 (3 vols).
British Library (Add MSS 28793-5).

Travel journals rel to Wales, Hadrian's Wall and
the west of England etc 1797-1802.
Fitzwilliam Museum, Cambridge.

Welsh travel journal 1800-5.
Cardiff Central Library.

Misc corresp, memoranda etc *c*1830-5.
Bath Reference Library. NRA 25737.

'Analysis of language' *c*1830.
Wellcome Institute, London.

Notebook 1834 and 'analysis of antiquities' 1839
(4 vols).
British Library (Add MSS 52490-3).

[657] **SKINNER, William** (1778-1857)
Bishop of Aberdeen 1816-57 and primus of the
Scottish episcopal church 1841-57.

Letters to him rel to provincial and diocesan
affairs 1816-50 (16 items); letters from Charles
Wordsworth and others rel to the Allen affair
1849 (23 items); corresp rel to a continental
bishopric 1825 (1 vol).
Scottish Record Office (CH 12).

Copies of his corresp, mainly letters to him 1838-
53 (91ff).
Lambeth Palace Library (MS 1541).

Corresp and papers rel to Scotch Episcopal
Friendly Society affairs 1810-15 (1 bundle).
Bishop of Aberdeen and Orkney. Enquiries to NRA
(Scotland) (NRA (S) 2698).

Letters from Sir William Dunbar *c*1844-53.
Bishop of Aberdeen and Orkney. Enquiries to NRA
(Scotland) (NRA (S) 1829). NRA 22244.

[658] **SMITH, Sir George Adam** (1856-1942)
Old Testament scholar; principal of Aberdeen
University 1909-35.

Corresp and papers rel to his appointments,
travels, publications and heresy case 1902 (12
boxes); official corresp and papers *c*1892-1934 (1
box); engagement books 1905-8, 1912-31 (1 box);
lectures, sermons, addresses etc (5 boxes).
National Library of Scotland (Dep 311). NRA
27274.

[659] **SMITH, Gervase** (*d* 1882)
Wesleyan methodist minister.

Corresp incl letters from Charles Prest 1863-6 and
others 1841-72 (*c*85 items).
Methodist Archives, Manchester.

[660] **SMITH, James** (1841-1928)
Bishop of Dunkeld 1890-1900; archbishop of St
Andrews and Edinburgh 1900-28.

Letters from Scottish bishops 1867-1926 (37
bundles), from other bishops (4 bundles), from
Rome 1900-27 (5 bundles) and from WF Brown
rel to his apostolic visitation of Scotland 1917-20
(1 bundle); corresp with Blairs and Scots colleges
abroad 1866-1927 (37 bundles); personal and
official corresp 1859-1925 (59 bundles); corresp
and papers as procurator 1876-90 (27 bundles),
rel to religious orders and schools 1902-19 (17

F

bundles) and to diocesan administration 1878-
1933 (24 bundles); misc papers 1857-1913 (17
bundles); diaries 1855-89 (3 vols); sermons 1863-
1903 (6 bundles).
Scottish Catholic Archives (ED 6).

[661] **SMITH, John** (*c*1766-1826)
Usher at Westminster School 1788-1805; vicar of
Newcastle upon Tyne 1805-26.

Corresp and papers incl corresp with the Spencer
Stanhope family 1782-1824 and letters from the
bishop of Durham 1807-23, account books etc
1789-1807 (7 bundles); diaries 1785-1824 (37
vols); sermons 1794-7 (*c*200 items).
Sheffield Central Library (Spencer Stanhope 60555-
9, 60636-9). NRA 0725.

Account book 1805-10 (1 vol); notes on
Sophocles' *Electra c*1785 (77ff).
Brotherton Library, University of Leeds (MSS 510,
533). Presented by JM Spencer-Stanhope 1942.
NRA 25809.

[662] **SMITH, John Pye** (1774-1851)
Congregational minister; theological tutor at
Homerton College 1806-50.

Collected corresp and papers 1809-50 (54 items);
diaries 1798-1804, 1830-42; notebook 1828;
sermon and lecture notes (30 vols, etc).
Dr Williams's Library, London (New College L18-
21). NRA 13042.

Letters from James Montgomery 1795-6 (30
items).
Sheffield Central Library. NRA 8514.

European travel journal 1816 (2 vols).
Bodleian Library, Oxford (MSS Eng misc e 1375-
6). Purchased 1984.

Autobiography 1832-43.
Wellcome Institute, London (MS 4638).

[663] **SMITH, Samuel** (1766-1841)
Dean of Christ Church, Oxford 1824-31; sub-
dean of Durham 1831-41.

Misc letters to him 1816-38 (12 items); corresp,
mainly with William van Mildert, rel to the
university of Durham 1832-4 (21 items).
Durham University Library. Purchased 1980. NRA
25113.

[664] **SMITH, Sydney** (1771-1845)
Rector of Foston, Yorks 1807-29; canon of St
Paul's 1831-45.

Collected corresp and misc papers, mainly letters
from him, 1798-1844 (*c*650 items); 'Advice to my
parishioners' (1 vol).
New College, Oxford (4429-39, 8730).

[665] **SMITH, Thomas** (1763-1831)
Vicar apostolic of the northern district 1821-31.

Corresp 1808-31 (521 items), mainly letters from
vicars apostolic, Robert Gradwell (30 items), John
Lingard (10 items), Pius VIII and others.
Bishop of Leeds.

[666] **SMITH, William** (1819-1892)
Archbishop of St Andrews and Edinburgh 1885-
92.

Letters from Scottish bishops 1853-92 (27
bundles), from other bishops 1877-92 (3 bundles)
and from vicars general and diocesan
administrators 1883-90 (8 bundles); corresp with
religious orders and schools 1880-*c*1892 (3
bundles) and rel to parish administration 1835-92
(21 bundles); general corresp 1856-92 (24
bundles); corresp and papers rel to Dunkeld
diocese *c*1883-8 (32 bundles), to Blairs and Scots
colleges in Rome and Valladolid 1883-92 (19
bundles), and to Mary Queen of Scots and her
beatification 1866-91, nd (12 bundles); diary and
papers rel to the provincial council at Fort
Augustus 1886 (13 bundles); personal diary 1866
and papers 1819-95 (10 bundles); misc and
printed papers (5 bundles).
Scottish Catholic Archives (ED 4).

[667] **SMITH, William Robertson** (1846-1894)
Theologian and semitic scholar.

Corresp with JS Black (719 items), his family and
others incl letters rel to his trials for heresy
(*c*1,280 items); papers (1 box) incl notebooks,
lectures, sermons, memoranda etc and trial papers
1877-80.
Cambridge University Library (Add 7449, 7476).

[668] **SOMERVILLE, Thomas** (1741-1830)
Minister of Jedburgh 1772-1830.

Corresp mainly with his son and daughter-in-law
1768-1830 (*c*76 items); misc papers (1 bundle).
Bodleian Library, Oxford (MS dep c 360). NRA
9423.

[669] **SOUTER, Alexander** (1873-1949)
New Testament and patristic scholar.

Letters, mainly from churchmen and scholars,
1892-1947 (20 vols).
Bodleian Library, Oxford (MSS Eng lett c 597-
616).

Working papers and notebooks incl lecture notes
taken as a student and texts for lectures and
articles (2 boxes).
King's College London.

[670] **SOUTHCOTT, Joanna** (1750-1814)
Religious fanatic.

Corresp and papers of and rel to her, mostly
taken down by Jane Townley and Anne
Underwood, 1792-1844 (25 vols) incl
communications and accounts of her visions,
letters from and copies by TP Foley.
British Library (Add MSS 26038-9, 27919, 32633-
7, 47794-47803, 57860, Eg MS 2399). Formerly
in the possession of Southcott's biographer, Alice
Seymour, at Rock Cottage, Blockley, mainly
presented by Mrs AM Stitt 1952.

Papers incl communications 1794-1871 (*c*440
items).
Blockley Antiquarian Society. NRA 21033. From
Rock Cottage 1971.

Corresp and papers of and rel to her (*c*125 items)
incl letters 1802-1966 (21 items), communications
1796-1844, nd (42 items), notebooks containing
collected MSS *c*1795-1891 (29 items), scrolls,
seals, notes, poems etc.
University of Texas Library. From the collection of
George Bennett, acquired in 1962. EP Wright, *A
catalogue of the Joanna Southcott collection at the
University of Texas,* 1968.

Communications and copy letters from Jane
Townley 1796-1842 (4 vols, 2 items).
Gloucestershire Record Office. NRA 20570. From
Rock Cottage, presented by Blockley Antiquarian
Society 1977.

[671] **SPENCER, George [Ignatius]** (1799-1864]
Passionist.

Letters to him 1808-64 (92 items); collected
letters from him 1839-64 (*c*200 items); journal
1817-64 (3 vols); commonplace book and
sermons.
*Archives of the English Province of Passionist
Fathers, London.*

Personal papers (5 boxes), incl family corresp
1808-34, mainly letters to his father (200 items),
student notebooks 1816-20 (12 vols), account of
Italy and Vienna 1820 (2 vols), sketchbooks from
1814 (*c*5 vols) and misc papers as rector of
Brington, Northants 1829.
British Library (Spencer papers).

[672] **SPOONER, William Archibald** (1844-1930)
Warden of New College, Oxford 1903-24.

Letters to him 1909-28 (5 items); corresp and
papers rel to the warden's lodgings 1903-4, nd (1
vol, 18 items); diaries 1881-1925 (2 vols, 1
bundle); autobiographical papers and
reminiscences (1 bundle); working papers rel to
Mark Pattison and Benjamin Jowett (1 bundle).
New College, Oxford.

[673] **SPURGEON, Charles Haddon** (1834-1892)
Baptist minister of the Metropolitan Tabernacle,
London 1861-92.

Letters from Baptist churches outside England (1
vol); proofs of books, articles and sermons incl
misc letters from him (5 boxes); transcripts and
photocopies of his letters (4 bundles); scrapbooks
(61 vols).
Spurgeon's College, London.

[674] **SRAWLEY, James Herbert** (1868-1954)
Canon and chancellor of Lincoln 1923-47.

Corresp and papers rel to the liturgy 1908-48 incl
letters from Edmund Bishop 1908-15 and RJ
Connolly 1917-48 (6 bundles); papers rel to the
archbishop's committee on the separate churches
of the East 1908-17 (7 items); misc papers rel to
Edmund Bishop 1914-53 (1 bundle); notebooks
rel to Robert Grosseteste and Lincoln cathedral (3
vols) and misc historical papers 1925-53 (1
bundle, 10 items); sermons, addresses,
memoranda and draft articles 1893-1939 (24
items).
Lincolnshire Archives Office (Misc Dep 53). NRA
27631.

[675] **STACEY, George** (1786-1857)
Quaker minister; clerk of the London Yearly
Meeting of the Society of Friends.

Family and other corresp and papers *c*1815-40
(150 items).
Society of Friends Library, London (Temp MSS
130). Deposited by PH Stacey 1970, 1973.

[676] **STALEY, Vernon** (1852-1933)
Provost of St Andrew's cathedral, Inverness 1901-
11; rector of Ickford 1911-33.

Corresp with bishops and others rel to ritualism,
his publications etc 1880-1930 (*c*70 items) and
misc papers.
Pusey House, Oxford.

[677] **STANLEY, Arthur Penrhyn** (1815-1881)
Dean of Westminster 1864-81.

Family corresp, incl letters from his sister Mary
1849-*c*1862 and to him on his mother's death
1862 (2 bundles); diary *c*1839-41 (1 vol)
transcribed by his sister Mary; misc papers 1823-
8 incl some rel to his ordination (1 vol, 11 items);
sermons on special occasions 1835-82 (1 vol).
Cheshire Record Office (DSA 80-91 *passim*).
Deposited by Lady Kathleen Stanley 1953. NRA
17206.

'Recollections' (1 vol); letters to his sister Louisa
1844-74 (1 vol); corresp of his wife (8 vols) incl
letters to Queen Victoria 1863-74 (1 vol).
Westminster Abbey.

F*

Misc letters, mainly to him and his wife 1847-87
(1 vol).
Bodleian Library, Oxford (MS Eng lett d 91).

Letters to him, mainly invitations and
acknowledgements 1862-79 (39ff).
Lambeth Palace Library (MS 1680).

Family corresp 1831-41, mainly letters to his
sister Mary; corresp with Julius and Augustus
Hare 1832-49 and sermons.
Pusey House, Oxford.

Sermons and addresses (2 boxes).
Balliol College, Oxford (MSS 411-12). RAB
Mynors, *Catalogue of the manuscripts of Balliol
College, Oxford*, 1963.

Pyrenean travel journal 1828 (2 vols).
John Rylands University Library of Manchester
(Eng MS 1090).

Notes of Thomas Arnold's lectures 1831-4; notes
for his *Life* of Arnold; classical notebook 1833.
Rugby School. NRA 5282.

[678] **STANLEY, Edward** (1779-1849)
Rector of Alderley, Cheshire 1805-37; bishop of
Norwich 1837-49.

Diaries 1805-27 (10 vols).
Cheshire Record Office (P143).

Copies of his letters to his wife Catherine 1835 (1
vol), letters from her 1809, 1814 (3 items) and
sketch books 1817, 1828, nd (3 vols).
Cheshire Record Office (DSA). Mainly deposited
by Lady Kathleen Stanley 1953. NRA 17206.

[679] **STANTON, Richard** (1820-1901)
Oratorian.

Letters from FW Faber 1848-62 (20 items);
corresp with HE Manning 1872 (4 items); novice
papers with those of FW Faber (1 bundle);
memoirs 1820-1900 (2 vols).
The Oratory, London. NRA 16631.

Letters from JH Newman 1845.
The Oratory, Birmingham.

[680] **STEVENS, Thomas** (1809-1888)
Rector of Bradfield 1843-82 and warden of St
Andrew's College, Bradfield 1847-81.

Letter books rel to Bradfield College and parish,
farming, estate and personal affairs 1849-81 (18
vols); school exercises 1818 (1 bundle) and
Oxford bills etc 1836-9 (1 bundle).
Berkshire Record Office (D/ESv (M)). Deposited
by Mrs B Stevens 1963. NRA 10469.

[681] **STEVENSON, Joseph** (1806-1895)
Jesuit; historian and archivist.

Corresp 1839-94 (1 box, 8 bundles) incl letters
from bishops 1848-94 and other clergy, EI

Purbrick 1869-88, Lords Bute, Clifford and
Dormer, the Duke of Norfolk and others 1846-93
and the Record Commission 1847-92; diary;
historical transcripts and research notes (c30
notebooks, 3 folders); personal papers (1 folder).
Society of Jesus, London.

[682] **STOCK, Joseph** (1740-1813)
Bishop of Killala 1798-1810, of Waterford and
Lismore 1810-13.

Diaries of the rebellion at Killala 1798 and of his
visitation of Waterford 1811 (2 vols).
Trinity College, Dublin (MSS 948, 1690).

[683] **STONE, Darwell** (1859-1941)
Principal of Dorchester Missionary College 1888-
1903, of Pusey House, Oxford 1909-34.

Corresp as spiritual adviser to religious
communities etc 1903-33 (11 boxes); papers rel to
Dorchester Missionary College and overseas
missions to 1933 (10 boxes); corresp and papers
rel to Pusey House 1904-39 (6 boxes); papers rel
to offices held by him 1912-35 (20 boxes), to
ecclesiastical controversies 1904-36 (14 boxes) and
to funds for ordination candidates (16 boxes);
sermons, lectures, speeches and publications (13
boxes); diaries and papers collected by FL Cross
for his *Life* (14 boxes); misc papers 1890-1934 (14
boxes).
Pusey House, Oxford (DSt). NRA 25887.

[684] **STONOR, Edmund** (1831-1912)
Titular archbishop of Trebizond 1889;
chamberlain to Pius IX.

Corresp and papers rel to papal diplomatic
missions and administration of the English
College 1863, 1867; private corresp 1854-1906 (74
items); misc personal papers incl two treatises (9
items).
English College, Rome (Scritture 123).

[685] **STOPFORD, Edward Adderley** (1810-
1874)
Archdeacon of Meath 1844-72.

Letters from churchmen and statesmen 1836-73
(26 items); letters from him to his wife 1836-71
(75 items).
Representative Church Body Library, Dublin (MS
81). Presented by RJ Stopford 1961. NRA 11578.

[686] **STORY, George** (1738-1818)
Wesleyan methodist minister.

Papers incl letters to him, sermon and lecture
notes c1764-92 (18 vols, 8 items).
*William R Perkins Library, Duke University,
Durham, N Carolina.*

[687] **STRAIN, John Menzies** (1810-1883)
Vicar apostolic of the eastern district, Scotland
1864-78; archbishop of St Andrews and
Edinburgh 1878-83.

Letters from Rome 1863-83 (14 bundles), from
Scottish bishops 1835-83 (53 bundles), from
vicars general 1856-76 (13 bundles), from English
and other bishops 1859-83 (13 bundles), from
Scots colleges abroad 1856-83 (17 bundles) and
from mission procurators 1860-82 (4 bundles);
corresp with priests and parishes 1810-83 (56
bundles), with lawyers 1862-83 (12 bundles) and
rel to the administration of Dunkeld diocese
1866-83 (13 bundles); administrative and financial
corresp and papers 1836-83 (10 bundles); poor
school committee papers (1 bundle); journal 1857-
9 (1 vol); misc personal papers etc (3 bundles).
Scottish Catholic Archives (ED 3).

[688] **STRONG, Thomas Banks** (1861-1944)
Dean of Christ Church, Oxford 1901-20; bishop
of Ripon 1920-5, of Oxford 1925-37.

Corresp and papers rel to the revision, copyright
and printing of the Prayer Book 1901-29 (6 files)
and as a delegate of the Oxford University Press
1911-29 (1 file), and misc corresp and papers
1919-29 (1 file).
Oxford University Press Archives. NRA 27789.

[689] **STUART, Janet Erskine** (1857-1914)
English provincial 1894-1911 and superior-general
1911-14 of the Society of the Sacred Heart.

Collected letters, mainly from her (11 boxes);
misc educational and other papers (2 boxes, c8
bundles); morality plays (2 boxes).
Society of the Sacred Heart, Roehampton.

Papers rel to her election as superior general etc
(1 box); copies of letters from churchmen (1
bundle) and other papers rel to her as superior
general.
*Central Archives, Society of the Sacred Heart,
Rome.* Photocopies at Roehampton.

[690] **STUART, William** (1755-1822)
Bishop of St Davids 1793-1800; archbishop of
Armagh 1800-22.

Corresp and misc family papers 1792-1822 (c335
items, 10 bundles) incl letters from the Duke of
Bedford 1806-7 (15 items), Charles Brodrick
1802-16 (25 items) and TL O'Beirne 1803-14 (11
items).
Bedfordshire Record Office (WY 990-6). NRA
19616.

[691] **STUBBS, William** (1825-1901)
Bishop of Chester 1884-8, of Oxford 1888-1901.

Letters to him 1865-72, 1895 (c8 items), with
misc papers, some rel to Lambeth Palace Library
1862-9 (c20ff).

Lambeth Palace Library (MS 1680). Presented by
LM Stubbs 1942.

Letters from EB Pusey 1865-81 (11 items).
Ascot Priory. Copies at Pusey House, Oxford.

[692] **SYMONDS, Thomas** (1773-1845)
Vicar of Eynsham 1826-45 and of Stanton
Harcourt 1827-45.

Letters to him some rel to parochial affairs 1798-
1845 (3 vols); misc personal and official papers
1796-1845 (1 vol); accounts and business papers
1787-1845 (2 vols); notebooks rel to parish affairs
etc 1803-45 (2 vols); biblical and historical papers
(6 vols).
Bodleian Library, Oxford (MSS Don b 34-5 and
passim, MS Top Oxon b 275). NRA 27381.

[693] **SYMONS, Benjamin Parsons** (1785-1878)
Warden of Wadham College, Oxford 1831-71;
vice-chancellor of Oxford University 1844-8.

Letters from the Duke of Wellington 1844-8 (30
items), with draft replies 1845-6 (2 items); letters
from EB Pusey and others 1828-70 (9 items).
Bodleian Library, Oxford (MS Eng lett d 193).
NRA 10089.

[694] **TABRAHAM, Richard** (1792-1878)
Wesleyan methodist minister.

Corresp, mainly letters to him, c1820-75 (c500
items).
Methodist Archives, Manchester.

[695] **TAFT, Zechariah** (1772-1848)
Methodist preacher.

Corresp of Taft and his wife 1802-49 (76 items)
incl letters from Jabez Bunting 1812-28 (5 items)
and rel to women preachers.
Methodist Archives, Manchester.

[696] **TAIT, Archibald Campbell** (1811-1882)
Bishop of London 1856-68; archbishop of
Canterbury 1868-82.

Corresp and papers mainly as bishop of London
and archbishop of Canterbury 1802-91 (441 vols)
incl diaries 1834-82 (74 vols) and sermons 1836-82
(83 vols).
Lambeth Palace Library. Partial list: NRA 8476.

[697] **TALBOT, Edward Keble** (1877-1949)
Superior of the Community of the Resurrection,
Mirfield 1922-40.

Corresp and papers 1882-1949 (10 boxes) incl
letters from or rel to him, mainly to his family,
retreat notes, addresses, conference papers,
sermons etc.

Borthwick Institute, York (Mirfield Deposits 7 and 13). NRA 18541.

[698] TALBOT, George (1816-1886)
Chamberlain to Pius IX.

Letters from HE Manning, JH Newman, NPS Wiseman and others 1846-63; diary, Rome 1845-52 (4 vols).
English College, Rome (Scritture 76, Libri 817-20).

Letters from France 1861 (1 bundle).
Vatican Archives, Rome (Spogli Talbot).

[699] TALBOT, James Robert (1726-1790)
Vicar apostolic of the London district 1781-90.

Corresp and papers c1764-91 (c325 items), incl letters from William Gibson 1782-91 (77 items), Christopher Stonor 1781-9 (34 items) and priests in English colleges at Douai, St Omer and Rome, corresp rel to missions in the London district 1783-8 (17 items), the Catholic committee 1787-9 32 items) and foreign seminaries 1764-89 (c50 items).
Westminster Diocesan Archives (A42, 48-9). NRA 28616.

Student notes on logic c1763 and annotated dictates (2 vols).
Westminster Diocesan Archives (St Edmund's College Ware, series 9). NRA 16303.

[700] TALBOT, Neville Stuart (1879-1943)
Bishop of Pretoria 1920-33; assistant bishop of Southwell 1934-43.

Letters from his brother EK Talbot 1908-42 (157 items).
Borthwick Institute, York (Mirfield Deposit 13). NRA 18541.

Sermon notes and misc papers (4 boxes).
Nottinghamshire Record Office.

[701] TATLOW, Tissington (1876-1957)
Canon of Canterbury 1926-57.

Papers as secretary of the joint conference on Faith and Order 1912-39 (2 vols).
Lambeth Palace Library (MSS 1793-4).

[702] TAYLER, John James (1797-1869)
Unitarian; principal of Manchester New College, London 1853-69.

Letters etc from his congregation at Manchester 1832, 1835 (4 items); notes on his reading (1 vol); lectures (6 vols); sermons, addresses etc 1820-67 (20 vols etc).
Manchester College, Oxford. NRA 19870.

[703] TAYLOR, William (1816-1886)
Free Church of Scotland minister, Pulteneytown, Wick 1844-50.

Corresp 1855-60 (1 bundle); commonplace book (1 vol); notebooks rel to Egyptian vocabulary, Hebrew etc (6 vols).
New College, Edinburgh.

[704] TEMPLE, Frederick (1821-1902)
Archbishop of Canterbury 1896-1902.

Personal and family corresp 1834-1909 (17 bundles, c250 items) mainly letters to him and his wife from their son William; official corresp 1857-96 (1 bundle, c100 items) incl letters to him rel to the controversies over *Essays and Reviews*, 1861 and his appointment as bishop of Exeter, 1869 (1 bundle, c35 items); diary of self-examination 1843-9 (1 vol).
Rt Revd FS Temple. NRA 28747.

Papers as bishop of London 1885-97 (37 boxes) incl papers rel to clergy 1885-92 (3 boxes), to rural deaneries and the appointment of rural deans (23 boxes) and rel to the Clergy Discipline Act etc 1888-92 (1 box).
Lambeth Palace Library (Fulham papers).

Corresp and papers as archbishop 1897-1902 (60 vols).
Lambeth Palace Library. See *Index to the letters and papers of Frederick Temple*, 1975.

Letters to him as archbishop (27 items).
Pusey House, Oxford (Conybeare papers).

Letterbook as principal of Kneller Hall 1850-1 (1 vol).
Lambeth Palace Library (MS 1798).

Sermons 1866-9 (2 vols).
Rugby School. NRA 5282.

[705] TEMPLE, William (1881-1944)
Archbishop of York 1929-42, of Canterbury 1942-4.

Corresp and papers mainly as archbishop of Canterbury c1898-1951 (109 vols) incl engagement diaries 1907-44 (26 vols) and sermons and speeches c1898-1944 (c3 vols).
Lambeth Palace Library.

Corresp and misc papers of him and his wife 1888-1945 (3 bundles, c350 items) incl letters from his father mainly rel to theological, philosophical and other intellectual questions 1888-1902 (c320 items) and misc corresp and papers as bishop of Manchester 1921-9 (1 bundle).
Rt Revd FS Temple. NRA 28747.

Corresp rel to ecclesiastical controversies etc 1918-44 (1 bundle), misc receipts, letters from him etc 1928-39 (11 items).
Borthwick Institute, York (Bishopthorpe papers). NRA 7540.

Notes for Lent and Garter Day addresses 1942 (1 bundle).
Canterbury Cathedral Library.

[706] **THIRLWALL, Newell Connop** (1797-1875)
Bishop of St Davids 1840-74.

Corresp incl letters from him to Miss Elizabeth Johnes 1864-75 (*c*400 items), with letters from her.
National Library of Wales. Transferred from the muniment rooms at The Palace, Abergwili. See *Annual Report* 1971-2, p84.

Letters to him from Welsh clergy and others 1840-72 (59 items).
National Library of Wales. Purchased. See *Annual Report* 1963-4, p41 and 1967-8, p40.

Letters to him (1 vol).
Rare Book and Manuscript Library, Columbia University, New York. Copies, location of originals untraced.

[707] **THOM, John Hamilton** (1808-1894)
Minister of Renshaw Street Unitarian Chapel, Liverpool 1831-54, 1857-66.

Corresp of him and his wife with the Rathbone family and others 1829-93 (145 items); journal 1830-4 (1 vol).
Liverpool University Library (Rathbone papers). NRA 7187.

Misc corresp and papers 1831-94 (41 items); sermons, mainly MS and printed copies, 1842-77 (8 vols).
Liverpool Record Office (288 ULL). NRA 3491.

[708] **THOMAS, Owen** (1812-1891)
Calvinistic methodist minister, Liverpool 1865-91.

Letters to him, mainly from clergy 1842-91 (1 vol) and from Lewis Edwards 1849-83 (2 vols); letters to him and his wife from her father, William Roberts 1846-63 (71 items); personal and family corresp 1802-91 (165 items); misc papers incl biographical material rel to John Jones and Henry Rees.
National Library of Wales. Presented by J Saunders Lewis 1964.

Letters from Lewis Edwards, mainly rel to articles for *Y Traethodydd*, 1844-8 (1 vol); letters from Edward Morgan 1865-70 (14 items); corresp 1855-79 (1 vol).
National Library of Wales (Presbyterian Church of Wales MSS, Bala College Group). NRA 28416.

Pocket book, sermons, notes, MS of *Cofiant Henry Rees*, collected MSS *c*1767-1890 (*c*19 vols).
National Library of Wales (MSS 624-40, 1206, 4836).

[709] **THOMAS, William** (1834-1879)
Unitarian minister at Bwlchyfadfa and Llwynrhydowen 1860-79.

Diaries 1850, 1852-3,1855; account of his life at Carmarthen College and Glasgow University 1853-60; notes about the school at Llandyssul 1865-75, misc notes 1871-8; cuttings books incl material rel to the ejection of the congregation from the old chapel in 1876 (2 vols).
Old Chapel, Llwynrhydowen.

[710] **THOMPSON, James Matthew** (1878-1956)
Fellow of Magdalen College, Oxford 1904-38.

Letters to him, mainly rel to the controversy over his *Miracles in the New Testament* 1907-50 (2 vols); diary 1902; theological papers, lecture notes etc *c*1916-20 incl outline of his proposed Bampton lectures 1920 (1 vol).
Bodleian Library, Oxford (MSS Eng lett d 181-2, Eng th d 51). Presented by his son JDA Thompson 1960-1.

[711] **THOMSON, William Aird** (1773-1863)
Minister, Middle Parish, Perth 1808-43, Free Church, Perth 1843-63.

Letters from Thomas Chalmers, Alexander Dunlop, Robert Paul and others, mainly rel to church politics 1832-6 (44 items); letters to him and his daughter Margaret from JR Omond 1831-45 (18 items).
Orkney Archives (Omond papers). Presented by Brigadier JS Omond 1954. NRA 19068.

[712] **THORNTON, Lionel Spencer** (1884-1960)
Member of the Community of the Resurrection, Mirfield 1915-60.

Notebooks and papers on theology and church history 1929-57 (9 vols, 1 bundle, *c*20 items), notes for lecture courses, retreats and on 'The seal of the Spirit' (9 vols); sermons 1921-45 (12 items); MSS of his theological works (4 items) and misc papers, mainly printed.
Borthwick Institute, York (Mirfield Deposit 8). NRA 18541.

[713] **THOROLD, Anthony Wilson** (1825-1895)
Bishop of Rochester 1874-90, of Winchester 1890-5.

Notebook as assessor of proceedings in the trial of Edward King 1889-90 (101ff).
Lambeth Palace Library (MS 1918).

[714] **THORP, Charles** (1783-1862)
Archdeacon of Durham 1831-62 and warden of Durham University 1833-62.

Letters and papers rel to the foundation of Durham University (5 vols).
Durham University Library.

[715] **THRING, Edward** (1821-1887)
Headmaster of Uppingham School 1853-87.

Letters from him (3 files); MSS of his writings on
education etc (15 files); family papers (2 files);
diaries 1853-61, 1885-7 (2 vols); sermons (1 box);
misc papers (1 file).
Uppingham School.

[716] **THURSTON, Herbert** (1856-1939)
Jesuit; author.

Corresp rel to the Jesuits, freemasonry,
spiritualism etc (7 files and boxes); general and
collected corresp 1890-1939 (14 boxes); papers rel
to miracles, St Ignatius's *Spiritual Exercises* etc
(16 files).
Society of Jesus, London.

[717] **TIERNEY, Mark Aloysius** (1785-1862)
Chaplain to the Dukes of Norfolk and RC
mission priest at Arundel 1824-62; canon
penitentiary of Southwark Cathederal 1852-62.

Corresp, research papers and collected MSS (87
vols etc) incl letters to him 1835-57 and draft
replies (1 box), corresp on the restoration of the
Jesuit order and old chapter disputes 1822-7 (2
bundles), working notebooks (25 vols), collected
and copied MSS made for him or John Kirk (30
vols), annotated copies of Charles Dodd, *Church
history of England* with proofs of Tierney's
edition, MSS of *Correspondence between the Messrs
Bodenham and the Rev MA Tierney* and *Letter to
the King* (9 bundles), draft 'Reply to Cardinal
Wiseman' and papers as a student and teacher at
St Edmund's College, Ware 1812-19 (1 bundle).
Southwark Diocesan Archives. NRA 27760.
Bequeathed in 1862 to Thomas Grant, bishop of
Southwark and partially described in HMC, *Third
R, App*, 1872, pp233-7.

Letters to him and copies of letters from him
1831-59 (28 items); corresp with the Howard
family (*c*20 items); working papers, drawings for
and MSS of *History and antiquities of the castle and
town of Arundel* and *Sussex archaeological
collections* 1834-60 (9 vols, 3 files).
Duke of Norfolk. FW Steer, *Arundel Castle
archives,* i-iv, 1968-80 *passim; Bibliotheca
Norfolkiana,* 1961 *passim.*

Letterbook 1847-52; corresp with EE Estcourt,
FC Husenbeth, John Lingard and Robert
Lythgoe; letters from Thomas Grant; copies of
Stonyhurst MS Anglia A/1-4.
Society of Jesus, London.

Catalogue of his books and papers (1 vol).
The Oratory, London. NRA 16631. HMC, *Third
R, App* 1872, p237.

[718] **TODD, James Henthorn** (1805-1869)
Regius professor of Hebrew, Trinity College,
Dublin, 1849-69.

Corresp 1827-63 (*c*220 items) incl letters from
Lord JG Beresford 1836-59 (12 items), CR
Elrington 1836-8 (26 items), Samuel Kyle 1836-8
(12 items) and Edward Stopford 1834-9 (14
items).
Trinity College, Dublin (MS 2214). Deposited by
Dr EJ Gwynn 1938. NRA 20234.

Letter book rel to the repeal of the celibacy
statute for fellows 1840; volume of extracts from
his diary 1843-4; account book as bursar 1852-5;
college board notebook 1857-61; misc notes and
working papers.
Trinity College, Dublin. NRA 20234.

Letters from John O'Donovan and others rel to
antiquarian matters 1836-58 (*c*2 vols).
National Library of Ireland (MSS 5443, 5941).
*Manuscript sources for the history of Irish
civilisation,* 1965.

Letters from EB Pusey 1841-3 (11 items);
commentary on Ezekiel.
Pusey House, Oxford.

[719] **TOLLER, Thomas Northcote** (1756-1821)
Minister of the Independent Church, Kettering
1775-1821.

Letters to him *c*1777-1818 (17 items); account of
his answers to invitations from London
congregations to leave Kettering and his replies to
requests that he should remain 1799-1800;
shorthand lecture and sermon notes, misc papers
*c*1775-1828.
Northamptonshire Record Office (1978/301).

[720] **TOMLINE, Sir George Pretyman** (1750-
1827), 5th Bt 1823
Bishop of Lincoln 1787-1820, of Winchester
1820-7.

Personal, family and official corresp and papers
incl letters from William Pitt mainly rel to affairs
of church and state 1774-1805 (80 items), letters
from George Rose mainly to him 1782-1809 (220
items) and corresp with his wife 1789-1816 (*c*120
items), with other family papers and papers of
William Pitt.
Suffolk Record Office, Ipswich. Deposited by
Captain GMT Pretyman 1953. NRA 0174.

Corresp amongst papers of William Pitt (*c*12 files)
incl letters from Shute Barrington and Beilby
Porteus 1801, 1807 (1 file), Hannah More 1800-3
(1 file), William Paley 1795-1802 (1 file), William
Pitt 1780-99 (1 file) and William Wilberforce
1787-1806 (1 file).
Kent Archives Office (U1590/S5). NRA 25095.

See also HMC, *Papers of British Cabinet Ministers
1782-1900,* 1982 *sub* William Pitt.

[721] **TONER, John** (1857-1949)
Bishop of Dunkeld 1914-49; apostolic
administrator of the Glasgow archdiocese 1920-2.

General corresp as apostolic administrator 1920-2
(3 boxes) and papers rel to education in Dunkeld
diocese 1912-19 (2 boxes).
Glasgow Archdiocesan Archive.

[722] **TORRY, Patrick** (1763-1852)
Bishop of Dunkeld and Dunblane 1808-52 and of
St Andrews 1842-52.

Corresp 1794-1851 (*c*100 items) incl letters from
John Skinner 1795-1814, Alexander Jolly 1809-32,
Michael Russell 1842 and GH Forbes 1849-51 and
copies of letters from him 1836-49.
Scottish Record Office (CH 12).

Corresp, mainly rel to diocesan affairs, 1799-1851
(*c*30 items).
Bishop of St Andrews, Dunkeld and Dunblane.
Enquiries to NRA (Scotland) (NRA (S) 2706).

[723] **TOWNSEND, Thomas Stewart** (1801-
1852)
Bishop of Meath 1850-2.

Letters from Lord JG Beresford, Samuel Hinds
and others about Irish church affairs 1836-52
(43ff).
Lambeth Palace Library (MS 1727).

[724] **TRAIL, Samuel** (1806-1887)
Professor of systematic theology, Aberdeen
1867-87.

Letters from Lord Arbuthnott, Duncan Mearns,
Hercules Scott and others 1828-45 (2 vols);
account book 1836 (1 vol); notebooks 1867-87 (2
vols); printed extracts from the *Confession of
Faith* with MS annotations *c*1871 (1 vol);
scrapbook rel to his moderatorship 1874-5 (1 vol).
Aberdeen University Library. NRA 22895.

[725] **TREGELLES, Samuel Prideaux** (1813-
1875)
Biblical scholar.

Collections of MSS, copy and proofs rel to his
edition of the Greek NT (8 boxes).
St Andrews University Library (MSS 36252-9).

Letters to him 1861 (2 items) and to his wife 1876
(2 items); letters to Sir JFT Crampton from
scholars supporting Tregelles's request to collate
the Codex Sinaiticus 1860 (20 items).
British Library (Add MS 61835).

[726] **TRENCH, Richard Chenevix** (1807-1886)
Archbishop of Dublin 1863-86.

Letters from his cousin and agent Thomas Cooke
Trench 1866-70 (16 items).

Representative Church Body Library, Dublin (MS
327). Presented by CEF Trench 1985. NRA
28015.

Misc corresp 1842-86 (13 items).
Rt Revd FS Temple. NRA 28747.

[727] **TROY, John Thomas** (1739-1823)
RC bishop of Ossory 1776-84; archbishop of
Dublin 1784-1823.

Corresp and papers 1759-1823 (20 boxes) incl
general corresp, letter books 1761-99 (6 vols),
diary 1777 (1 vol) and papers rel to diocesan
administration, education, devotional practices,
the Armagh inquiry 1776-81 and the 1798
rebellion.
Diocesan Archives, Archbishop's House, Dublin.

[728] **TUCKER, Josiah** (1712-1799)
Dean of Gloucester 1758-99.

Corresp and papers 1776-91.
St John's College, Oxford (MS 294). Given by
Miss MAR Tucker 1947. NRA 7453.

[729] **TUCKWELL, William** (1829-1919)
Fellow of New College, Oxford 1848-58;
headmaster of Taunton College 1864-77.

Scrapbooks, mainly of corresp and papers rel to
Taunton College 1857-1916 (3 vols); meditations
and sermon notes (3 vols); MSS of his
biographical works 1904-11 (4 vols); misc literary,
historical, theological and other corresp and
papers, some printed, 1872-1913.
King's College, Taunton. NRA 28728.

[730] **TUKE, Henry** (1755-1814)
Quaker minister.

Corresp mainly with his family (*c*10 bundles) incl
letters from JD Lambert 1790-1 (1 bundle), his
father 1768, 1791-1815 (1 bundle) and his wife
1778-94 (1 bundle); literary MSS and related
corresp (2 bundles).
Borthwick Institute, York. Deposited by Anthony
Tuke 1969. NRA 14940.

[731] **TUKE, Samuel** (1784-1857)
Quaker minister.

Corresp, mainly with his family (*c*10 bundles) incl
letters from WH Alexander 1841-9 (1 bundle).
Borthwick Institute, York. Deposited by Anthony
Tuke 1969. NRA 14940.

[732] **TURNER, William** (1714-1794)
Unitarian minister of Westgate Chapel, Wakefield
1761-92.

Letters to him, mainly from Theophilus Lindsey
1771-94, (58 items).

Dr Williams's Library, London (12.44). NRA
13168.

Letters from Theophilus Lindsey 1771-7 (14
items).
*Literary and Philosophical Society of Newcastle
upon Tyne.* NRA 28899.

[733] **TURNER, William** (1761-1859)
Minister of Hanover Square Unitarian Chapel,
Newcastle upon Tyne 1782-1841.

Letters to him 1784-1840 (78 items).
*Literary and Philosophical Society of Newcastle
upon Tyne.* NRA 28899.

[734] **TURNER, William Edward** (1836-1911)
Quaker minister; editor of the *British Friend*
1891-1901.

Travel journals 1865-75 (3 vols); addresses 1866-8
(1 vol); papers incl account of European tour and
addresses rel to war c1856-70 (40ff).
Society of Friends Library, London (Temp MSS
36/1, Port 8 126-30).

[735] **TYERMAN, Luke** (c1820-1889)
Wesleyan methodist minister.

Corresp c1833-86 (c230 items), mainly letters
from LH Wiseman 1860-4 (7 items) and others
(c205 items); diary (2 vols); historical materials,
mainly biographies of early methodist clergy (24
vols); lecture notes (4 vols); sermons (c200 items).
Methodist Archives, Manchester.

[736] **TYRELL, George** (1861-1909)
Modernist theologian.

Corresp and papers 1898-1909 among those of his
biographer Maude [Dominica] Petre, incl corresp
with his Jesuit superiors 1901-6, misc corresp
1900-8, corresp rel to his death 1909-33 and
literary MSS 1904-9 (3 vols).
British Library (Add MSS 52367-82 *passim*).
Presented by Mrs Margaret Clutton, sister of
Maude Petre, 1964.

Corresp with Friedrich von Hügel, mainly rel to
modernism, 1897-1909 (5 vols).
British Library (Add MSS 44927-31). Presented by
Maude Petre 1937.

[737] **ULLATHORNE, William Bernard** (1806-
1889)
Vicar apostolic of the western district 1845-8, of
the midland district 1848-50; bishop of
Birmingham 1850-88.

Corresp and misc papers, mainly as bishop, 1833-
89 (c1,100 items) incl corresp with Lord
Shrewsbury 1833-52, Mother Francis Raphael
1843-89, the Propaganda 1847-86, Ambrose
Phillips de Lisle 1848-66, JH Newman 1848-54,

NPS Wiseman 1848-60 and James Brown 1852-66
and reports from the Vatican Council 1869-70.
Archbishop's House, Birmingham. NRA 8129.

Corresp and papers rel to the communities of
Dominican nuns at Stone, Stoke and elsewhere
1843-88 (c525 items) incl letters from him at
Rome during and after the Vatican Council 1869-
70 (c40 items); papers rel to diocesan
administration 1856-84 (29 items); drafts of his
autobiography and other works, sermons, books
and printed papers 1838-80 (c20 items); sermons,
retreat lectures etc delivered at Stone (22 items)
and misc personal and family papers etc 1847-89
(31 items).
St Dominic's Convent, Stone. NRA 27580.

Corresp 1834-82 (1 box), mainly letters from the
Benedictine chapter 1846-81.
Downside Abbey.

Corresp rel to Prior Park College, Bath etc 1836-
67 (95 items); letters from HA Vaughan 1875-81
(7 items).
Westminster Diocesan Archives (St Edmund's
College Ware, series 7, 15). NRA 16303.

Corresp 1846-9 incl letters from Thomas Brindle
and NPS Wiseman mainly rel to Prior Park
College (c100 items); letters from Rome.
Bristol Record Office (Clifton diocesan records).

Misc corresp and papers 1812-88 incl letters to
him from EW Pugin 1874, sermon notes,
memoranda etc (1 bundle).
St Francis of Sales Church, Yoxall (Joseph Parker
papers). NRA 9681.

Account of his work in the western district 1845-7
(1 vol).
Bishop of Clifton.

[738] **UNDERHILL, Evelyn** (1875-1941)
Religious writer.

Corresp and papers incl sermons and articles
1888-1969 (6 boxes).
King's College London.

[739] **VALTON, John** (1740-1794)
Methodist preacher.

Letters from John Wesley and other corresp
1771-93 (17 items); autobiography; journals 1763-
89 (c6 vols).
Methodist Archives, Manchester.

[740] **VAN MILDERT, William** (1765-1836)
Bishop of Llandaff 1819-26, of Durham 1826-36.

Corresp, journals and papers as regius professor
of divinity at Oxford, dean of St Paul's and
bishop of Durham (c600 items).
Van Mildert College, Durham. Deposited by his
sister's descendant JE Grant-Ives Esq.

Visitation notes and misc corresp, sermons, verses etc, with other family papers 1782-1843 (*c*140 items).
Durham University Library (MS Accessions 49-102). Deposited by Captain and Mrs Grant-Ives.

Letters from Samuel Smith rel to Durham University 1832-4 (10 items).
Durham University Library (Samuel Smith papers). Purchased 1980. NRA 25113.

[741] **VAUGHAN, Herbert Alfred** (1832-1903)
Rector of St Joseph's College, Mill Hill 1866-72; bishop of Salford 1872-92; archbishop of Westminster 1892-1903; cardinal 1893.

Corresp rel to the foundation and administration of St Joseph's College 1866-1903, mainly letters from him to successive rectors from 1872, associated accounts 1866-7 and papers rel to higher education, college administration and St Joseph's Missionary Society (*c*8 boxes); corresp and papers rel to missionary education 1855-72 incl notebook of investigative interviews in Europe and England *c*1855-8 (320pp) and memorials 1863-72 (162pp); fund raising records 1863-72 incl letters of introduction (1 box) and notes of itineraries, donors and donations (5 vols); corresp and papers rel to the purchase of *The Tablet* 1866-71 (35 items); spiritual diary 1895-1901 (1 vol); sermon and retreat notes and devotional works 1855-1901 (6 boxes); testamentary papers 1903 (1 bundle); press cuttings 1868-1903 (19 vols).
St Joseph's College, Mill Hill.

Official papers 1893-1903 (9 boxes).
Westminster Diocesan Archives.

Misc papers rel to training of priests *c*1870-8 (1 vol, 2 bundles); notes on the diocese of Salford 1872-92 (1 vol); letters from Rome 1879-80 (1 bundle); sermon notes 1880 (1 vol).
Bishop of Salford.

[742] **VENABLES, Richard** (1775-1858)
Archdeacon of Carmarthen 1832-58.

Letters mainly from his family and solicitors rel to personal, legal and business affairs etc 1810-57 (*c*440 items); diaries 1808-24 (15 vols).
National Library of Wales. Deposited by Sir Michael Dillwyn-Venables-Llewellyn Bt. See *Annual Report* 1970-1, p62.

[743] **VENABLES, Richard Lister** (1809-1894)
Rector of Whitney 1834-43; vicar of Clyro 1847-73.

Letters from his family, mainly rel to personal and business affairs etc 1835-93 (*c*1,200 items); diaries 1828-93 (79 vols); sermon notes 1836-81 (5 bundles).

National Library of Wales. Deposited by Sir Michael Dillwyn-Venables-Llewellyn Bt. See *Annual Report* 1970-1, pp62-3.

[744] **VENN, Henry** (1725-1797)
Vicar of Huddersfield 1759-71; rector of Yelling 1771-97.

Collected letters from him mainly to members of his family 1764-96 (*c*550 items) incl letters to his son John 1777-96 (106 items).
Church Missionary Society, London (Venn MSS C1-16A). Bequeathed by Dr JA Venn 1958. NRA 2694.

[745] **VENN, Henry** (1796-1873)
Honorary secretary of the Church Missionary Society 1841-73.

Letters from various correspondents *c*1805-73 (*c*95 items) incl Charles Simeon *c*1825-*c*1835 (6 items), Lord Teignmouth 1827-43 (9 items) and William Wilberforce 1819-32 (26 items); letters 1813-43 (34 items); corresp with his family 1813-73 (287 items, 2 bundles); personal and travel diaries 1810-71 (8 vols, 1 bundle); CMS diary 1849-50 (1 vol); autobiographical papers and accounts of his children (1 vol, 2 items); personal and travel accounts 1818-56 (6 vols).
Church Missionary Society, London (Venn MSS C30-6, F10-22, 35-40). Bequeathed by Dr JA Venn 1958. NRA 2694.

[746] **VENN, John** (1759-1813)
Rector of Clapham 1792-1813.

Letters from his father 1777-96 (106 items), Charles Simeon with copies of replies 1782-97 (17 items), the Thornton family 1789-95 (1 bundle) and others 1778-1810 (32 items); general corresp 1783-1803, 1813 (158 items); copies of letters to his family 1778-1813 (6 vols); diaries 1777-1813 (9 vols); autobiographical papers collected by his children incl copies of his letters (5 vols).
Church Missionary Society, London (Venn MSS C1, 19-22, 68, F3-6). Bequeathed by Dr JA Venn 1958. NRA 2694.

[747] **VON HÜGEL, Friedrich** (1852-1925)
Theologian.

Letters to him 1874-1925 (*c*1,100 items); diaries 1877-1924 (43 vols); misc notes (1 box).
St Andrews University Library.

[748] **WADE, Nugent** (1809-1893)
Rector of St Anne Soho 1846-90 and canon of Bristol 1872-93.

Personal and ecclesiastical corresp 1827-70 incl letters rel to Irish church affairs and ritualism *c*1830-50; diary 1829-40.

Pusey House, Oxford. Deposited by Miss Elmira Wade. NRA 0250, 19807.

[749] **WALDEGRAVE, Samuel** (1817-1869)
Bishop of Carlisle 1860-9.

Family corresp 1826-69; journal at Cheam School 1834-5 (1 vol); account book 1844-57 (1 vol); diary 1868 (1 vol); visitation notebook (1 vol); sermon notes.
Earl Waldegrave. Access restricted. NRA 28249.

[750] **WALKER, James** (*c*1770-1841)
Bishop of Edinburgh 1830-41 and primus of the Scottish episcopal church 1837-41.

Corresp rel to provincial, diocesan and personal affairs 1790-1840 incl letters from WF Hook, Alexander Jolly and MH Luscombe (*c*85 items); sermons 1789-1838 (41 items); misc personal papers 1793-1837 (14 items).
Scottish Record Office (CH 12).

[751] **WALMESLEY, Charles** (1722-1797)
Vicar apostolic of the western district 1780-97.

Letters from Rome 1778-97 (1 vol *passim*); corresp and related papers 1772-96 (7 vols *passim*).
Bristol Record Office (Clifton diocesan records).

Prayers (1 vol); copies of collected letters 1786-97 (1 vol).
Bishop of Clifton.

[752] **WALPOLE, George Henry Somerset** (1854-1929)
Bishop of Edinburgh 1910-29.

Letters from EW Benson 1882-96, CG Lang 1909 and others 1882-1924 (1 vol).
Scottish Record Office (CH 12/28).

Official journal *c*1910-26 (1 vol).
Bishop of Edinburgh. Enquiries to NRA (Scotland) (NRA (S) 2703).

[753] **WALSH, Thomas** (1777-1849)
President of Oscott College 1818-26; vicar apostolic of the midland district 1826-48, of the London district 1848-9.

Corresp and papers 1828-49 (418 items), mainly letters to him, incl corresp with Lord Shrewsbury 1837-48 (24 items), Ambrose Phillipps de Lisle 1835-45 (9 items) and with the Propaganda 1830-9 (20 items), appointments and faculties (7 items) and personal, financial and misc papers (37 items).
Archbishop's House, Birmingham. NRA 8129.

Bills, receipts and notes rel to the building of the new college at Oscott 1819-39.
Oscott College, Sutton Coldfield.

[754] **WALSH, William Joseph** (1841-1921)
President of St Patrick's College, Maynooth 1880-5; RC archbishop of Dublin 1885-1921.

Corresp and papers 1880-1921 (*c*150 boxes) incl general corresp, memoranda, reports, sermons, notes, draft for a book on bimetallism and papers rel to the administration of St Patrick's College, education policy, relations with government, the land question, home rule and Sinn Fein.
Diocesan Archives, Archbishop's House, Dublin.

[755] **WARD, Bernard Nicholas** (1857-1920)
President of St Edmund's College Ware 1893-1916; bishop of Brentwood 1917-20.

Corresp and papers 1890-1919 (*c*1,600 items, 5 vols) incl general corresp and papers as president 1893-1917 (*c*420 items) and rel to higher education *c*1890-1914 (*c*140 items) and the *Edmundian* 1914-19 (*c*235 items), copies of letters sent 1916-17 (*c*700 items), diaries 1890-1916 (4 vols) and visitors book 1906-11.
Westminster Diocesan Archives (St Edmund's College Ware, series 13). NRA 16303.

[756] **WARD, Wilfrid Philip** (1856-1916)
RC biographer and apologist.

Corresp rel to modernism, the Synthetic Society, anglican orders and other religious, political and literary topics 1845-1925 (*c*3,300 items), mainly letters to him from AJ Balfour, Henri Brémond, Lord Halifax, Friedrich von Hügel, George Tyrell and others; notebooks, diaries, subject files, press cuttings etc (4 boxes).
St Andrews University Library. See MJ Weaver, 'A working catalogue of the Ward family papers', *Recusant History*, 15, 1976, pp43-71.

[757] **WARD, William George** (1812-1882)
RC convert; theologian and philosopher.

Letters from FW Faber, EB Pusey and NPS Wiseman (14 items); notebooks (2 vols).
St Andrews University Library. See Weaver, *op cit*.

Theological lectures, literary MSS and misc personal papers 1840-98 (7 items, 1 vol); Cave fund account book 1866-9.
Westminster Diocesan Archives (St Edmund's College Ware, series 5, 20). NRA 16303.

[758] **WARDLAW, Ralph** (1779-1853)
Congregational minister of North Albion Street Chapel 1803-19, of West George Street Chapel, Glasgow 1819-53.

Letters from William Urwick and other corresp and papers rel to the dispute between the Irish Evangelical Society and the Congregational Union of Ireland 1840-7 (71 items).
Dr Williams's Library, London (New College 494). NRA 13042.

[759] **WATKINSON, William Lonsdale** (1838-1925)
Wesleyan methodist minister.

Letters from Marshall Hartley and others 1886-1920 (*c*73 items).
Methodist Archives, Manchester.

[760] **WATSON, Charles** (1794-1866)
Minister of Burntisland 1820-37.

Letters and related papers from Thomas McCrie 1819-34 (1 vol); diaries, notebooks and journals 1817-66 (21 vols); family prayers (3 vols); scrapbook 1816-31.
New College, Edinburgh.

[761] **WATSON, Edward William** (1859-1936)
Canon of Christ Church, Oxford and regius professor of ecclesiastical history 1908-34.

Letters from WS Sanday *c*1895-9, William Stubbs 1884-8 and John Wordsworth 1888-1908 (26 items).
Bodleian Library, Oxford (MS Eng lett e 44).

Papers as secretary of the archbishop's committee for the translation of the Athanasian Creed 1904-18.
Lambeth Palace Library (MS 1469).

[762] **WATSON, Joshua** (1771-1855)
Treasurer of the National Society 1811-42 and of the Society for Promoting Christian Knowledge 1814-30.

Letters to him 1802-52 and papers rel to Ely Chapel, Holborn 1813-41 (127ff).
Lambeth Palace Library (MS 1562). Presented by AB Webster 1954.

Papers as joint secretary of the Westminster Association 1814-16 (2 vols, 93ff).
Lambeth Palace Library (MSS 1787-9). MSS 1787-8 presented by Canon Charles Inge 1950.

Letters from Christopher Wordsworth 1840-8 (85ff).
Lambeth Palace Library (MS 2147).

Letters from Edward Churton 1842-51 (24 items).
Pusey House, Oxford. NRA 29544.

[763] **WEBB, Benjamin** (1819-1885)
Vicar of St Andrew, Wells Street, London 1862-85.

Letters to him 1850-85 (196ff).
Lambeth Palace Library (MS 1750). Purchased 1961.

Letters from EB Pusey 1843-[60] (44 items).
Bodleian Library, Oxford (MS Eng lett e 91 aa). Presented by the Revd JF Mozley 1965.

G

Diaries 1837-85 (39 vols).
Bodleian Library, Oxford (MSS Eng misc e 406-41, f 97-9). Bequeathed by Professor CCJ Webb 1954.

Reports on churches for the Cambridge Camden Society 1839-41.
Lambeth Palace Library (MSS 1977-89 *passim*). Presented by Church House Library from the library of the Revd EJ Boyce, 1953.

[764] **WEEDALL, Henry** (1788-1859)
President of Oscott College 1826-43, 1853-9.

Corresp 1844-59, mainly letters to him (33 items).
Archbishop's House, Birmingham. NRA 8129.

'Records of St Mary's College, Oscott' from 1830 (1 vol); papers rel to college buildings and administration 1835-59.
Oscott College, Sutton Coldfield.

[765] **WELD, Thomas** (1750-1810)
Founder of Stonyhurst College.

Corresp mainly rel to Catholic and family affairs and refugees from the French Revolution, with related papers, 1767-1810 (397 items) incl corresp and papers about the Gordon riots 1780 (15 items); corresp and papers rel to Catholic emancipation and the Protestation oath 1778-92 (1 bundle) and the Trappist convent at East Lulworth 1794-1813 (18 items); 'Materials for the history of Bindon Abbey ...' (1 vol); diary 1772-7 (1 vol); accounts 1772-1809 (52 vols, 1 bundle); bills and receipts 1771, 1809, nd (15 bundles); misc papers 1767-98 (3 vols, 1 bundle).
Dorset Record Office. Deposited by Colonel JW Weld 1956, 1964. NRA 9928.

[766] **WELD, Thomas** (1773-1837)
Cardinal 1830.

Corresp, mainly with the Clifford family, Barons Clifford, accounts and misc papers 1819-*c*1840 (1 box); family settlements and a paper on his elevation to the cardinalate 1811-30 (1 bundle, 1 item).
Lord Clifford of Chudleigh. NRA 20060.

[767] **WELLS, Francis Ballard** (1811-1888)
Private secretary to archbishop Howley 1837-42; rector of Woodchurch, Kent 1841-88.

Letters to him and misc papers 1828-87 (*c*850 items).
West Sussex Record Office (Add MSS 7341-56). NRA 21168.

[768] **WESLEY, Charles** (1707-1788)
Methodist.

Family and other corresp *c*1735-88 (2 vols and *c*850 items) incl letters from John Bennet, Selina,

Countess of Huntingdon, Charles and Vincent Perronet and his brother John; letters from JW Fletcher 1752-78 (59 items); journal 1736-56 (1 vol etc); household and other accounts 1772-87 (5 vols); notebooks incl copy letters (5 vols); hymns *c*1749-86 (4 vols etc); shorthand sermons (1 vol); poems on the psalms, gospels etc and misc papers.
Methodist Archives, Manchester. From the collection of Thomas Jackson.

[769] **WESLEY, John** (1703-1791)
Founder of the Methodist movement.

Collected corresp and papers incl letters from Benjamin Ingham, George Whitefield and others 1726-88 (133 items), letters from him 1723-91 (706 items), register of letters received (1 vol), diaries and journals 1725-7, 1729-41 (8 vols), diary and accounts 1783-90 (1 vol), personal narrative of the Sophy Hopkey affair 1736-7, sermon register *c*1787-8 (1 vol), sermons, notes on St Matthew etc (1 vol), Dublin Society book, Holy Club notes, London Society lists, misc hymns, sermons, prayers, poems etc (*c*12 vols).
Methodist Archives, Manchester. Acquired from various sources including the Colman and Lamplough collections and Methodist Book Room.

Personal and family corresp and papers 1734-1864 (1,167 items) incl letters from Adam Clarke, Thomas Coke, JW and Mary Fletcher, Selina, Countess of Huntingdon, William Law, Vincent Perronet, Samuel Wesley and George Whitefield; Georgia diary 1736; press cuttings and printed material.
Emory University Library, Atlanta, Georgia. See *National union catalog* 79-775.

Corresp with members of his family, Adam Clarke and others 1738-91 (*c*140 items); diary 1790-1 (1 vol); notebook 1711/12; sermons 1725-41 (3 items).
Wesley College, Bristol. From the collections of George Morley and Adam Clarke. NRA 27694.

Journal of his journey from England to Georgia 1735-6 (1 vol).
Georgia University Library, Athens, Georgia (Egmont Papers).

[770] **WESTCOTT, Brooke Foss** (1825-1901)
Bishop of Durham 1890-1901.

Corresp, sermons and 'Memoir of archbishop Benson' 1898.
Cambridge University Library (Add 7683, 8315, 8317).

Letters from him, MSS of his theological works, sermons, addresses etc 1872-1901, nd (5 boxes).
Selwyn College, Cambridge. NRA 24353.

[771] **WHATELY, Richard** (1787-1863)
Archbishop of Dublin 1831-63.

General corresp, mainly letters to him, 1831-60 (86ff); part of a letter book 1835-6 (46ff); letters to NW Senior 1818-41 (18ff) and to CB Wale 1851-8 (58ff); corresp of Whately and his wife with Joseph Blanco White 1828-41 (86ff); misc papers (56ff).
Lambeth Palace Library (MS 2164). Presented by Miss R Whately 1968.

Letters from NW Senior, some rel to ecclesiastical and personal affairs, 1811-63 (85 items).
National Library of Wales (Senior papers). NRA 28427.

Copies of his letters to Edward Copleston 1829-45 (13 items) made by his chaplain John O'Regan; commonplace book 1814-17, copied by his chaplain *c*1850 (1 vol).
Lambeth Palace Library (MSS 3163-4). Presented by JWH O'Regan 1981.

Letters from Edward Hawkins 1846-9 and lectures by Whately and Hawkins (2 boxes).
Oriel College, Oxford.

[772] **WHITE, Henry Julian** (1859-1934)
Dean of Christ Church, Oxford 1920-34.

Corresp and papers among those of the Anglo-Continental Society 1891-1932 (5 vols) incl letter books as secretary 1912-19 (3 vols).
Lambeth Palace Library (MSS 2910, 2912, 2922-4).

Corresp and papers rel to his edition of the Vulgate NT with John Wordsworth *c*1882-*c*1934 incl letters from Wordsworth, the Clarendon Press, foreign scholars and others (*c*6 boxes and files), notebooks (*c*20 vols) and misc papers.
Christ Church, Oxford.

[773] **WHITE, John** (1867-1951)
Minister of the Barony, Glasgow 1911-34.

Corresp and papers mainly rel to the union of the Church of Scotland and the United Free Church of Scotland 1929 (88 boxes).
New College, Edinburgh.

[774] **WHITE, Joseph Blanco** (1775-1841)
Unitarian; theological writer.

Corresp, mainly letters to him from Edward Copleston and others 1809-44 (187 items); letters and papers rel to *El Espanol* 1810-14 (*c*32 items) incl letters from John Allen (7 items) and Lord Holland (19 items); private journal 1812-20 (1 vol); diaries 1816-39 (*c*12 vols); commonplace books 1818-22 (3 vols); account book 1813-30 (1 vol); notebooks on historical and theological subjects etc 1810-41 (*c*22 vols); MS autobiography, literary MSS, sermons, notes and

papers incl printed material, some in Spanish *c*1805-41.
Liverpool University Library. Bequeathed by the Revd JH Thom 1894. NRA 26823.

Letters from members of his family 1815-42 (1 vol, 47 items), from mainly Spanish correspondents 1811-30 (35 items), and from other correspondents 1820-39 (*c*55 items); journals 1822, 1835, 1838-9 (3 vols), commonplace books 1812-39 (5 vols); literary MSS, sermons, certificates etc 1791-1842 (2 vols, etc).
Manchester College, Oxford. NRA 19869.

Corresp, mainly letters from WE Channing, JS Mill, Robert Southey and others *c*1810-40 (*c*50 items).
Liverpool University Library (Rathbone papers). Presented 1958. NRA 7187.

[775] **WHITESIDE, Thomas** (1857-1921)
RC bishop 1894-1911 and archbishop of Liverpool 1911-21.

Papers as bishop and archbishop incl corresp (*c*20 boxes), visitation diaries and other records.
Archbishop of Liverpool.

Copies of his letters to Rome 1915-20 (1 vol).
Lancashire Record Office (Liverpool archdiocesan records).

[776] **WHITTAKER, John William** (*c*1790-1854)
Vicar of Blackburn 1822-54.

Letters to him 1814-39 mainly rel to Blackburn parochial affairs, industrial disturbances and catholic emancipation (*c*270 items).
Blackburn Public Library. NRA 11530.

Letters to him etc, mainly from his family, 1804-30 (*c*500 items).
Wigan Record Office (Edward Hall collection).

Family letters collected by him 1782-1838 (1 vol).
Manchester Central Library (MS f 929. 2 W 126).

Letters from John Rolph in Canada 1812-21 (12 items).
Public Archives of Canada (MG24 J48).

[777] **WICHE, John** (1718-1794)
Baptist minister, Maidstone 1746-94.

Corresp with Nathaniel Lardner 1761-8 (66 items) and Francis Blackburne 1766-84 (31 items).
Dr Williams's Library, London (12.45, 53). NRA 13168.

[778] **WILBERFORCE, Henry William** (1807-1873)
RC author and journalist.

Letters from his father William 1818-31 (46 items).
Wilberforce House Museum, Hull.

Letters to him and his family from HE Manning 1839-88 (71 items) and JH Newman 1836-84 (*c*114 items).
Ushaw College, Durham. NRA 13674.

Theological notebook 1831 (1 vol).
Oriel College, Oxford. NRA 27726.

[779] **WILBERFORCE, Robert Isaac** (1802-1857)
Archdeacon of the East Riding 1841-5; RC 1845.

Letters from JH Newman 1827-34 (47 items), HW Wilberforce 1830-54 (88 items), Samuel Wilberforce 1823-54 (*c*500 items) and others (119 items).
Mrs CE Wrangham.

Corresp and papers (1 vol) incl letters from WE Gladstone 1838-54 (18 items), JH Newman 1827-54 (51 items) and EB Pusey 1827-54 (17 items).
Miss Irene Wilberforce.

Letters from John Keble 1827-54 (51 items).
Keble College, Oxford. NRA 21028.

Letters from Edward Churton 1845-54 (103 items).
Pusey House, Oxford. NRA 29544.

[780] **WILBERFORCE, Samuel** (1805-1873)
Bishop of Oxford 1845-69, of Winchester 1869-73.

Large groups of letters to him, with some drafts and copies of his replies and original letters returned, 1822-73 (40 vols) incl corresp with Sir Charles Anderson 1825-73 (11 vols) and R Chenevix Trench 1838-73 (2 vols) and letters from WE Gladstone 1834-73 (4 vols, 124ff), John Keble 1836-65 (139ff), JH Newman 1831-41 (52ff) and CR Sumner 1830-62 (172ff); small groups of letters and single letters, mainly from public figures, 1822-73 (12 vols); corresp and papers rel to Oxford and Winchester dioceses and parochial affairs *c*1820-69 (3 vols, 45ff); corresp rel to the church overseas 1853-73 (2 vols); letters from his family 1814-65, nd (6 vols); letter books 1843-68 (8 vols); diaries 1823-73 (16 vols); notebooks rel to church affairs 1823-64 (14 vols); literary papers and corresp and accounts with publishers 1833-77 (6 vols, 93ff); misc papers mainly rel to church affairs *c*1818-*c*1869 (1 vol, 198ff).
Bodleian Library, Oxford (MSS Wilberforce). Purchased from the executors of Dr Octavia Wilberforce 1965. NRA 7132.

Letters from his brother RI Wilberforce, mainly 1830-49 (*c*200 items).
Mrs CE Wrangham.

Letters to him, mainly rel to missionary work in east Africa and British colonies, 1790-1872 (35 items).
William R Perkins Library, Duke University, Durham, N Carolina.

Lambeth Palace Library (MSS 1823-4). Purchased 1964.

Letters from GH Forbes 1865-74 (6 items); MS of *Four letters to the Rev William Nicholson* (1 vol); sermons, lectures, notes etc (10 vols).
National Library of Scotland (Dep 251). NRA 27272.

[799] WORDSWORTH, Christopher (1774-1846)
Master of Trinity College, Cambridge 1820-41.

Corresp 1803-45 (1 vol).
Lambeth Palace Library (MS 1822). Purchased 1964.

Corresp with his son Christopher 1821-46 (1 vol); misc corresp and papers 1811-46 (115ff).
Lambeth Palace Library (MS 2149-50). Presented by the Friends of Lambeth Palace Library 1967.

Letters from his brother William 1826-42; letters to HH Norris 1807-38 (101ff).
British Library (Add MS 46136). Presented by the Revd WA Wordsworth 1945.

Letters from William and Dorothy Wordsworth (29 items).
Wordsworth Library, Grasmere.

Diaries 1793-4, 1819-45; notes and notebooks rel to 17th cent history (3 bundles, 15 vols); accounts 1814-46 (2 vols); notebooks 1830-4, nd (5 vols etc).
Trinity College, Cambridge.

[800] WORDSWORTH, Christopher (1807-1885)
Headmaster of Harrow 1836-44; canon of Westminster 1844-68; bishop of Lincoln 1869-85.

Corresp with Jonathan and Joshua Watson and members of the Frere family 1821-67 (1 vol); corresp with EW Benson, WE Gladstone, EB Pusey and Samuel Wilberforce 1837-85 (1 vol); general corresp 18[22]-94 (7 vols); corresp with his father 1821-46 (1 vol).
Lambeth Palace Library (MSS 2140-9). Presented by the Friends of Lambeth Palace Library 1967.

Corresp rel to the school chapel 1836-9 (95 items), the restoration of Harrow church 1842 (28 items), the admission of free scholars 1843-4 (98 items) and misc corresp (69 items); lists of boys and their placings 1839 (1 vol); mark book 1841-3; entry book (1 vol); chapel account book 1837-46 (1 vol); sermons 1840-4 (2 vols); account of Harrow School, orders and statutes (3 items).
Harrow School. Mainly presented by his daughter Susan Wordsworth 1891.

Corresp and papers rel to charities 1861-74 (2 vols, *c*3 bundles), to lay conferences and the diocesan synod 1868-71 (2 vols, 5 bundles); misc papers mainly rel to diocesan affairs *c*1866-83 (1 box).

Lincolnshire Archives Office (Wordsworth papers). NRA 29309.

Misc corresp and papers with autobiographical material 1815-86 (267ff) and letters from his uncle William Wordsworth 1828-49.
British Library (Add MSS 46136-7).

Letters from William Wordsworth (5 items); memoranda book and other papers rel to his publication of William Wordsworth's *Memoirs*, 1815.
Wordsworth Library, Grasmere.

Undergraduate diary 1825 (1 vol).
Trinity College, Cambridge (0.11.9). Deposited by the Revd WA Wordsworth 1940.

Papers rel to the Anglo-Continental Society 1844-81 (1 vol) incl journal of a visit to Florence [1862] (30ff).
Lambeth Palace Library (MS 2908).

[801] WORDSWORTH, John (1843-1911)
Bishop of Salisbury 1885-1911.

Letter book of his and George Moberly's letters to clergy 1875-87 with some letters to him (1 vol).
Wiltshire Record Office. P Stewart, *Guide to the records of the bishop ... of Salisbury*, 1973, p19.

Letters to him rel to his edition of the Vulgate NT *c*1882-4 (1 bundle).
Christ Church, Oxford.

Misc letters and papers mainly rel to apostolic succession in the Anglican church 1889-99 (90ff).
Lambeth Palace Library (MS 2165).

Corresp and papers, with some of HJ White, mainly as an officer of the Anglo-Continental Society 1889-*c*1907 (5 vols) incl papers rel to reunion with Rome 1895-8 (1 vol), corresp and papers rel to the reformed Catholic Church of Italy 1889-1904 (1 vol) and papers as president of the Jerusalem and the East Mission Fund 1895-1907 (1 vol).
Lambeth Palace Library (MSS 2908-13).

General corresp as president of the Jerusalem and the East Mission Fund 1897-1911 (1 vol); corresp and papers concerning his visit to the eastern patriarchs 1897-9 (1 vol); misc corresp rel to the affairs of the Fund 1869-1908 (2 vols).
Lambeth Palace Library (MSS 2327-30). Presented by the Jerusalem and the East Mission Fund 1969.

Papers mainly rel to the Lambeth Conference 1897, the report of a sub-committee of the Upper House of the Convocation of Canterbury on the ornaments of the church and its ministers 1908, and a conference between the Anglican and Swedish churches 1909 (6 vols).
Lambeth Palace Library (MSS 1396-1401). Mainly presented by his widow 1911.

Letters to him rel to the report of the archbishop's commission on relations between the Anglican and Swedish churches 1911 (32ff).
Lambeth Palace Library (MS 1946).

Sermons (395 items).
King's College London.

[802] **WRAY, Cecil** (1805-1878)
Perpetual curate of St Martin in the Fields, Liverpool 1836-78.

Corresp 1826-78 (620ff) incl letters from GA Denison 1850-76, AP Forbes 1854-6, WF Hook 1838-42, John Keble 1850-60 and JM Neale 1846-65.
Lambeth Palace Library (MS 1604). From the papers of Claude Jenkins.

[803] **WRIDE, Thomas** (d 1807)
Methodist.

Corresp, incl letters from John Wesley and others 1771-1804 (34 items); misc notes, sermons and papers.
Methodist Archives, Manchester.

[804] **WRIGHT, George** (1776-1826)
Minister of Markinch 1801-18, of First Charge, Stirling 1818-26.

Corresp (1 vol); diaries (6 vols); lectures, sermons and notes (21 vols).
New College, Edinburgh.

[805] **WYNTER, Philip** (1793-1871)
President of St John's College, Oxford 1828-71; vice-chancellor of Oxford University 1840-4.

Corresp and papers rel to university affairs 1817-89 (4 vols) incl corresp rel to EB Pusey's sermon of 14 May 1843 (147ff), letters from the Duke of Wellington with draft replies 1841-4 (443ff) and letters from Lord Derby 1861-9 (80ff).
Bodleian Library, Oxford (MSS Dep d 3-6). NRA 27382.

Corresp with EB Pusey rel to the controversies over *Tracts for the Times*, Pusey's suspension from preaching etc 1835-45 (2 vols).
Pusey House, Oxford.

[806] **YOUNG, Robert** (1777-1813)
Minister of the Scots Church, London Wall 1803-13.

Letter book 1801-13 (1 vol); letters from his father (c100 items); autobiographical fragments c1812 (1 vol); collections for his congregation's history (1 vol).
Guildhall Library, London (MSS 4972-5).

[807] **ZOUCH, Thomas** (1737-1815)
Rector of Wycliffe 1770-93, of Scrayingham 1793-5; prebendary of Durham 1805-15.

Letters from William Lowther, 1st Earl of Lonsdale 1786-1815 (36 items) and from others 1796-1812 (10 items); historical and theological papers (30 vols and bundles); accounts and memoranda 1763-86 (3 vols).
Clwyd Record Office, Ruthin (DD/L). NRA 19944.

WINDSOR
The Aerary, St George's Chapel, Windsor Castle
  176, 186, 191, 533

WORCESTER
Hereford and Worcester Record Office 323

WORKSOP
Worksop College 482

YORK
Borthwick Institute of Historical Research, York
  University 253, 269, 293, 399, 510, 697, 700,
  705, 712, 730, 731, 792
Minster Library 276, 488

YOXALL
St Francis of Sales Church 737

Printed by HMSO, Edinburgh Press
Dd 0238896 C17 6/87 (241883)